BEYOND DEPORTATION

CITIZENSHIP AND MIGRATION IN THE AMERICAS
General Editor: Ediberto Román

Tierra y Libertad: Land, Liberty, and Latino Housing
Steven W. Bender

*No Undocumented Child Left Behind: Plyler v. Doe and the
Education of Undocumented Schoolchildren*
Michael A. Olivas

*Marginal Workers: How Legal Fault Lines Divide Workers and
Leave Them without Protection*
Ruben J. Garcia

*Run for the Border: Vice and Virtue in U.S.-Mexico
Border Crossings*
Steven W. Bender

*Those Damned Immigrants: America's Hysteria over
Undocumented Immigration*
Ediberto Román

Strange Neighbors: The Role of States in Immigration Policy
Carissa Hessick and Gabriel G. Chin

*Revoking Citizenship: Expatriation Policies in America from the
Colonial Era to the War on Terror*
Ben Herzog

*Beyond Deportation: The Role of Prosecutorial Discretion in
Immigration Cases*
Shoba Sivaprasad Wadhia

Beyond Deportation

The Role of Prosecutorial Discretion in Immigration Cases

Shoba Sivaprasad Wadhia

With a Foreword by Leon Wildes

To mary —
Thank you for your
leadership.

Shoba Sivaprasad Wadhia
10.08.2015

NEW YORK UNIVERSITY PRESS

New York and London

NEW YORK UNIVERSITY PRESS
New York and London
www.nyupress.org

References to Internet websites (URLs) were accurate at the time of writing.
Neither the author nor New York University Press is responsible for URLs
that may have expired or changed since the manuscript was prepared.

Library of Congress Cataloging-in-Publication Data
Wadhia, Shoba Sivaprasad, author.
Beyond deportation : the role of prosecutorial discretion in immigration cases /
Shoba Sivaprasad Wadhia.
pages cm — (Citizenship and migration in the Americas)
Includes bibliographical references and index.
ISBN 978-1-4798-2922-4
1. Deportation—United States. 2. Emigration and immigration law—
United States. 3. Prosecution—United States—Decision making. I. Title.
KF4842.W33 2015
342.7308'2—dc23   2014047910

New York University Press books are printed on acid-free paper,
and their binding materials are chosen for strength and durability.
We strive to use environmentally responsible suppliers and materials
to the greatest extent possible in publishing our books.

Manufactured in the United States of America

10 9 8 7 6 5 4 3 2 1

Also available as an ebook

For my parents, Geetha and R. Sivaprasad

CONTENTS

The INS had a long tradition of denying that it ever had a humanitarian program to benefit noncitizens. In official bar association liaison committee meetings with the New York district director of the INS that I attended before 1972, District Director Peter Esperdy, in response to a direct question, denied the existence of a "nonpriority" program or any other policy by which the INS might defer or decline the removal of eligible noncitizens. Although district directors had been routinely forwarding meritorious hardship cases to regional commissioners, this beneficial program was practiced *sub rosa* and was never publicly discussed or acknowledged.

In August 1971, John Lennon and Yoko Ono arrived in the United States on visitor visas. They retained me in January 1972 to assist them with their immigration problem. Yoko had an eight-year-old daughter, Kyoko, whose father, Yoko's former American husband Tony Cox, had absconded with her several years earlier and the child was nowhere to be found. John and Yoko had just secured a court order for the child's temporary custody in the U.S. district court in Saint Thomas, U.S. Virgin Islands, where Yoko and Tony had divorced, and the court granted Kyoko's temporary custody to her and John. Tony Cox then filed a new custody proceeding in Texas, where Yoko and John also appeared and secured a temporary custody order from that court as well. But once again, Tony Cox absconded with the child and needed to be located.

I approached the INS district director, Sol Marks, and requested an extension of stay to permit the Lennons to find Kyoko and secure her custody, which I felt was the strongest reason for an extension of stay I had ever heard. Upon checking with the Office of the INS Commissioner, Marks granted only a one-month extension and issued a warning that my clients "had better leave."

Unknown to us at the time, the commissioner had received a letter from Senator Strom Thurmond representing the Internal Security

Former Beatle John Lennon, left, with his attorney Leon Wildes, right. Photo courtesy of Leon Wildes.

Subcommittee of the Senate Judiciary Committee, advising that John Lennon's presence in the United States could be detrimental to President Richard Nixon's reelection plans. Lennon, who had an immense impact on young people, had been discouraging young Americans from serving in Vietnam, and the upcoming November election was to be the first time in U.S. history that eighteen-to-twenty-year-olds would be permitted to vote. This information was shared with District Director Marks and soon resulted in the institution of harsh deportation proceedings against John and Yoko as overstayed visitors. The INS assumed that Lennon would have no choice but to leave or be deported, since his old British marijuana conviction would leave him no other choice.

During the deportation proceedings and thereafter, District Director Marks was continuously interviewed in the media. As the official voice of the INS, he continuously claimed that "I am an enforcement officer and I have an obligation to remove *every* illegal alien. John Lennon is not being treated differently from any other illegal alien."

The case lasted five years. Among the steps that I took on Lennon's behalf was the filing of a federal action under the Freedom of Information Act. I demanded documentation of the INS "nonpriority" program, later known as "deferred action." Eventually, I secured a copy of the provision of law, in an unpublished INS Operation Instruction, as well as copies of 1,843 approved nonpriority cases. I published the provision and analyzed the cases in a series of articles on deferred action published in the *San Diego Law Review*. With John's encouragement, I was anxious to publicize my discovery and analyze the basis upon which the INS had exercised its prosecutorial discretion in past years. In addition, I learned that no nonpriority request had been made in the Lennon case itself. I felt that John and Yoko's plight merited prosecutorial discretion.

The New York U.S. attorney wrote to Federal Judge Owen and suggested that it was appropriate for the INS to consider an application for nonpriority classification for John Lennon. He also instructed that no INS officer previously involved with the case be allowed to participate. I drafted the nonpriority request, which was filed and processed through the Office of the Commissioner of Immigration, using the same procedure as the nearly two thousand similar cases. My application was granted, and thus John Lennon was granted nonpriority status. Two weeks later, he was granted lawful permanent resident status by an order of the Second Circuit Court of Appeals, notwithstanding his marijuana conviction, in 1976.

Imagine my gratification upon meeting Shoba Sivaprasad Wadhia, a talented young lawyer and professor who had taken up my favorite cause where I had left off. I was pleased as well when I later learned that she was producing a book essential to this vital area of developing law and policy. Her book capably examines prosecutorial discretion as it applies in the immigration context, its relation to prosecutorial discretion in the criminal process, the precise details of "deferred action," how it has been applied by the Obama administration, particularly in respect to its expanded use to assist young people, and the technical effect of judicial review and the Administrative Procedure Act in this area. She also outlines her efforts in securing and publicizing prosecutorial discretion programs and her recommendations for improving prosecutorial discretion in the immigration system. I am proud to say that I consider this work to be a major contribution to this vital area of developing law.

The U.S. government managed to deport about four hundred thousand unauthorized noncitizens in its most productive year, constituting less than 4 percent of the total unauthorized population in the United States. To accomplish its huge task, the immigration authorities must prioritize the use of government facilities and personnel and properly aim their limited resources at the highest priorities, assuming as well that their vital work is carried out with appropriate humanitarianism and professional skill. Wadhia's volume is a valuable contribution to our nation's admirable efforts to accomplish this noble task.

Leon Wildes
Senior Partner, Wildes & Weinberg
Adjunct Professor Emeritus, Benjamin N. Cardozo School of Law
Past National President American Immigration Lawyers Association

ACKNOWLEDGMENTS

I send my deepest appreciation to Michael A. Olivas, who inspired me to write this book and who has supported me unconditionally, beginning even before this book project was born. After reviewing my articles on prosecutorial discretion, Professor Olivas encouraged me to reflect on and refine those articles to produce a book. In an all too generous email, Professor Olivas noted, "I am in your debt, more than I even knew, and your work on the various [prosecutorial discretion] issues is inspiring. We are all lucky to have someone as careful and thorough as you doing this kind of work, so we all can learn. I hope you will stitch all these pieces into a book-length manuscript, which would advance the cause and your own work much more than having a series of articles in various places. You are three-fourths of the way there now."

I am grateful for the support of Leon Wildes, who gave his blessing for this book and who graciously agreed to author the foreword. In particular, I will remember the day Mr. Wildes and I spent together in his New York office and at the Fig & Olive for a long lunch, fully engaged in conversation about John Lennon's case, the evolution of my book, and the personal events and family that have brought and continue to bring meaning to our lives.

I truly appreciate the support and assistance from Clara Platter, Dorothea S. Halliday, Deborah Gershenowitz, and Constance Grace of New York University Press for managing the editing process that began with a book proposal and ended on a book shelf. I also thank Ediberto Román, general editor of the press's Citizenship and Migration in the Americas series, for his generous support and the anonymous peer reviewers whose feedback on my proposal and manuscript improved this book.

I am thankful for the past and current mentors who have shaped me professionally. I am grateful to T. Alexander Aleinikoff for accepting me as his research assistant in 1997 and later connecting me to the late

Michael A. Maggio, whose passion and commitment to legal excellence were unwavering and life changing. I cannot imagine what kind of lawyer I might be without the years I spent with Maggio Kattar. I value the time I spent at the National Immigration Forum under the leadership of Frank Sharry and the opportunities I had to learn the language of immigration politics and its relationship (or lack thereof) to the law. I thank Phillip J. McConnaughay, former dean of Pennsylvania State University Dickinson School of Law, for hiring me in 2008 to start the Center for Immigrants' Rights and continuously supporting my work as a teacher and scholar.

Stephen H. Legomsky has been a constant mentor whose support and review of my scholarship has always been supportive and thorough. From the first day he engaged me with special generosity. I will especially remember Professor Legomsky's visit to Penn State and our breakfast at Teaism in Washington, D.C. I appreciate the feedback from professors and scholars on my previous work around immigration prosecutorial discretion, among them Hiroshi Motomura, David A. Martin, Jill Family, and Lenni Benson. I also benefited from the feedback I have received at various workshops including the Immigration Law Teachers' Workshop and Clinical Writers' Workshop.

I am fortunate to have received excellent research assistance from law graduates and students, especially Rachel Lok Keung, Nicole Comstock, Stephen Coccorese, and Sihan Wang. I also appreciate the work of law student editors at *Connecticut Public Interest Law Journal, Harvard Latino Law Review, University of New Hampshire Law Review, Texas Law Review, Georgetown Immigration Law Journal,* and American Immigration Council who worked on previous articles of mine that have developed into this book.

There are not enough cheers for the fearless Margaret Stock, who took on one of the greatest tasks by reviewing my manuscript in draft form—thank you and again. This book is largely improved because of her work. I will not forget receiving thoughtful edits on the very same night she won the MacArthur Fellowship (and on many other occasions) or our quiet dinner in State College the night before she spoke about immigration issues at Penn State Law.

I am grateful to the late Sara Nehman, who left such an impression on my childhood and also taught me to love music and practice wisely.

ACKNOWLEDGMENTS | XV

I am so indebted to my wise and calm husband Hemal, exuberant daughter Devyani, and "cutest toddler" awardee Neelesh for loving and supporting me unconditionally as I practice the art of packing lunches, doing laundry, and playing law professor–lawyer with love and patience (almost) every day. And how fortunate I am to have my twin sister Latha—you are a special gift. Finally, I owe so much to my mother Geetha and father Siva (aka "Dr. Siva")—everything I accomplish begins with you. I am so fortunate to have you as parents and to have known and loved your own parents.

Introduction

Envision a young man named Roman who is brought to the United States as a toddler, grows up in an all-American household along the Eastern Shore, completes his schooling and attends college, and marries his high school sweetheart, a U.S. citizen. Certain marks on Roman's record, such as a criminal conviction many years previous, are sufficient to make him deportable from the United States and leave him with no avenue for appeal or protection.

In the past twenty years, immigration laws have been shaped to leave people like Roman without options to reside in the United States lawfully with their families. These laws have classified particular mis-behaviors as "deportable" offenses since the eighteenth century.[1] However, the existence of an immigration system that deprives judges of an opportunity to weigh positive equities such as a marriage to a U.S. citizen, rehabilitation, or meaningful contributions to a family or community is more contemporary, and has created a humanitarian crisis that demands a robust prosecutorial discretion policy. Even without such a crisis, the use of prosecutorial discretion to protect people from removal in compelling cases is critical.

"Prosecutorial discretion" refers to a decision by a government employee or attorney or the immigration agency (as opposed to a judge) to abstain from enforcing the immigration laws against a person or group of persons. In the immigration context, the decision to exercise prosecutorial discretion favorably is pivotal for the individual because such discretion functions as a form of protection from removal, though the immigration "status" conferred is itself tenuous. A prosecutorial discretion grant is also important to an agency seeking to focus its priorities on the "truly dangerous" in order to conserve resources and to recognize that some individuals with exceptional qualities lack a legal way to remain in the United States.

Beginning in late 2010, the Department of Homeland Security (DHS) published a medley of memoranda to outline its civil enforcement "priorities" and also identify the various factors that U.S. Immigration and Customs Enforcement (ICE) employees and attorneys should consider in deciding whether prosecutorial discretion is appropriate. In the wake of stalled congressional reforms and an election year, prosecutorial discretion surfaced as an attractive government tool to deal with noncitizens with strong equities who lack a legal immigration status or eligibility for formal relief by a judge.

Public interest over prosecutorial discretion peaked in June 2012 when President Barack Obama announced a policy termed Deferred Action for Childhood Arrivals, or DACA.[2] DACA is a sort of deferred action that itself is a form of prosecutorial discretion in immigration law. DACA has enabled thousands of young people to work, study, and drive in the United States with dignity and without the constant fear of arrest and possible deportation.[3] Critics labeled the memoranda on prosecutorial discretion and the DACA program in particular as excessive and politically motivated. Whether or not prosecutorial discretion has earned visibility for political reasons, understanding prosecutorial discretion and the important role it plays in U.S. immigration law is essential.

My preoccupation with prosecutorial discretion began when I was a twenty-two-year-old law student at Georgetown University Law Center and then a law clerk for the late Michael Maggio, a prominent immigration lawyer with a small firm in downtown Washington, D.C. As a law clerk and later attorney at Maggio Kattar P.C., I worked on the cases of many worthy individuals who were not eligible for benefits under current immigration law and faced deportation. The stories of my clients and my desire to protect them from harm or deportation, keep their family together, or obtain a visa based on their exceptional talents were overwhelming. My most striking cases involved clients like Roman whose only prayer was prosecutorial discretion. I handled only a few such cases, but they were life changing and both tested my capacity to obtain prosecutorial discretion to protect a deserving person from deportation and highlighted the powerlessness I felt operating inside a broken immigration legal system.

Following the attacks of September 11, 2001, I evolved from a zealous attorney for noncitizens faced with complex issues to a legislative lawyer influencing immigration policy in front of the "political" branches, advocates, and affected communities. Amid the hours spent inside my office drafting comments in response to a new agency rule, analyzing the latest big bill on immigration reform, or facilitating a meeting among the interested stakeholders and government officials, I gradually learned how much political reality shapes progress on immigration. In the decade after 9/11, agency officials and policymakers were loath to use "prosecutorial discretion" or related tools to focus resources on high priorities and instead preferred to enforce the immigration law at all costs. I was conscious of the need to educate the immigration agency about the tool of prosecutorial discretion, and the heavy dose of political will required before the agency would pronounce and implement a policy on such discretion even with this education.

My interest in prosecutorial discretion is also personal. I was the first child born to my parents in the United States. Early in life, I absorbed sharp ideas about equal opportunity and social justice. I am the daughter of immigrant parents who personify the American Dream and instilled the pursuit of excellence in their children; I am also a wife and the mother of two small children born in the United States. My family relationships and opportunities to pursue education and a fulfilling career have created a happiness that I believe every person deserves. Cumulatively, these experiences have confirmed my belief that any person who has aspired to build or sustain a productive life in the United States must be protected or at least measured by the government before an immigration charge is brought or executed against him or her.

I am grateful to have the opportunity to produce a book that is essential to the discourse on immigration law and policy—the first to comprehensively describe the history, theory, and application of prosecutorial discretion in the immigration arena. This book examines how prosecutorial discretion interacts with the resource constraints of the agencies and the humanitarian circumstances faced by immigrants who lack a legal way to reside in the United States. Ultimately, I advocate for a bolder standard on prosecutorial discretion, greater mechanisms for accountability when such standards are ignored, improved transparency about the cases involving prosecutorial discretion, and recognition of "deferred action" in the law as a formal benefit. As this book goes to print, the administration expects to announce a prosecutorial discretion policy that could in fact align with or enhance the ideas proposed in chapter 8.

This book is divided into eight chapters. Chapter 1 offers a necessary introduction to the structure of the immigration process and a short history of the overhaul of the immigration agencies following 9/11. This chapter not only provides a background to the jargon that permeates the chapters that follow but also illustrates why prosecutorial discretion matters and how it fits into the overall immigration framework.

Chapter 2 provides details on a famous case involving prosecutorial discretion, the deportation case of John Lennon and the efforts undertaken by his attorney, Leon Wildes, to encourage the immigration agency to publish its policies about prosecutorial discretion. The Lennon case is significant because it triggered the publication of the immigration agency's first guidance on "deferred action," a form of prosecutorial discretion that has been used as a remedy for individuals facing compelling circumstances for many years. This chapter also summarizes early guidance on prosecutorial discretion issued by the immigration agency.

Chapter 3 explains how immigration prosecutorial discretion is related to the criminal system by defining criminal prosecutorial discretion and identifying the points at which prosecutorial discretion is exercised in the modern criminal system and examining how immigration prosecutorial discretion compares to that in the criminal system. The use of prosecutorial discretion in the criminal justice system has been widely cited by the agency and courts to describe immigration prosecutorial discretion.

Chapter 4 provides a detailed analysis of "deferred action," one of the most precious forms of prosecutorial discretion. It also details how victims of domestic violence, sexual assault, and other crimes have long used deferred action as a tool for protection from deportation. Finally, to satisfy the readers who love numbers, this chapter scrutinizes data provided by the immigration agencies regarding deferred action, and underscores how deferred action operates like a formal resolution.

Chapter 5 examines the role of prosecutorial discretion in immigration matters during the Obama administration, summarizes related policies during this time period and the events that led to the DACA program, and considers why prosecutorial discretion was both visible and divisive among legislators, policymakers, and immigration advocates during this time. Finally, this chapter examines how the absence of legislative action on immigration provoked support for prosecutorial discretion.

Chapter 6 examines the immigration agency's historical position against judicial review over immigration prosecutorial discretion decisions and the philosophy behind judicial review. This chapter describes the standards outlined in the Administrative Procedure Act and Immigration and Nationality Act for judicial review of agency actions and applies these standards to a portion of federal circuit court decisions involving administrative discretion. This chapter illustrates that noncitizens possibly do have a right to challenge a prosecutorial discretion decision in federal court.

Chapter 7 considers the degree to which the immigration agency (and DHS in particular) has publicized information about its prosecutorial discretion programs, and my personal journey in seeking statistics and trends in prosecutorial discretion decisions from the agency. As this chapter explains, transparency in prosecutorial discretion matters because it improves the possibility that justice will be served for people whose roots and presence are in the United States and promotes other administrative law values like consistency and acceptability to the public.

Chapter 8 provides recommendations for improving prosecutorial discretion in the immigration system. It also highlights the limitations of prosecutorial discretion in solving immigration problems that demand a legislative solution.

This book is limited to discussing DHS's exercise of prosecutorial discretion and does not discuss other immigration adjudications before DHS or the Executive Office for Immigration Review. Notably, many scholars have written extensively about immigration adjudications in these contexts.[4] While the focus of this book is on the important role of prosecutorial discretion in immigration law, I want to underscore my view that broader legislative reforms are necessary in the immigration system. Prosecutorial discretion itself is a limited benefit that by its nature is aimed at decision making on a case-by-case basis in light of broader policy decisions about where to focus resources. Given the sheer size of the unauthorized immigrant population in the United

States, prosecutorial discretion is not the most effective long-term tool because while broad exercises of prosecutorial discretion have historically enabled large numbers of the unauthorized population to reside in "limbo" inside the United States, the affected individuals have remained vulnerable to future removal and in many cases have been without permission to travel or work or the ability to live with dignity. Moreover, when DHS's exercise of prosecutorial discretion results in the nonenforcement of the immigration laws against millions of unauthorized immigrants, public criticism is sharpened.

Legalizing unauthorized noncitizens working and residing in the United States by creating legal avenues to regularize their status is more effectively achieved through legislative reforms and is a subject of much debate by members of Congress, the administration, mainstream and ethnic media, labor unions, civil rights groups, economists, and faith-based groups, among others.[5] On June 27, 2013, the U.S. Senate passed a "comprehensive" immigration bill that among other provisions would provide a path to citizenship for the majority of the undocumented population, allow noncitizens to work and travel with a new temporary legal immigration status, modernize the family-based and employment-based immigration system by reducing the delays that have separated family members and delayed workers from being employed, and improve protections for children and the mentally disabled. It remains to be seen whether a similar bill will pass in the House, what might happen when the House and Senate go to "conference," and whether a comprehensive immigration reform bill will become law, but prospects are grim as this book goes to print.

Even with broad statutory reforms, the role of immigration prosecutorial discretion is critical to ensuring that individuals with compelling equities and desirable qualities are protected from removal, while individuals who present true dangers to the community or national security are targeted for removal. I hope this book provokes reasoned discussion about where prosecutorial discretion fits within the larger structure of immigration law and policy and why it matters even if Congress passes comprehensive immigration reform.

1

Primer

*Understanding How Prosecutorial Discretion Functions
in the Immigration System*

A principal feature of the removal system is the broad discretion exercised by immigration officials. . . . Federal officials, as an initial matter, must decide whether it makes sense
to pursue removal at all. . . . Discretion in the enforcement
of immigration law embraces immediate human concerns.
Unauthorized workers trying to support their families, for
example, likely pose less danger than alien smugglers or
aliens who commit a serious crime. The equities of an individual case may turn on many factors, including whether the
alien has children born in the United States, long ties to the
community, or a record of distinguished military service.[1]

This chapter introduces the reader to the complexity of the immigration
design and the extent to which prosecutorial discretion operates within
this design. Likewise, it underscores the significant role of DHS in exercising prosecutorial discretion and the fact that all three major agencies,
USCIS, CBP, and ICE, have the authority to use this discretion. Finally,
this chapter provides the reader with an understanding of the largely
humanitarian and economic reasons why prosecutorial discretion exists.
   Prosecutorial discretion has been a main ingredient of the immigration system since its creation. As described in greater detail in chapter
3, many of the principles of immigration prosecutorial discretion are
similar to the criminal context, where "prosecutorial discretion" is more
well known and widely used. A favorable exercise of prosecutorial discretion in immigration law identifies the agency's authority to refrain
from asserting the full scope of the agency's enforcement authority in
a particular case.[2] Historically, this discretion has been applied to both
individuals and groups.[3]

The theory behind immigration prosecutorial discretion is seemingly simple and twofold. The first part of the theory is economic. Specifically, the number of noncitizens who are technically "deportable" under the immigration laws is much larger than the number that the immigration agency can successfully handle with its available resources. Estimates suggest the immigration agency has the resources to remove about four hundred thousand people, or less than 4 percent of the deportable population living in the United States each year.[4] Because the government has limited resources, permitting the agency and its officers to refrain from asserting their maximum enforcement authority against particular populations or individuals is cost-saving and arguably allows the agency to focus its work on the "truly" dangerous.[5]

The second part of the theory of prosecutorial discretion is humanitarian. Some individuals who are in technical violation of the law may nonetheless have redeeming qualities such as a loving marriage, continued valuable employment, U.S. citizen children, faithfulness to prayer, or good moral character. Other candidates for prosecutorial discretion may be the victims of a natural disaster or domestic violence or witnesses in a labor or civil rights dispute and for these reasons should be protected from removal. Allowing such persons to live free from apprehension, detention, or removal is partially a reward for their good deeds or a means of alleviating their hardships and, in part, a judgment by society that some people are morally deserving and more likely to contribute to society in the future. This compassion-based formula is complicated when a person has committed a transgression that feels "criminal" or is labeled as such.

A closely tied and possible third part to the theory is somewhat more political and describes the creation of prosecutorial discretion policy when statutory attempts to fix broken immigration laws stall or fail. While it is important to understand the relationship between legislative reforms and a prosecutorial discretion policy, the relationship should not be overstated. As a general matter, prosecutorial discretion is not typically "caused" by congressional inaction, although immigration advocates become more public and demanding of an administration to provide a temporary solution using prosecutorial discretion in the wake of such inaction.

Current Immigration Structure

The September 11, 2001, attacks launched a national discussion on border security and immigration law. A wide variety of stakeholders, among them congressional members, leaders in the White House and executive branch, individuals who favor restrictions on immigration, and public policy think tanks, linked the 9/11 attacks to failures in the U.S. immigration system, pointing to border vulnerabilities and deficiencies in the Department of State and Immigration and Naturalization Service (INS). What followed was a quick but passionate debate in Congress about overhauling INS, then a component of the Department of Justice (DOJ), and moving many of its units into a new cabinet-level agency.[6]

With the passage of the Homeland Security Act of 2002, INS was abolished by statute and a new "Department of Homeland Security" took charge of immigration services, enforcement, and related policy-making (including visa policies).[7] The "services" unit known as U.S. Citizenship and Immigration Services (USCIS) is responsible for processing affirmative applications and petitions such as lawful permanent residence ("green card"), asylum, and citizenship applications.[8] USCIS houses a citizenship office, legislative affairs office, and asylum and refugee affairs office, among other units.[9]

The immigration "enforcement" unit comprises two divisions: Customs and Border Protection (CBP) and Immigration and Customs Enforcement (ICE).[10] CBP is responsible for border enforcement and in this capacity apprehends, detains, and inspects goods and people at and between ports of entry.[11] ICE is charged with interior enforcement and in this role investigates, arrests, detains, and removes noncitizens.[12] Attorneys within ICE also represent the U.S. government in removal proceedings before the Executive Office for Immigration Review, a unit within DOJ.[13] Throughout this book I refer to DHS, INS, or both as "the agency" or "the immigration agency." If I refer to an agency outside of these two units, such as the DOJ, I identify it by name.

Following the post-9/11 reorganization, the immigration court system was retained within DOJ under a unit called the Executive Office for Immigration Review (EOIR), while the function of issuing visas remained at the State Department.[14] The Homeland Security Act resulted in additional jurisdictional and substantive changes with regard to the care and custody of unaccompanied minor children, oversight of individual and systemic abuses or misconduct by DHS officers and contractors, and related matters.[15] For example, noncitizens in immigration custody who feel they are being verbally or physically abused by an official working at the immigration facility may file a complaint with the DHS Office for Civil Rights and Civil Liberties.

Despite the transfer and merger of core immigration units into DHS, and absence of a particular individual to oversee the arguably competing missions and cultures of the new immigration units, the principle of prosecutorial discretion survived the move.[16] When Congress amended the Immigration and Nationality Act (INA) to reflect the transfer of core immigration functions to a new DHS, it crafted a broad statute to recognize the executive functions of the secretary of homeland security to administer the immigration laws, which as a legal matter has been viewed as including the use of prosecutorial discretion. Section 103(a) of the INA, as amended by the Homeland Security Act, reads:

> The Secretary of Homeland Security shall be charged with the administration and enforcement of this chapter and all other laws relating to the immigration and naturalization of aliens, except insofar as this chapter or such laws relate to the powers, functions, and duties conferred upon the President, Attorney General, the Secretary of State, the officers of the Department of State, or diplomatic or consular officers: *Provided, however*, That determination and ruling by the Attorney General with respect to all questions of law shall be controlling.[17]

This summary of the revised government immigration structure is terse but provides an important foundation for understanding the current locations and individuals who possess the great power of prosecutorial discretion. Specifically, CBP, ICE, and USCIS all have jurisdiction to exercise prosecutorial discretion.[18] Each of these units employ thousands of professionals, some of whom are lawyers and many of whom are "frontline" officers who handle routine functions like inspections at the airport (CBP), detention at a local jail (ICE), and adjudication of an asylum application (USCIS). These officers may exercise prosecutorial discretion in a variety of ways. For example, a USCIS officer may exercise prosecutorial discretion positively by deciding not to issue a Notice to Appear or NTA against a person whom she has also deemed ineligible for a family-based benefit. An ICE officer may exercise favorable prosecutorial discretion by granting a temporary stay of removal, joining in a motion to terminate removal proceedings, granting an order of supervision, or canceling an NTA.[19] A CBP officer may exercise prosecutorial discretion encouragingly by granting "parole" or "entry" to a person who does not have valid travel documents to be "admitted" into the United States. In fact, there are at least twenty-five different forms of prosecutorial discretion.

Prosecutorial discretion may also be exercised during different points in the enforcement process, including, but not limited to, at the point of interrogation, arrest, charging, detention, trial, and removal.[20] In other words, prosecutorial discretion could be exercised positively well before a person is even in the situation of facing an immigration judge or DHS officer for removal. Arguably, prosecutorial discretion is applied to the vast majority of America's undocumented population in this way, meaning that DHS does not attempt to arrest, detain, and "try" every undocumented noncitizen before deciding whether or not to exercise prosecutorial discretion favorably. Such an attempt would be inefficient because it would be costly to the administration and also undermine one of the central theories of immigration prosecutorial discretion. Imagine the case of an undocumented parent who is living in a small American town, working "under the table," and supporting two U.S. citizen children at home and has resided in this town for more than seven years. In this situation, DHS may decide not to arrest or detain this parent as a matter of prosecutorial discretion and instead focus on an undocumented person living in the same town who is operating a "cover" real estate business that is actually being used to traffic young girls for sexual favors. In less clear cases where DHS encounters a noncitizen whom it can technically arrest, it may exercise prosecutorial discretion favorably with a warning such as "I am not going to write this up now, but if your husband does not file papers for you by next month, I am going to send you in front of the judge." The authority to exercise prosecutorial discretion is not limited to "prosecution" in the immigration realm, but can affect a person even after immigration charges have been filed against him or her or when an individual has been fully "prosecuted" and ordered removed from the United States.

To understand the various types of prosecutorial discretion in the immigration system, one must understand the process of deportation. Many noncitizens charged with violating U.S. immigration laws are served with an NTA.[21] Once the NTA is filed by DHS with the immigration court within EOIR, jurisdiction is transferred from DHS to EOIR and removal (deportation) proceedings are commenced.[22] Immigration judges preside over removal proceedings and received 310,455 removal proceedings in fiscal year 2012.[23] As with criminal law, the decision about whether or not to bring charges against a person is a pivotal discretionary point in the process as it determines if the person will face "trial" (called "removal proceedings"). In removal proceedings, most cases revolve not around whether the noncitizen is removable as charged, but rather around whether he or she is eligible for one of the various forms of relief from removal, such as asylum, cancellation of removal, or adjustment of status.[24] Most of these statutory reprieves include a discretionary component and, as a practical matter, enable the immigration judge to deny relief even when a noncitizen meets all of the statutory criteria for such relief.[25] At the removal hearing, an immigration judge will normally sustain or dismiss charges made by ICE against the noncitizen and, if appropriate, determine if a noncitizen is eligible for formal relief from removal.[26]

Once removal proceedings have begun, an immigration judge may also adjudicate certain procedural requests such as motions to administratively close, postpone, dismiss, or reopen a removal proceeding.[27] DHS's decision to commence removal proceedings by filing an NTA with the immigration court represents the defining moment during which prosecutorial discretion can be exercised to save the government the resources of an administrative hearing and possible appeals, and also recognizes the equities and humanitarian situations faced by noncitizens who are ineligible for formal immigration relief.[28] In some cases, *placing a person in removal proceedings* is an act of favorable prosecutorial discretion, especially when the person qualifies for relief that can be granted only by an immigration judge. In these cases, the foundation for such discretion turns less on saving government resources and more on recognizing individual equities that enable the person to seek formal relief.

Noncitizens generally have a right to pursue judicial review following a final order of removal unless one of the statutory exceptions applies. Under the immigration statute, noncitizens are barred from seeking review in immigration cases involving most crimes, many discretionary decisions, and most expedited removal orders.[29] Legal scholars and judges have long examined the role of judicial review in immigration matters, and also criticized the impacts of the "plenary power" doctrine,[30] and statutory deletions of judicial review for certain immigration cases.[31]

The power of DHS to exercise prosecutorial discretion is distinct from the authority of DOJ, which following 9/11 was narrowed considerably but, interestingly, placed the immigration court structure, EOIR, on independent footing for the first time in years. Before DHS was created, EOIR and INS were separate entities within the same agency, DOJ. While the optics of the immigration court's independence might look more like a "win" for judges seeking to exercise formal discretion robustly in appropriate cases before them, the reality is that Congress stripped much of this formal discretion in the 1990s. These statutory changes are detailed in chapter 2, but for the moment it should be noted how this paradigm of less discretionary authority at EOIR and a new DHS to house immigration services and enforcement has caused prosecutorial discretion to take the lead in discretionary powers.[32]

2

The Early Years

The Deportation Case of John Lennon and Evolution of
Immigration Prosecutorial Discretion

If, in our two hundred years of independence, we have in
some measure realized our ideals, it is in large part because
we have always found a place for those committed to the
spirit of liberty and willing to help implement it. Lennon's
four-year battle to remain in our country is testimony to his
faith in this American dream.[1]

While prosecutorial discretion has long existed in the immigration
context, it operated for decades in secrecy and away from the public.
Indeed, few people today are aware of the debt that immigration prosecutorial discretion owes to an unlikely hero—the member of the Beatles
known as John Lennon. Lennon's case brought the issue of immigration prosecutorial discretion into the public eye for the first time. This
chapter details the immigration case of John Lennon and the efforts
undertaken by his attorney, Leon Wildes, to encourage the immigration agency to publish its policies about prosecutorial discretion. This
chapter also chronicles the prosecutorial discretion guidance published
by the agency between 1975 and 2007, following the Lennon case as the
immigration agency began to acknowledge its use more publicly.

Thanks to Lennon, his wife Yoko Ono, and Wildes, the use of prosecutorial discretion in immigration cases went "public."[2] Lennon and
Ono retained immigration lawyer Wildes to represent them in their
immigration case. Wildes was then a young attorney in New York who
had discovered a talent for handling "impossible" cases after successfully winning several cases involving visa denials by consular officers
after lawyers referred them to him.[3] His first encounter with John Lennon was preceded by a phone call from a law school classmate who

represented the Beatles as a lawyer for Apple Records.[4] Wildes did not know who the Beatles were, let alone John Lennon " 'The night I met the Lennons to discuss their legal situation, I went home and told my wife that I had met with Jack Lemmon and Yoko Moto.' His wife instantly—and exuberantly—corrected him."[5]

Lennon and Ono had entered the United States in 1971 as tourists so they could locate Kyoko, Ono's daughter from a previous relationship.[6] While Ono had been awarded custody over Kyoko by a family court, the situation was complicated by the fact that the child's father had kidnapped Kyoko and could not be found.[7] After the Lennons' visas expired, Immigration and Naturalization Service (INS) district director of New York Sol Marks sent them a letter warning of deportation proceedings if they did not leave the United States.[8] Wildes was tasked with extending their stay in the United States. In light of Wildes's longtime relationship with Marks and the compelling reasons behind Lennon and Ono's desire to remain in the country temporarily, Wildes would ordinarily have secured a series of temporary extensions for the couple until Kyoko was found; such extensions were commonly granted at the time. However, the politics of John Lennon's case made multiple extensions of his immigration status a monumental challenge.[9] The political landscape was volatile: Lennon was an opponent of the Vietnam War and attracted young people to his cause, eighteen-year-olds were allowed to vote in the U.S. election for the first time in history, and Richard Nixon faced a difficult reelection campaign and saw Lennon as a source of trouble.[10] This political situation played a dramatic role in Lennon's immigration case, and led Wildes to argue that INS was deporting Lennon for political reasons. Wildes later discovered through correspondence from Senator Strom Thurmond, Sol Marks, and the Senate Internal Security Committee just how well orchestrated was the campaign to deport Lennon.[11]

As a legal strategy, Wildes first pursued visa petitions based on "exceptional ability" in the arts and sciences for Ono and Lennon.[12] Wildes reflects upon preparing these petitions: "We decided to file two outstanding-artist petitions. We started contacting people for reference letters. By simply mentioning my clients' names, I could get through to nearly everyone. Yoko said she would be happy to get letters from Andy Warhol, Clive Barnes, Jasper Johns, Stanley Kubrick, Elia Kazan, Claes

Oldenburg, Leonard Bernstein, and Virgil Thomson. If you're a collector of signatures, you would have valued my files at a million dollars!"[13] After Wildes filed the artist petitions with INS, John Lennon and Yoko Ono were placed in deportation (now removal) proceedings. INS did not adjudicate the visa petitions, and yet Wildes knew that he could not pursue permanent residency or "green cards" in deportation proceedings until INS had first made a decision on the visa petitions.[14] Wildes was able to delay the deportation proceedings pending the decision by INS on the artist petitions, both of which were eventually granted. The next stage of the immigration case was for the immigration judge to preside over Ono and Lennon's green card applications in deportation proceedings. One legal wrinkle in Lennon's case was a British drug conviction for possession of cannabis resin. Lennon believed the drugs had been "planted" by a man who wanted to prove that all musicians were out to trouble the youth of England,[15] but the facts behind Lennon's crime were irrelevant so long as his conviction made him excludable under U.S. immigration law. At the time of Lennon's case, the immigration statute made possession of marijuana or any narcotic a ground for exclusion and therefore a bar to obtaining a green card.[16] Wildes succeeded in securing a national expert to testify at the immigration proceeding that cannabis resin was neither marijuana nor a narcotic (and therefore not a ground for exclusion under the immigration statute), but the immigration judge was unconvinced.[17]

For the first and only time in his thirty-eight-year career with INS in New York, Sol Marks held a press conference to announce his decision in the case of Lennon and Ono.[18] At the press conference, Marks announced that Ono would receive a green card and that Lennon would be denied his green card and deported based on his drug conviction.[19] When Wildes asked about Marks's ability to exercise prosecutorial discretion by not instituting proceedings against Lennon or by placing his case in "nonpriority" or "deferred action" status,[20] Marks stated publicly that INS lacked any such authority.[21] Wildes shared with me that Marks issued the same statement publicly on many occasions, and reversed his position only at the time he was formally deposed under oath.

Wildes appealed the decision on Lennon's deportation order to the Board of Immigration Appeals and lost, and thereafter filed another appeal in the federal court of appeals for the Second Circuit.[22] On October 7, 1975, the court found that Lennon's drug conviction did not render him "excludable" under the immigration statute, and vacated the denial of his green card and his deportation order on these grounds.

As part of his legal strategy, Wildes conducted groundbreaking research on the "nonpriority" program, and eventually filed an application for "nonpriority status" for Lennon. Wildes learned that INS had for many years been granting "nonpriority" status to prevent the deportation of noncitizens with sympathetic cases, but INS had never publicized the practice. INS was forced to provide data on the program. Wildes relied on the data provided by INS and also information in Lennon's file to craft a compelling argument for Lennon's nonpriority status.[23] He also received a letter from the former INS associate commissioner, E. A. Loughran, in which Loughran defines a nonpriority case as "one in which the Service in the exercise of discretion determines that adverse action would be unconscionable because of humanitarian factors."[24] Wildes prepared an affidavit for Lennon's nonpriority case detailing the medical hardships Yoko Ono (now a green card holder) would suffer if Lennon were deported; he describes this today as one of the "nicest pieces of work I did in the Lennon case."[25] Lennon was eventually granted nonpriority status in September 1975, but this status later became unnecessary after he secured a green card.[26]

Thanks to Wildes's work on the Lennon case, INS migrated information about the nonpriority program from the INS "Blue Sheets," which indicated policy that was closed to the public, to the "White Sheets," signifying the newly public nature and the existence of the program.[27] The published guidance was contained in a policy document called "Operations Instructions" and stated: "In every case where the district director determines that adverse action would be unconscionable because of the existence of appealing humanitarian factors, he shall recommend consideration for nonpriority."[28] The Operations Instruction also listed factors that should be considered in determining whether a case should be designated for nonpriority status: "When determining whether a case should be recommended for nonpriority category, consideration should include the following: (1) advanced or tender age; (2) many years' presence in the United States; (3) physical or mental condition requiring care or treatment in the United States; (4) family situation in the United States effect of expulsion; (5) criminal, immoral or subversive activities or affiliations- recent conduct."[29]

Just one year after the INS publicly revealed its Operations Instruction on nonpriority status or what is known today as deferred action, INS General Counsel Sam Bernsen published a legal opinion about the use of prosecutorial discretion in immigration cases.[30] In this opinion, Bernsen identified decisions dating back to 1909 in which the agency had exercised prosecutorial discretion.[31] The Bernsen opinion runs eight pages and is strikingly assertive in describing the broad authority of the immigration agency to exercise prosecutorial discretion, the preference for such discretion to be instituted before removal proceedings begin, and the intolerance for situations where individuals are selectively prosecuted for political or discriminatory reasons.[32]

On the heels of the Lennon case, federal courts were faced with the query about whether deferred action operated as a sort of immigration benefit or if it functioned purely as a management tool for the agency. How this question is answered determines whether individuals must be given adequate notice about the existence of deferred action, the opportunity to challenge a decision on deferred action if they believe they were denied it as an abuse of discretion, and other related safeguards. As discussed in chapter 4, deferred action is distinguishable from the various other tools the agency uses to exercise prosecutorial discretion.

The federal courts' reaction to this issue following the Lennon case deserves some discussion. In Lennon, the Second Circuit held that the nonpriority category was an "informal administrative stay of deportation."[33] In a second case, called *Soon Bok Yoon v. INS*, the Fifth Circuit also concluded that nonpriority status was not a right.[34] Soon Bok was a native and citizen of Korea who entered the United States as a visitor and was later placed in deportation proceedings, at which she alleged the immigration judge should have informed her about every discretionary form of relief available including nonpriority status. The court disagreed and held "nonpriority status is in the nature of a voluntary stay of the agency's mandate pendente lite, issued in large part for the convenience of the INS. . . . The decision to grant or withhold nonpriority status therefore lies within the particular discretion of the INS, and we decline to hold that the agency has no power to create and employ

Fig. 2.1. Former Beatle John Lennon, middle, with his attorney Leon Wildes, left, and wife Yoko Ono, right, in New York. Photo by Bob Gruen, courtesy of Leon Wildes.

such a category for its own administrative convenience without standardizing the category and allowing applications for inclusion in it."[35]

But other courts disagreed. Diverging from the position held by the courts in *Lennon* and *Son Book Yoon*, the Eighth Circuit recognized the Operations Instructions differently. *Vergel v. INS* involved a native and citizen of the Philippines who entered the United States as a visitor with a four-year-old girl, Maria, who was born with cerebral palsy.[36] Vergel had nursed and cared for Maria for nearly four years, until the little girl was strong enough to enter the United States. Vergel continued to care for Maria inside the country long after her visa expired, and Vergel was eventually placed into deportation proceedings and ordered deported. Notably, the Eighth Circuit continued Vergel's case after advising the agency to consider her for deferred action: "It appears that deportation will cause severe hardship not only to Ms. Vergel but also to the invalid child involved. Thus, there is a substantial basis upon which the District Director could place petitioner in a 'deferred action category' allowing her to remain in this country on humanitarian grounds."[37] The Eighth Circuit issued a similar decision in another case involving David, a man from the Philippines who lawfully entered the United States as the spouse of a temporary worker, and was pursued by INS after it discovered that David had unlawfully worked at a convalescent home for eight days at a wage of $2.90 per hour.[38] David was placed into deportation proceedings and granted voluntary departure; following his administrative proceedings, he filed a petition for review in federal court.[39] While the *David* court found no reason to reverse the decision of the INS or BIA on legal grounds, it did question the agency's wisdom in deporting a man like David, who was married to a registered nurse, educated, and a person who had in good faith applied for (but was denied) labor certification.[40] The court reflected upon David's equities: "While waiting for the anticipated certification because of [David's] financial situation and the critical need for such help in the area, he rendered assistance, granted, without the certificate, for a period of eight days. . . . It should be obvious that deportation will cause severe hardship on petitioner and his wife. . . . [W]e think there is presented here a substantial basis upon which a district director could place petitioner in a 'deferred action category' allowing him to remain in this country on humanitarian grounds."[41] In both *Vergel* and *David*, the Eighth Circuit identified humanitarian factors as a foundation upon which INS could grant the petitioners deferred action status.[42] The Eighth Circuit's conclusion is significant to the extent that it contains an implication that applying for nonpriority or deferred action status is a "right."[43]

In 1979 and on the heels of *Vergel* and *David*, the Ninth Circuit in *Nicholas v. INS* held that the Operations Instruction on deferred action operated like a substantive rule.[44] The case itself involved George Bernard Nicholas, a native and citizen of the Bahamas who married a U.S. citizen and was the father of two children, also U.S. citizens.[45] Among other challenges, Nicholas alleged that the INS district director's verbal denial of his request for nonpriority status "represented such a departure from established patterns as to constitute a reversible abuse of discretion."[46] The court concluded that the Operations Instruction on deferred action constituted a substantive benefit, noting, "Delay in deportation is expressly the remedy provided by the Instruction. It is the precise advantage to be gained by seeking non-priority status. Clearly, the Instruction, in this way, confers a substantive benefit upon the alien, rather than setting up an administrative convenience."[47] Turning to the language of the Operations Instruction, the court in *Nicholas* focused on the "shall" and concluded: "(1) The sole basis for granting relief is the presence of humanitarian factors; (2) The Instruction is directive in nature; and (3) The effect of such relief upon a deportation order is to defer it indefinitely. . . . It is obvious that this procedure exists out of consideration for the convenience of the petitioner, and not that of the INS. In this aspect, it far more closely resembles a substantive provision for relief than an internal procedural guideline."[48]

INS was conscious about the courtroom battle over what to call the Operations Instructions and why it mattered. In the agency's view, resolution came when it reworded the prelude of the Operations Instruction to read, "A Service Director may, in his or her discretion recommend, deferral of (removal) action, an act of administrative choice to give some cases lower priority and in no way an entitlement in appropriate cases."[49] By recasting the Operations Instruction as a measure of pure administrative convenience, the agency sought to minimize potential litigations and may have even avoided a Supreme Court decision to resolve the circuit conflict.[50] Had the Operations Instruction stayed on the books with the word "shall" and given the fact that at least one court found that the Instruction operated as a sort of immigration benefit, it is possible that the Supreme Court would have attempted to decide the question so that every federal circuit court could treat judicial challenges similarly.

In 1996, the Operations Instructions were moved into a new publication titled "Standard Operating Procedures."[51] The Operations Instructions were eventually rescinded in 1997 through a memorandum issued by former INS Acting Executive Associate Commissioner Paul Virtue.[52] Titled "Cancellation of Operations Instructions," the memo identified a series of Operations Instructions that were rescinded as a consequence of the 1996 immigration laws.[53] Virtue recalls that, in canceling the Operations Instructions, there was no intention by the agency to eliminate deferred action relief.[54] Rather, the purpose of canceling the rule was "housekeeping"—there was an internal effort to take the Operations Instructions and place them into policy manuals such as the Standard Operating Procedures manual.[55]

After the Operations Instruction on deferred action was removed, the factors outlined in the Instruction for "deferred action" continued to be utilized by agency officials. As described in one leading treatise on immigration law and procedure, "[w]hile the deferred action program is still an internal administrative arrangement, with no provision for an application or participation by the alien, it is appropriate for the alien or the alien's counsel to call to the attention of the district director the circumstances of a particular case, with appropriate documentation, and to request that consideration be given to placing it in deferred action status."[56] The treatise's inclusion of the description and process for applying deferred action further underscores the agency's recognition of deferred action even after the Operations Instructions were formally rescinded.

The 1996 Immigration Laws and Prosecutorial Discretion

Legislative amendments to the Immigration and Nationality Act in 1996 heightened the need for renewed guidance on prosecutorial discretion.[57] For example, the 1996 immigration laws mandated detention for "arriving aliens," including asylum seekers, and removed the authority for immigration judges to decide if arriving aliens should be released on bond.[58] The laws also expanded the categories of people who could be mandatorily detained without a bond hearing,[59] and expanded the list of activities that could be classified as an "aggravated felonies." This new definition was to be applied retroactively.[60] In addition, the 1996 immigration laws meaningfully limited individual review in a federal court by enforcing statutory bars to review on certain noncitizens with criminal histories or with discretionary denials, among others.[61]

Imagine the scenario of Mark, a lawful permanent resident who is now an adult who graduated from a U.S. high school and college, married a U.S. citizen, and works full-time in a professional job to support his family. For Mark, a bar fight fifteen years ago resulting in an assault conviction can result in mandatory detention and deportation without any consideration by an immigration judge for the equities in his case. The 1996 laws left many people like Mark without any chance to apply for relief or a second chance from a judge. The literature criticizing the 1996 immigration laws, and its consequences, is plentiful.[62] The harshness of the 1996 laws caused increased pressure to grant prosecutorial discretion.

With the backdrop of the 1996 laws came a flurry of debate and correspondence among members of Congress, the attorney general, and INS about the role of prosecutorial discretion in immigration law. In a letter dated November 4, 1999, twenty-eight members of Congress urged the agency to issue guidelines on prosecutorial discretion in recognition of the impact of the 1996 immigration laws in sympathetic cases:

> [C]ases of apparent extreme hardship have caused concern. Some cases may involve removal proceedings against legal permanent residents who came to the United States when they were very young, and many years ago committed a single crime at the lower end of the "aggravated felony" spectrum but have been law-abiding ever since, obtained and held jobs and remained self-sufficient, and started families in the United States. Although they did not become United States citizens, immediate family members are citizens. There has been widespread agreement that some deportations were unfair and resulted in unjustifiable hardship. If the facts substantiate the presentations that have been made to us, we must ask why the INS pursued removal in such cases when so many other more serious cases existed.[63]

This letter was cosigned by both Republican and Democratic members of the House, including a few architects of the 1996 laws.[64]

In a response to the congressional letter, Assistant Attorney General Robert Raben wrote to Massachusetts Congressman Barney Frank, advising him about INS's long-standing use of prosecutorial discretion in immigration law, and describing pending INS guidance about the situations in which prosecutorial discretion should be exercised.[65] Raben's letter underscored the inadequacy of prosecutorial tool as a magic wand for solving all of the problems in the congressional letter outlined above: "Guidelines on prosecutorial discretion—no matter how comprehensive or how carefully implemented—remain an inadequate substitute for the more thorough evidentiary processes previously available under the INA, wherein the experienced immigration judge could review evidence and elicit testimony. . . . I urge you to reject the notion that prosecutorial discretion, even wisely exercised, can provide an adequate substitute for sound administrative adjudication."[66]

Amid these events came a written memorandum from Owen ("Bo") Cooper, the INS general counsel, to former INS Commissioner Doris Meissner.[67] The purpose of the Cooper memo was to enable INS to study the use of prosecutorial discretion and provide a legal foundation for any guidance on prosecutorial discretion produced by INS in the future.[68] The memo itself reads like a short lesson plan, describing the principle, purpose, and limitations of prosecutorial discretion, and also identifying criminal law jurisprudence as a leading source.[69] The Cooper memo explains that while immigration officers are not "prosecutors" in the literal sense, they nevertheless enjoy broad prosecutorial authority over enforcement decisions.[70]

On November 7, 2000, her last day as INS commissioner, Doris Meissner issued what became the gold standard for the next decade on the role of prosecutorial discretion in immigration law.[71] The Meissner prosecutorial discretion memo has been repeatedly cited by attorneys and government agencies alike, and in many ways superseded the legendary Operations Instruction on deferred action. The Meissner Memo is more expansive than the Operations Instruction to the extent that it identifies a range of possible actions (one of which is deferred action) to which prosecutorial discretion may apply.[72]

The Meissner Memo details the cost-related arguments behind prosecutorial discretion. "Like all law enforcement agencies, the INS has finite resources, and it is not possible to investigate and prosecute all immigration violations . . . the Service must make decisions about how best to expend its resources. Managers should plan and design operations to maximize the likelihood that serious offenders will be identified."[73] The Meissner Memo recognizes the humanitarian theory behind prosecutorial discretion by listing a number of largely compassionate factors that may be considered by an immigration officer in deciding whether to exercise prosecutorial discretion.[74] While the list at first appears long and unachievable, the memo suggests that an individual need not show every factor to qualify and clarifies that an officer's decision must be based on a "totality of the circumstances, not on any one factor considered in isolation."[75] The nonexhaustive list of factors identified by Meissner includes (1) immigration status, (2) length of residence in the United States, (3) criminal history, (4) humanitarian concerns, (5) immigration history, (6) likelihood of ultimately removing the alien, (7) likelihood of achieving enforcement goal by other means, (8) whether the alien is eligible or is likely to become eligible for other relief, (9) effect of action on future admissibility, (10) current or past cooperation with law enforcement authorities, (11) honorable U.S. military service, (12) community attention, and (13) resources available to the INS.[76] Notably, the Meissner Memo instructs that discretionary judgments must be made astutely and consistently. Specifically, Meissner notes, "Service officers are not only authorized by law but expected to exercise discretion in a judicious manner at all stages of the enforcement process—from planning investigations to enforcing final orders—subject to their chains of command and to the particular responsibilities and authority applicable to their specific position."[77] This language suggests that, while the act of discretion is an option, exercising such discretion in a fair and evenhanded manner is an obligation. This is similar to the obligatory language of the former Operations Instruction on deferred action.[78]

The foregoing summary explains how the 1996 laws affected individual lives and hampered the ability for immigration judges to exercise discretion as part of their adjudicatory function. It further shows how Congress and the public placed pressure on the administration to exercise prosecutorial discretion in the wake of these laws. Another part of this story relates to the politics that lay between congressional reaction to the 1996 laws and disappointment about how the administration was handling the harsh consequences of these laws. This hostility is well encapsulated in the transcript of an immigration symposium held in the fall of 2000 at which scholars, impacted families, Barney Frank, and Bo Cooper were all featured.[79] At the time of the symposium, INS was working on its prosecutorial discretion memo and Representative Frank had introduced legislation to mitigate some human consequences of the 1996 immigration laws. With regard to the congressional criticism INS received about prosecutorial discretion, Cooper recounted how "many in Congress began to say, 'Well, it's not that the laws are too harsh, it's just that the INS is not making careful decisions about how to enforce them." In many respects that seems to me to be an inadequate argument."[80] He went on to outline what he anticipated to be then forthcoming guidance by INS. Meanwhile, Congressman Frank was not shy in calling the Illegal Immigration Reform and Immigrant Responsibility Act of 1996 (IIRAIRA) "a lousy law" and blaming the lack of movement to ameliorate the 1996 laws on a lack of political will, and critiquing INS for not taking a stronger position on prosecutorial discretion after the laws were immediately passed. Congressman Frank remarked, "INS was terrified and they did go scoop up some people whom no rational person would have scooped up, because they were afraid of Congress yelling at them. Next the horror stories came out."[81] Congressman Frank also pointed out the hypocrisy displayed by select members of Congress who led the efforts to pass IIRAIRA, urged INS to not use any discretion immediately after the bill was passed, and then turned around to criticize INS for failing to exercise discretion when the horror stories grew.[82]

The narrative surrounding the 1996 law is revealing because it illustrates the conflict between congressional acts that eliminate discretion and the desire of the executive branch to use prosecutorial discretion to cure some of the most heart-wrenching cases. Looking back, some scholars view the 1996 laws not as an elimination of discretion altogether but as a transfer of administrative discretion from the immigration judges to lower agency officials.[83] As noted by immigration scholars Adam Cox and Cristina Rodríguez: "[I]t is important to see that the Executive still has de facto delegated authority to grant relief from removal on a case-by-case basis. The Executive simply exercises this authority through its prosecutorial discretion, rather than by evaluating eligibility pursuant to a statutory framework at the end of removal proceedings. In fact, because these decisions are no longer guided by the INA's statutory framework for discretionary relief, the changes may actually have increased the Executive's authority."[84] Cox and Rodríguez conclude that the scope of DHS's prosecutorial discretion may have increased as a consequence of the 1996 immigration laws. If their conclusion is accurate, exercising prosecutorial discretion in a manner that incorporates the various humanitarian-related factors once utilized in the formal adjudicatory context is even more important than before.

Guidance on Prosecutorial Discretion Following the Demise of INS and Creation of DHS

Prosecutorial discretion policy remained strong following the demise of INS and creation of DHS. Notably, Congress confirmed in INA § 103(a) the authority of the DHS secretary to "perform such other acts as he deems necessary for carrying out his authority under the provisions of this chapter."[85] Likewise, guidance documents by USCIS, CBP, and ICE affirmed the concept of prosecutorial discretion, and in some cases referenced or explicitly reaffirmed the Meissner Memo. For example, in January 2003, former USCIS Executive Associate Commissioner Johnny N. Williams issued a memo to regional directors and service center directors discussing their authority to refrain from bringing charges against noncitizens who are both a beneficiary of immigration benefits and potentially in violation of immigration laws as a consequence of their unlawful presence.[86] The Williams memo reminds officers that they may refrain from charging such noncitizens and calculate humanitarian and other factors when making such a determination.[87] The Williams memo also instructs officers to review the Meissner Memo.[88] And in September 2003, former USCIS Associate Director for Operations William Yates issued a memo to regional directors and service center directors discussing their authority to issue charging documents to noncitizens, and reminding directors that every decision must be made in accordance with the Meissner Memo.[89]

In October 2005, former ICE Principal Legal Advisor William J. Howard issued a memo to all OPLA (Office of the Principal Legal Advisor) chief counsel highlighting the limited resources of ICE and stating that "the universe of opportunities to exercise prosecutorial discretion is large."[90] The Howard Memo lists scenarios for which an officer's "favorable" exercise of discretion would be appropriate, and discourages the issuance of charging papers to noncitizens with viable family petitions or green card applications and those with sympathetic factors, such as citizen children with serious medical conditions.[91] The Howard Memo also offers possible scenarios for deferring enforcement even after charging papers have been filed.[92] Overall, the Howard Memo preserves many of the same principles found earlier in guidance on prosecutorial discretion and concludes, "Prosecutorial discretion is a very significant tool . . . to deal with the difficult, complex and contradictory provisions of the immigration laws and cases involving human suffering and hardship."[93]

Prosecutorial discretion guidance continued to flow from the immigration agency. In December 2006 former DRO (Detention Removal Office) Director John P. Torres published a memorandum instructing select ICE senior leaders about the exercise of prosecutorial discretion when making detention or custody decisions about noncitizens with severe medical conditions. This guidance outlines the following examples of medical conditions that should "trigger or flag" a need for prosecutorial discretion: advanced chronic conditions with complications, advanced immunological diseases, pending/recent organ transplants, end-stage/terminal illness, and extreme mental illness, among other examples.[94]

In November 2007, former ICE Assistant Secretary Julie Myers issued guidance to all field office directors and special agents in charge, advising them to release apprehended nursing mothers absent national security or public safety or other investigative interests.[95] This guidance was issued following a heart-gripping story involving a twenty-six-year-old nursing mother from Honduras who was arrested by the immigration agency and separated from her U.S.-born baby for several days while in detention.[96] In the memo, Myers reminds officers that "[t]he process for making discretionary decisions is outlined in the [Meissner Memo]. . . . Field agents and officers are not only authorized by law to exercise discretion within the authority of the agency but are expected to do so in a judicious manner at all stages of the enforcement process."[97] The agency continued to publish guidance on prosecutorial discretion during the Obama administration, the bulk of which is analyzed in chapter 5.

Categorical Grants of Prosecutorial Discretion

Historically, prosecutorial discretion has been exercised not only on an individualized basis but also categorically.[98] One of the most widely used categorical forms of prosecutorial discretion is "Extended Voluntary Departure," which allows classes of people to stay in the United States after a humanitarian crisis, such as a civil war or political upheaval in a home country. Extended Voluntary Departure (EVD) has been granted to nationals from at least fifteen countries.[99] EVD was first utilized in 1960, when INS granted it to certain Cubans,[100] and it was subsequently used to protect nationals from Chile, Cambodia, Vietnam, Ethiopia, Uganda, and other countries.[101] Today, the program is called "Deferred Enforcement Departure" (DED) and is managed by the secretary of homeland security. According to the Congressional Research Service:

> The discretionary procedures of DED and EVD continue to be used to provide relief the Administration feels is appropriate, and the executive branch's position is that all blanket relief decisions require a balance of judgment regarding foreign policy, humanitarian, and immigration concerns. Unlike [Temporary Protected Status], aliens who benefit from EVD or DED do not necessarily register for the status with USCIS, but they trigger the protection when they are identified for deportation. If, however, they wish to be employed in the United States, they must apply for a work authorization from USCIS.[102]

Immigration "parole" is another discretionary form of relief that has been applied to special groups. Parole has been part of the immigration system for decades and was later codified in the Immigration Nationality Act beginning in 1952.[103] When one is "paroled" into the United States, one is permitted into the United States but is treated as if one is "at the border" for immigration purposes.[104] Parole is currently defined in the INA as follows:

> The Attorney General may . . . in his discretion parole into the United States temporarily under such conditions as he may prescribe only on a case-by-case basis for urgent humanitarian reasons or significant public benefit any alien applying for admission to the United States, but such parole of such alien shall not be regarded as an admission of the alien and when the purposes of such parole shall, in the opinion of the Attorney General, have been served the alien shall forthwith return or be returned to the custody from which he was paroled and thereafter his case shall continue to be dealt with in the same manner as that of any other applicant for admission to the United States.[105]

Although parole has a statutory basis, the agency's decision to grant parole to groups of people and also to individuals for humanitarian reasons is viewed as prosecutorial discretion. One notable and early example of such parole took place in 1956, when President Dwight D. Eisenhower invoked the parole power to permit thousands of Hungarian "Freedom Fighters" to enter the United States.[106] President John F. Kennedy also exercised prosecutorial discretion through parole to allow thousands of Cubans and Hong Kong Chinese to enter the country.[107] The need for parole during this time was elevated by the fact that the INA set a relatively small quota for these nationals from these countries (e.g., there were far more Chinese nationals in need of refuge than the maximum number allotted by statute) and the absence of a statutory vehicle for admitting refugees. In fact, both President Eisenhower and President Kennedy pushed Congress to enact refugee-related legislation during their tenures, but in the wake of congressional inaction and the immediate needs faced by the populations targeted for parole, they continued to exercise prosecutorial discretion. As expressed by President Eisenhower at a press conference in January 1957, "The Attorney General will continue to parole Hungarian refugees into the United States until such time as the Congress acts. This action, in my opinion, is clearly in the national interest. It will prevent a stoppage of the flow of these refugees and will permit the United States to continue, along with the other free nations of the world, to do its full share in providing a haven for these victims of oppression."[108]

Indeed, the United States has a long history of using parole to protect refugees. In 1980, Congress passed the Refugee Act, creating for the first time a statutory framework for refugees. Specifically, the Refugee Act created an "asylum" process by which persons in the United States could apply for protection and an overseas "refugee" process by which persons outside the United States could apply for similar protection.[109] The Refugee Act has been codified in the INA and defines a refugee as someone who has suffered persecution or has a well-founded fear of persecution because of political opinion, nationality, group membership, race, or religion.[110] Even after the Refugee Act was enacted by Congress, parole has continued to operate as a powerful tool for permitting individuals and groups to enter and remain in the United States in a tenuous status.[111] As described by immigration scholar and former

INS General Counsel David Martin, "[P]arole has also been used in hundreds of thousands of cases each year to allow arriving aliens at the port of entry to establish physical presence in the United States, without detention and without the initiation of immigration-court proceedings, even though these persons appear to be inadmissible. Humanitarian parole, granted so that an inadmissible person may receive urgent medical care, for instance, or may be united with a dying relative, furnishes one important example."[112]

"Parole in Place" (PIP) is another form of parole that allows people who have not been formally admitted into the United States to become eligible to apply for a green card or "adjust status" while in the United States. While PIP is a remedy that is adjudicated individually on a case-by-case basis, the DHS has used it to protect certain classes, such as family members of U.S. military personnel. The benefits of PIP can be appreciated only with the understanding that typically people who have not been formally admitted or paroled into the United States are ineligible to obtain visas or adjust status (receive a green card) in the United States and instead must travel to a consulate overseas to receive their visa.[113] The negative consequence that comes from such travel under the current paradigm is striking because a departure from the United States triggers inadmissibility bars that run from three years to forever. As described by military and immigration expert Margaret Stock, "PIP attempts to avoid the separation of military families by allowing some family members—in meritorious cases only—to adjust their status inside the United States and thereby avoid a lengthy separation that might harm the military member's morale, readiness, or ability to complete his or her service."[114] On November 15, 2013, USCIS issued policy to clarify the use of PIP for immediate family members of U.S. military members. The memorandum states in part, "The fact that the individual is a spouse, child or parent of an Active Duty member of the U.S. Armed Forces, an individual in the Selected Reserve of the Ready Reserve or an individual who previously served in the U.S. Armed Forces or the Selected Reserve of the Ready Reserve, however, ordinarily weighs heavily in favor of parole in place. Absent a criminal conviction or other serious adverse factors, parole in place would generally be an appropriate exercise of discretion for such an individual."[115] In reality, PIP is a form of prosecutorial discretion.

"Deferred action" serves as a final illustration of how the agency has used different forms of prosecutorial discretion to protect classes of people. In 2005, the USCIS announced deferred action for select foreign academic students affected by Hurricane Katrina.[116] In 2009, USCIS announced deferred action for the widows of U.S. citizens for two years.[117] In an official press release, DHS Secretary Napolitano is quoted as saying: "Granting deferred action to the widows and widowers of U.S. citizens who otherwise would have been denied the right to remain in the United States allows these individuals and their children an opportunity to stay in the country that has become their home while their legal status is resolved."[118] Deferred action has also been used to protect victims of domestic abuse, sexual assault, and other crimes.[119] The Violence Against Women Act (VAWA) was enacted by Congress in 1994 and amended three times to include statutory remedies for abused spouses, parents, and children; victims of crimes and domestic abuse; and victims of human trafficking.[120]

The historical use of prosecutorial discretion as a tool for protecting victims and others is detailed in chapter 4. The examples identified in this chapter are not exhaustive but demonstrate how the immigration agency has long used prosecutorial discretion and the authority under the INA to protect classes of people temporarily. They also illustrate how prosecutorial discretion has been used to shelter classes of people, many of whom were later protected by legislation.

3

Lessons from Criminal Law

How Immigration Prosecutorial Discretion Compares to the Criminal System

The prosecutor has more control over life, liberty, and reputation than any other person in America. His discretion is tremendous. He can have citizens investigated and, if he is that kind of person, he can have this done to the tune of public statements and veiled or unveiled intimations. Or the prosecutor may choose a more subtle course and simply have a citizen's friends interviewed. The prosecutor can order arrests, present cases to the grand jury in secret session, and on the basis of his one-sided presentation of the facts, can cause the citizen to be indicted and held for trial. He may dismiss the case before trial, in which case the defense never has a chance to be heard. Or he may go on with a public trial. If he obtains a conviction, the prosecutor can still make recommendations as to sentence, as to whether the prisoner should get probation or a suspended sentence, and after he is put away, as to whether he is a fit subject for parole. While the prosecutor at his best is one of the most beneficent forces in our society, when he acts from malice or other base motives, he is one of the worst.[1]

Prosecutors have long been viewed as powerful officials who exercise tremendous discretion over ordinary person's life. While scholars have written extensively about the history, power, and abuse of criminal prosecutorial discretion,[2] the literature has been less engaged with how prosecutorial discretion in the criminal system is related to such discretion in the immigration law system, a mostly civil system that possesses criminal-law-like features such as interrogation, arrest, detention, the filing of charges, and in some cases a hearing before an immigration judge with the government serving as the "prosecutor" and the non-citizen serving as the "defendant." This chapter explains how immigration prosecutorial discretion relates to the criminal system by (1) describing the history of the American criminal prosecutor, (2) defining criminal prosecutorial discretion and identifying the discretion points at which prosecutorial discretion is exercised in the modern criminal system, and (3) examining how the immigration prosecutorial discretion compares to the criminal system.

The History of Prosecutions in America

The public understands modern criminal prosecution as something the government does, but this has not always been the case. When prosecutions were first developed in England and through the middle of the nineteenth century, they operated as a type of legal matter initiated by private parties as opposed to the government.[3] Just as a person today can initiate a civil case, hundreds of years ago victims could initiate criminal prosecutions. Criminal prosecutions were also viewed as a way to limit the power of the Crown.[4] This system was adopted by colonial America, giving complete control of the prosecution to the crime victim.[5] As described by Professor Juan Cardenas, "Before the American Revolution, the crime victim was the key decisionmaker in the criminal justice system. Police departments and public prosecutors' offices did not exist as they are known today. Law enforcement was the general responsibility of the private citizen."[6]

Greater public interest concerns and the chaos involved in victims handling prosecutions challenged the value of private prosecutions.[7] The first public prosecutor was an "attorney general" appointed in Virginia in 1643. In a process modeled after the English system, the attorney general was authorized to initiate prosecutions.[8] Over time, the model of elected public prosecutors emerged, as did a federal prosecution system. The Judiciary Act of 1789 created the first federal Office of the Attorney General and provided for district attorneys, though without a clear configuration or hierarchy.[9] The position of attorney general began as a part-time post filled by one person. The duty of the attorney general was "to prosecute and conduct all suits in the Supreme Court in which the United States shall be concerned, and to give his advice and opinion upon questions of law when required by the President of the United States, or when requested by the heads of any of the departments, touching any matters that may concern their departments."[10] Since 1870, the Department of Justice has housed more than ninety U.S. attorneys who serve as federal prosecutors. In addition, district attorneys in each state prosecute state crimes. In most states, there is one district attorney and several "assistant" district attorneys in each district. Private prosecutors still exist in a limited form, as the government allows a private attorney to perform a prosecutorial function in certain cases.[11]

By the early 1900s, American prosecutors became powerful figures in the criminal law structure.[12] Even though prosecutors were elected and were more visible to the public, prosecutors were not always perceived as benevolent. The unresolved characterization of prosecutors was that they wielded too much power and without any oversight would be able to abuse their discretion or act inconsistently in cases bearing similarly relevant facts. Alongside the growth of prosecutorial power was growth in police power. Police worked side by side with public prosecutors and often exercised a great deal of discretion.

Beginning in the 1920s, "crime commissions" were developed to study the criminal justice system.[13] President Herbert Hoover created one of the most popular crime commissions, the National Commission on Law and Observance and Enforcement (popularly known as the Wickersham Commission, named after the former Attorney General George W. Wickersham). The commission's study was published in fourteen volumes and included topics like the causes of crime, police misconduct, and prosecution. The study identified abuses with police and prosecutorial power and discretion and made practical recommendations to resolve these problems.[14] For example, the Wickersham Commission found that elected prosecuting attorneys failed to improve "checks" on the discretionary decisions of the prosecutor.[15] Furthermore, it identified the plea bargaining stage as an "abuse" of the criminal process and recommended greater oversight at the state level by a "director of public prosecutions."[16] In 1931, the Wickersham Commission wrote, "In every way the prosecutor has more power over the administration of justice than the judges, with much less public appreciation of his power.

We have been jealous of the power of the trial judge, but careless of the continual growth of the power of the prosecuting attorney."[17]

Criminal Prosecutorial Discretion

Today, prosecutorial discretion is a main feature of the criminal justice system and is exercised by prosecutors in various ways. When a prosecutor declines to bring charges or chooses to file lesser charges, he or she is exercising prosecutorial discretion favorably. One of the most important stages is after an arrest, when the prosecutor decides whether to charge a person with committing a crime. This decision is so powerful because a charge may lead to detention, public humiliation, and/or a conviction. The authority for prosecutorial discretion in criminal law can be found in the U.S. Constitution and has further been affirmed by the U.S. Supreme Court,[18] and by the U.S. Attorney's Office.[19] For example, in *U.S. v. Armstrong*, the U.S. Supreme Court held,

> The Attorney General and United States Attorneys retain "broad discretion" to enforce the Nation's criminal laws. *Wayte* v. *United States*, 470 U.S. 598, 607 (1985) (quoting *United States* v. *Goodwin*, 457 U.S. 368, 380, n. 11 (1982)). They have this latitude because they are designated by statute as the President's delegates to help him discharge his constitutional responsibility to "take Care that the Laws be faithfully executed." U.S. Const., Art. II, §3; see 28 U.S.C. §§516, 547. As a result, "[t]he presumption of regularity supports" their prosecutorial decisions and, "in the absence of clear evidence to the contrary, courts presume that they have properly discharged their official duties." *United States* v. *Chemical Foundation, Inc.*, 272 U.S. 1, 14-15 (1926). In the ordinary case, "so long as the prosecutor has probable cause to believe that the accused committed an offense defined by statute, the decision whether or not to prosecute, and what charge to file or bring before a grand jury, generally rests entirely in his discretion." *Bordenkircher* v. *Hayes*, 434 U.S. 357, 364 (1978).[20]

The theory behind criminal prosecutorial discretion is tied to the availability of resources and the public interest. The economic reasons are articulated well by former Attorney General Robert H. Jackson before the Conference of United States Attorneys in 1940: "No prosecutor can even investigate all of the cases in which he receives complaints. If the Department of Justice were to make even a pretense of reaching every probable violation of federal law, ten times its present staff would be inadequate."[21] While some may believe that any person who violates a criminal law should be prosecuted, the growth of criminal statutes over the past century and the preservation of outdated laws mean that the federal government must target some crimes over others. Angela Davis describes how outdated laws such as fornication and adultery and minor infractions like gambling in the context of "placing small bets during a Saturday night poker game in a private home" may warrant a favorable exercise of criminal prosecutorial discretion.[22] The growth in criminal statutes is staggering and sometimes referred to as "overcriminalization." As described by one scholar and former attorney at the Justice Department:

> Today, the fact of the matter is that if someone were to look hard enough, they'd likely discover that we're all criminals, whether we know it or not, and regardless of whether we have any intent to violate the law. . . . Today, however, buried within the 51 titles of the United States Code and the far more voluminous Code of Federal Regulations, there are approximately 4,500 statutes and another 300,000 (or more) implementing regulations with potential criminal penalties for violations. There are so many criminal laws and regulations, in fact, that nobody really knows how many there are, with scores more being created every year. And that's just federal offenses. Every new law gives prosecutors more power, and many of these laws, unfortunately, contribute to the overcriminalization problem.[23]

While prosecutorial discretion is not viewed as the only solution to the "overcriminalization problem," it is an important tool used in the criminal justice system to place Saturday night poker players on the back burner. More ambitious solutions that have been proposed include revamping the criminal laws and modifying the sentencing guidelines.

The "public interest" basis for criminal prosecutorial discretion considers the impact of prosecution on the community and victim and factors such as the victim's age and health. The relationship between the crime victim and the prosecutor is a complex one. Angela Davis advises that while prosecutors should support crime victims, their obligations are broader and may potentially conflict with the victims' goals.[24] Beyond the impact on a victim are factors that relate to the personal circumstances of the accused. For example, the U.S. Attorneys' Manual identifies "extreme youth, advanced age [and] mental and physical impairment" of the accused as potential reasons to decline prosecution.[25] Likewise, Attorney General Eric Holder noted recently that many of the "low-level" drug offenders placed into the criminal justice system are of a young age. The "public interest" prong of criminal prosecutorial discretion also considers the political reasons that influence prosecutorial decisions. For example, Senator David Vitter (R-LA) confessed to committing the crime of paying a prostitute to have sex with him. He was never arrested or charged, nor did he spend one day in jail.[26] By exercising prosecutorial discretion to not arrest Senator Vitter, the federal government avoided embarrassment and what some would argue advanced the public interest so that he could carry out his job as a senator.

As introduced in the preceding paragraph, the government has published guidelines on prosecutorial discretion in the U.S. Attorneys' Manual (USAM). The USAM is an internal guide of policy and procedures for U.S. attorneys, assistant attorneys, and district attorneys responsible for prosecuting violations of federal law. Within the chapter pertaining to the criminal division is a section on the principles of the prosecution function. These guidelines were first published in 1980 by Attorney General Benjamin R. Civiletti and remain the seminal memoranda.[27] In determining whether prosecution should be declined because no substantial federal interest would be served by prosecution, the USAM advises attorneys to consider the seven following factors: (1) federal law enforcement priorities, (2) nature and seriousness of the offense, (3) deterrent effect of prosecution, (4) sufficiency of evidence to prove culpability, (5) prior criminal history, (6) willingness to cooperate with investigations or prosecutions of others, and (7) potential sentence and related consequences if convicted.[28] The USAM notes that not every factor needs to be complied with for a federal prosecutor to decline prosecution.[29] Many of these factors are personal and based on the facts of each individual case, such as the age of the victim and the history of the accused. The very first factor, federal enforcement priorities, rests more specifically on the economic reasons for targeting limited law enforcement resources on the most serious offenders or the government's highest priorities. In discussing the nature and seriousness of an offense, the USAM notes that "[i]t is important that limited federal resources not be wasted in prosecuting inconsequential cases or cases in which the violation is only technical."[30] Illustrating this point, Davis comments on the discretion used by police each time someone commits a traffic violation.[31] She argues that few people would be supportive of a law that required police officers to issue tickets to every person who committed a traffic violation.[32] Davis also argues that the populace would assent that officers should preserve their limited resources for "more serious offenses" rather than traffic-related ones.[33]

Discretionary Points and Standards for Criminal Prosecutorial Discretion

Now that the legal authority for and theory of criminal prosecutorial discretion has been established, this section addresses at what point or points in the criminal process prosecutorial discretion can be exercised. There are many stages of the criminal process. Police play a significant role in the criminal process and carry significant discretion because they have the power to arrest, search, seize, and interrogate. The police officer may also play a role in recommending charges to the prosecutor or making a decision about whether to investigate alleged misconduct. Kenneth Culp Davis, emphasizing the central role of police in the justice process, estimated that about half of the discretionary decisions made by criminal justice agencies are made by police: "The police are among the most important policymakers of our entire society. And they make far more discretionary determinations in individual cases than any other class of administrators; I know of no close second."[34]

Once an arrest has been made, most of the discretionary power shifts to the prosecutor. The Vera Institute for Justice has identified the following "discretion points" at which a prosecutor may exercise discretion:

- Initial screening—when a reviewing prosecutor decides whether to accept a case for prosecution and, in some instances, how to charge the offense

- Pretrial release or bail procedure—whether a defendant is held in detention while the case is pending and whether a defendant is offered or awarded bail
- Dismissal—whether a case or charge is dismissed at any point after initial screening by a prosecutor or a judge
- Charge reduction—whether the seriousness or the number of charges are reduced at any point after initial screening
- Guilty plea—whether a defendant pleads guilty
- Sentencing—whether a prosecutor's decisions affect the length or nature of a convicted person's penalty[35]

This section describes some of the stages outlined above: charging, grand jury, plea bargains, and sentencing. Following an arrest, the prosecutor decides *whether* to file charges and *what kind* of charges to file. The prosecutor must decide whether to decline prosecution in a case where he or she has evidence that amounts to probable cause that a crime has been committed. If a prosecutor decides not to bring charges, the person is free to go.[36] Several scholars have identified the charging stage as the most powerful: "The decision to charge an individual with a crime is the most important function exercised by a prosecutor. No government official can affect a greater influence over a citizen than the prosecutor who charges that citizen with a crime. In many cases, the prosecutor determines the fate of those accused at least in those cases where the evidence or statutory sentencing structure renders the ultimate outcome of the prosecution largely a foregone conclusion."[37] Even in an instance where the criminal charge is filed but no conviction results, the impact this filing can have on the accused is life changing and results in "potential pretrial incarceration, loss of employment, embarrassment and loss of reputation, the financial cost of a criminal defense, and the emotional stress and anxiety incident to awaiting a final disposition of the charges,"[38] in addition to potential contact with immigration authorities. A decision to charge can also result in prolonged incarceration because many convictions carry "mandatory minimum" sentences.

The USAM guidelines advise government attorneys to give this calculation careful thought. The American Bar Association's Criminal Justice Section has also issued guidelines focused on charging decisions:

(b) The prosecutor is not obliged to present all charges which the evidence might support. *The prosecutor may in some circumstances and for good cause consistent with the public interest decline to prosecute, notwithstanding that sufficient evidence may exist which would support a conviction.* Illustrative of the factors which the prosecutor may properly consider in exercising his or her discretion are:

  (i) the prosecutor's reasonable doubt that the accused is in fact guilty;

 (ii) the extent of the harm caused by the offense;

(iii) the disproportion of the authorized punishment in relation to the particular offense or the offender;

(iv) possible improper motives of a complainant;

 (v) reluctance of the victim to testify;

(vi) cooperation of the accused in the apprehension or conviction of others; and

(vii) availability and likelihood of prosecution by another jurisdiction.[39]

While the standards published by the USAM and ABA are clear about the responsibility prosecutors have in deciding whether and what kind of charges to bring against the accused, critics have argued that the USAM is not a legally binding document and that as a practical matter "there is generally not a lot of soul searching about the decision to prosecute."[40] As illustrated by criminal law scholar Abbe Smith, "Unfortunately, I have witnessed many examples of this behavior, too many to count. In one memorable case, there was compelling evidence that the perpetrator of a serious physical assault was someone other than the defendant. The case carried a mandatory minimum prison sentence of five years. After discussions with the prosecutor—and disclosure of more defense evidence than is usually my practice—the prosecutor conceded that he did not know who committed the crime. However, instead of declining to prosecute, he shrugged and said 'Let's just let the jury decide.'"[41]

Another relevant point in the criminal process is the grand jury stage. Importantly, federal courts must utilize the grand jury process for felony charges. This means that the citizen-jurors together must decide whether there is probable cause that a defendant committed a felony offense.[42] While it may appear that the grand jury serves as an important "check" to the arresting police officer and prosecutor in determining whether a formal charge should be made, some scholars argue that it is the prosecutor who actually controls the grand jury process.[43] As described by Professor Kevin Washburn, "Despite the widespread belief that the grand jury's role is to serve as a check on the prosecutor, the grand jury is widely criticized for failing to live up to this role. The criticism is reflected in a cliché common among academics and practitioners that a skillful prosecutor could convince a grand jury to indict 'a ham sandwich.'"[44]

A further point in the criminal process is plea bargaining. Prosecutors wield a great amount of power during the plea bargaining phase,[45] which Angela Davis describes as a negotiation between the prosecutor and the defense attorney in which the former may offer to dismiss a charge in exchange for a defendant's plea to another charge.[46] Plea bargaining allows the prosecutor to succeed in cases without the expense of trial and further provides the prosecutor with an opportunity to prevail in some of the cases that he or she may have lost had they gone to trial.[47] Davis offers the example of someone who is guilty of breaking into a home and stealing several items—in this case, a prosecutor might consider the charge of first degree burglary, second degree burglary, or destruction of property and then offer second degree burglary in exchange for the prosecutor's agreement to dismiss all other charges.[48] It is striking that 97 percent of federal convictions and 94 percent of state convictions are the result of guilty pleas as opposed to trials.[49] Justice Anthony Kennedy remarked, "The reality is that plea bargains have become so central to the administration of the criminal justice system that defense counsel have responsibilities . . . that must be met to render the adequate assistance of counsel that the Sixth Amendment requires."[50] The plea bargaining stage of the criminal process is so critical that the Supreme Court has extended the Sixth Amendment right to counsel to the plea bargaining process.[51]

A final point in the criminal system worthy of discussion is sentencing and imprisonment. America has the largest incarceration system in the world, with a nationwide cost of eighty billion dollars in 2010 alone.[52] In many instances, prosecutors have the power to determine whether a person is incarcerated and for how long because of the increased prevalence of "mandatory minimum" sentencing laws. Mandatory minimum sentencing laws impose a specified time frame for imprisoning a defendant based on his or her offense. In this way, the charge and the plea are directly tied to the time a defendant spends incarcerated. As confirmed by Angela Davis, "Because almost all criminal defendants ultimately plead guilty, the charging and plea bargaining decision of prosecutors essentially predetermine the outcome in criminal cases with mandatory minimums."[53] In a speech to the American Bar Association House of Delegates in August 2013, Attorney General Holder rolled out a plan for reforming the criminal justice system and underscored the special role of prosecutorial discretion.[54] Specifically, Holder said that he would instruct federal prosecutors to exercise their prosecutorial discretion by charging defendants in certain low-level drug cases in such a way that would avoid a mandatory minimum prison sentence.[55] As described by Holder, "federal prosecutors cannot—and should not—bring every case or charge every defendant who stands accused of violating federal law. Some issues are best handled at the state or local level."[56]

Criminal Prosecutorial Discretion: Theory versus Practice

Having described the procedural points at which a prosecutor may exercise discretion and the various legal authorities and documents that have been produced in support of criminal prosecutorial discretion, one remaining question is whether the theory of criminal prosecutorial discretion is properly tied to the practice of how it is exercised. A study by the Vera Institute of Justice provides an "on the ground" view of the factors that drive prosecutors to exercise discretion. Titled "The Anatomy of Discretion," the Vera study is the culmination of a two-year research project using data from two large county prosecutors' offices and authored by Bruce Frederick and Don Stemen.[57] The Vera study demonstrates the following findings about the factors that influence prosecutorial discretion decisions:

- Strength of the evidence was the primary consideration at screening and continued to influence decisions throughout the processing of a case.

- Seriousness of the offense influenced decisions throughout the processing of a case.
- Victims' characteristics, circumstances, wishes, and willingness to testify affected prosecutors' evaluations of both the strength of the evidence and the merits of the case.
- In deciding whether or how a case should proceed, prosecutors were guided by an overarching philosophy of doing justice—or "the right thing." Most participants described justice as a balance between the community's public safety concerns and the imperative to treat defendants fairly. In considering that balance, survey respondents overwhelmingly considered fair treatment to be more important than public protection.
- In addition to considering legal factors, prosecutors evaluated defendants' personal characteristics and circumstances to judge whether the potential consequences of case dispositions would be fair.[58]

Though the findings by Vera suggest that prosecutors are driven by the "public interest" broadly speaking, the study goes on to identify less grand factors that influence prosecutorial decision making. As described by Frederick and Stemen: "While prosecutorial discretion is generally seen as very broad and unconstrained, prosecutors often rely on a small number of salient case characteristics, and their decision making is further constrained by several contextual factors. These contextual constraints—rules, resources, and relationships—sometimes trump evaluations of the strength of the evidence, the seriousness of the offense, and the defendant's criminal history. Chief prosecutors and criminal justice policy makers should be alert to the potential for contextual factors to influence and possibly distort the exercise of prosecutorial discretion."[59]

A 1987 study by Celesta Albonetti examined the factors influencing a government attorney's decision to prosecute.[60] Relying on a data set of 6,014 felony cases generated by the Superior Court of Washington, D.C., Albonetti concludes that a government attorney's decision to prosecute is driven by a "generalized preference for avoiding uncertainty, many of which may be related to the public interest."[61] Albonetti found that the existence of exculpatory evidence, the presence of corroborative or physical evidence, the number of witnesses, the presence of the defendant at the scene of the crime, stranger (as opposed to intimate or acquaintance) relationships, the innocence and credibility of the witness, and the use of a weapon were statistically significant to the probability of prosecution.[62]

Professional advancement also influences prosecutorial decision making. As described by Albonetti: "There is little ambiguity within the prosecutor's office regarding the criteria of successful movement within the profession and the hierarchically arranged office. Prosecutorial success, which is defined in terms of achieving a favorable ratio of convictions to acquittals, is crucial to a prosecutor's prestige, upward mobility within the office, and entrance into the political arena."[63] Similarly, Abbe Smith argues that prosecutors are under pressure to "win" because it affects both external benefits and internal ones, like salary and promotion.[64] It is difficult to understand how a prosecutor can be expected to refrain from filing charges against an individual who is accused of committing a crime when his or her salary is driven by the number of convictions he or she secures. On the other hand, the ABA's Criminal Justice Section advises, "In making the decision to prosecute, the prosecutor should give no weight to the personal or political advantages or disadvantages which might be involved or to a desire to enhance his or her record of convictions."[65]

Beyond the scope of this book are the racial disparities that exist in the criminal justice system at the time of charging and throughout the criminal process. Many scholars have described these disparities in rich detail.[66] Attorney General Holder also addressed racial disparities in sentencing when he remarked, "We also must confront the reality that, once they're in that system, people of color often face harsher punishments than their peers." He said, "This isn't just unacceptable—it is shameful."[67]

How Immigration Prosecutorial Discretion Compares to the Criminal System

As in the criminal justice system, prosecutorial discretion is a main feature of the immigration system and may be exercised in a variety of ways. While an immigration officer is not a prosecutor in the technical sense, he or she has the same authority to decline to bring charges or choose which charges to bring against a noncitizen. The legal authority for immigration prosecutorial discretion has been affirmed by the U.S. Supreme Court.[68] For example, in *Arizona v. United States*, the Supreme Court noted: "A principal feature of the removal system is the broad discretion exercised by immigration officials. Federal officials, as an initial matter, must decide whether it makes sense to pursue removal at all."[69]

The authority for immigration prosecutorial discretion has also been confirmed by the Immigration and Naturalization Service (INS).[70] While INS memoranda have been well summarized in chapter 2, they are revisited in this chapter for the single purpose of examining how they demonstrate that INS guidelines resemble criminal prosecutorial discretion policies. For example, the 1976 legal opinion by Sam Bernsen noted the following analogy between criminal law and administrative law when discussing prosecutorial discretion: "Prosecutorial discretion refers to the power of a law enforcement official to decide whether or not to commence or proceed with action against a possible law violator. This power is not restricted to those termed prosecutors, but is also exercised by others with law enforcement functions such as police and officials of various administrative agencies. The power extends to both civil and criminal cases."[71] Similarly, former general counsel for the INS Bo Cooper drafted a memorandum on prosecutorial discretion noting that "[t]he idea that prosecutor is vested with broad discretion in deciding when to prosecute, and when not to prosecute, is firmly entrenched in American law."[72]

The immigration agency has relied heavily on the guidelines established for criminal prosecutorial discretion to formulate its thinking on immigration prosecutorial discretion.[73] For example, the INS memorandum from Doris Meissner on prosecutorial discretion relies on the U.S. Department of Justice's USAM's Principles of Federal Prosecution.[74] At that time, INS was part of the Department of Justice. As explained earlier, the Principles of Federal Prosecution governing the conduct of U.S. attorneys use the concept of a "substantial Federal interest."[75] Based on this principle, the Meissner Memo states that "[a]s a general matter, INS officers may decline to prosecute a legally sufficient immigration case if the Federal immigration enforcement interest that would be served by prosecution is not substantial."[76] Referencing the USAM, the Meissner Memo lists some beneficial aspects of such principles: "Such principles provide convenient reference points for the process of making prosecutorial decisions; facilitate the task of training new officers in the discharge of their duties; contribute to more effective management of the Government's limited prosecutorial resources by promoting greater consistency among the prosecutorial activities of different offices and between their activities and the INS' law enforcement priorities; make possible better coordination of investigative and prosecutorial activity by enhancing the understanding between the investigative and prosecutorial components; and inform the public of the careful process by which prosecutorial decisions are made."[77] As in the criminal system, the theory behind immigration prosecutorial discretion is tied to economic and humanitarian reasons. The guidelines identified in chapter 2 and the more recent documents outlined in chapter 5 all premise immigration prosecutorial discretion on resources and compassion.[78] As an example, one memorandum published by U.S. Immigration and Customs Enforcement in June 2011 lists both adverse factors such as the seriousness of the crime, the person's criminal history, and whether a person is a repeat offender, as well as humanitarian factors like a close family relationship, presence in the United States since childhood, and a serious medical condition, which the officer should consider in determining whether or not prosecutorial discretion should be exercised favorably.

The concept of "overcriminalization" also exists in the immigration system. The Immigration and Nationality Act includes a robust list of infractions that constitute violations of immigration law, and subject a person to deportation. These offenses can be captured in roughly five different categories: health, moral-related, immigration control, crime-related, and national security-related. The spectrum of conduct leading to deportation is broad and striking and includes failure to file a change of address card within ten days of moving,[79] crimes involving "moral turpitude,"[80] being present in the United States without admission,[81] and the accrual of more than 180 days of "unlawful presence."[82]

As with criminal law, there are several discretionary points in the immigration enforcement process. These discretionary points include:

- Interrogation
- Apprehension or arrest
- Civil detention

- Charging and charge reduction
- Proceedings
- Removal from the United States

Many of the discretionary points resemble similar points in the criminal law system but have a different legal standard because the immigration system is considered "civil." Immigration officers enjoy broad authority to interrogate and arrest noncitizens for suspected immigration violations.[83] Moreover, there are several different kinds of officers who have authority to prepare, issue, and file charges against a noncitizen who is alleged to be in violation of the immigration laws.[84] In this way, the act of bringing charges against a noncitizen is not limited to the "prosecutor" but instead can be performed by a variety of officers at different ranks and units within the Department of Homeland Security (DHS). Specifically, U.S. Citizenship and Immigration Services (USCIS), U.S. Customs and Border Protection (CBP), and U.S. Immigration and Customs Enforcement (ICE) all have authority to issue or file a Notice to Appear (NTA).[85] The NTA is the immigration agency's charging document that informs the noncitizen about his or her status and the charges from the government's point of view.[86] Within the charging process officers may take (or refrain from taking) a wide variety of actions in their discretion. Many of the recent memoranda from DHS name these discretionary points as a valid exercise of prosecutorial discretion. To illustrate, the Morton Memo states that prosecutorial discretion applies to "deciding to issue, reissue, serve, file, or cancel a Notice to Appear (NTA)."[87]

To demonstrate how discretion might be exercised during the charging process, an ICE officer can arrest a young woman because he believes she is present in the United States without permission but, upon discovering that she is the mother of a U.S. citizen, choose not to issue an NTA. Even after an NTA issued, this same officer or another employee in DHS can choose not to file the NTA with an immigration court as a matter of prosecutorial discretion. Even after the NTA is filed with the immigration court, an ICE trial attorney can move the immigration court to dismiss removal proceedings by removing the NTA and case from the court's docket.

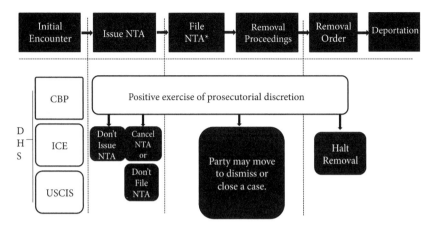

* Jurisdiction vests with EOIR

Fig. 3.1. Prosecutorial discretion in the Notice to Appear (NTA) process.[88]

Data published by the Office of Immigration Statistics within DHS reveal that DHS issued 233,958 NTAs in 2012, and that 140,707 of these NTAs were issued by ICE. Notably, 40,049 of these NTAs were issued by USCIS; 31,506 were issued by the Border Patrol within CBP; and 21,696 were issued by the Office of Field Operations, a unit within CBP.[89] Likewise, data obtained through the Freedom of Information Act indicate that CBP issued 64,000 NTAs during fiscal years 2011 and 2012 to nationals from over forty-five countries.[90] Likewise, data from USCIS reveal that more than 97,000 NTAs were issued during fiscal years 2011 and 2012.[91] While these data sets lack information about whether the NTAs issued were actually *filed* with the immigration court or instead *cancelled* as a matter of prosecutorial discretion, they do uncover significant evidence about the breadth of players at DHS who use their discretionary authority to issue charging documents to noncitizens. During the charging process, ICE attorneys may review an NTA before it is filed with the immigration court or upon review decide that it is not prudent to file an NTA, but this is not a required practice or rule in immigration law.[92]

The charging process is complex not only because a range of players can and do exercise discretion to issue, cancel, or file charges against a noncitizen, but also because some noncitizens may actually *benefit* from an NTA and removal proceedings. To understand this phenomenon, it should be explained that the Immigration and Nationality Act stipulates that categories of people such as those "arriving" at a border without documents or false documents, non–green card holders who are already inside the United States but who have been convicted of an aggravated felony, and those inside the United States who entered without authorization after receiving an order of removal on their record may be deported (removed) by an immigration officer *without* an NTA or formal removal proceeding before an immigration judge.[93] If an NTA is filed, the person therefore benefits from having a formal hearing at which he or she may challenge removability or apply for relief before an immigration judge. Another class who may benefit from an NTA are those who are eligible for reprieve from removal before the immigration judge through a form of relief known as cancellation of removal.[94] Whereas DHS and the Department of Justice both enjoy jurisdiction to grant various forms of relief from removal such as a green card, waivers of inadmissibility, and asylum, cancellation of removal is a special remedy that is available only in removal proceedings. Take the example of Maria, an undocumented mother of three young U.S. citizen children, one of whom suffers from autism. Maria has resided in the United States for twenty years, acted as the primary caregiver for her children, worked at a private school teaching Spanish, and received no negative mark on her record beyond the charge of being present without admission. Maria might qualify for cancellation of removal but cannot apply for this relief unless she is before an immigration judge as a result of having been placed into removal proceedings.

The immigration system does not have the same kind of plea bargaining stage as exists in the criminal system, but there is a type of plea bargaining called "voluntary departure."[95] Voluntary departure is a term of art that enables DHS to permit a noncitizen to depart the United States at his or her own expense in lieu of a removal order.[96] Another form of plea bargaining is a "stipulated order of removal,"[97] which means that the noncitizen "agrees" to a formal order of removal, makes no application for relief, and waives his or her right to a hearing before the immigration judge. While the stipulated order of removal program offers more efficiency to the government by avoiding a separate immigration court proceeding and related government resources, scholars have questioned the program's disproportionate impact on individuals who are incarcerated and without counsel.[98]

Notably, there is no "sentencing" stage in the immigration system. Thus, unlike criminal prosecutors, DHS officials do not exercise prosecutorial discretion during a separate sentencing phase. Moreover, if a noncitizen is "convicted" of a violation of immigration law and ineligible for any kind of relief such as cancellation of removal, asylum, or a green card, then he or she is ordered deported or detained until the appropriate travel documents are secured to deport him or her. Throughout the immigration process, a noncitizen may be detained by DHS.[99] There is no "statute of limitations" on immigration charges, nor is there a limit on how long a noncitizen may be detained pending a charge of removal, during the removal process, or even after a removal order is granted.[100] Thus, DHS wields enormous prosecutorial power to decide whether a noncitizen should be detained in a prison, placed on "alternatives" to detention, released on a bond, or freed on his or her own recognizance. Many of the guidance documents published by the immigration agency recognize the role prosecutorial discretion plays during the detention process.[101] One more recent prosecutorial discretion memo from ICE formalizes a policy that supports keeping parents who are targeted by ICE out of detention.[102] According to one agency official, "[The memo] clarifies that ICE officers and agents may, on a case-by-case basis, utilize alternatives to detention for these individuals particularly when the detention of a non-criminal alien would result in a child being left without an appropriate parental caregiver."[103] While the statute, regulations, and agency all support prosecutorial discretion during the detention process, Congress has identified categories of people who "shall" be detained during the enforcement process. For example, noncitizens who have been convicted of an aggravated felony "shall be detained" by the immigration agency pending removal.[104] Meanwhile, the U.S. Supreme Court and several federal courts have concluded that prolonged detention without a bond hearing violates due process.[105] Moreover, DHS retains discretion even when statutes use the word "shall."

As this section shows, the points at which prosecutorial discretion may be exercised during the immigration enforcement process bear many of the same features as in criminal law. Even where the stages themselves are labeled differently, such as plea bargaining in criminal law and voluntary departure in immigration law, the concepts are quite similar. In fact, immigration advocates drew a sharp parallel between the mandatory minimum system in criminal law and the mandatory detention provisions of the immigration statute following the August 2013 announcement by Attorney General Holder of reforms to the criminal justice process.[106] As described by one immigration lawyer: "Our current immigration deportation laws similarly impose mandatory minimum sentences for thousands of immigrants convicted of 'aggravated felonies'—a category so broad as to encompass crimes that are neither aggravated nor felonies. These mandatory minimum sentences under immigration law, however, do not result in jail sentences, but rather permanent exile from the U.S., for even long term lawful permanent residents and refugees, without any consideration of the individual circumstances of their cases."[107] The lawyer was thus analogizing the harsh consequences in the criminal system of mandatory minimums to the mandatory banishment that occurs in the immigration system and arguing for the necessity of discretion.

While there are similarities between the function of prosecutorial discretion in the criminal justice system and that in the immigration system, the following section elucidates two sharp differences. First, immigration is a civil system and is driven by a set of rules and procedures that are quite different from those in the criminal system. At the early stages, DHS employees function as police officers and prosecutors in many cases as they hold the power to interrogate, arrest, and bring charges against a noncitizen. Even without charges, a noncitizen can be held in custody for forty-eight hours or longer "in the event of an emergency or other extraordinary circumstance in which case a determination will be made within an additional reasonable period of time."[108] The practical consequence is that a noncitizen can be arrested and held in a prison by ICE without any charges so long as the agency has identified an "extraordinary circumstance" under which to hold him or her. Similarly, neither the regulations nor the Immigration and Nationality Act contain a time frame for serving an arrested noncitizen with charging papers or filing such papers with the immigration court. In many cases, immigration defendants will not see a judge until the Notice to Appear is filed with the court and the initial hearing is scheduled. Furthermore, unlike the criminal system, the civil immigration system does not include a grand jury to secure felony charges. Finally, people who are charged with violations of immigration law are not guaranteed a right to court-appointed counsel.[109] As illustrated sharply in a study analyzing immigration counsel in New York City, "A noncitizen arrested for jumping a subway turnstile of course has a constitutional right to have counsel appointed to her in the criminal proceedings she will face, notwithstanding the fact that it is unlikely she will spend more than a day in jail. If, however, the resulting conviction triggers removal proceedings, where that same noncitizen can face months of detention and permanent exile from her family, her home, and her livelihood, she is all too often forced to navigate the labyrinthine world of immigration law on her own, without the aid of counsel."[110] The practical effect is that many noncitizens or unlawfully held U.S. citizens navigate the removal process and related court hearings without counsel.[111] Finally, a noncitizen who has not yet been admitted into the United States bears the burden of proving that he or she is "clearly and beyond doubt" entitled to be admitted.[112] Likewise, the government need only prove deportability only by "clear and convincing evidence" for a person who has been deemed "admitted" into the United States and charged with deportability.[113] Insofar as prosecutorial discretion in immigration law comes with far fewer safeguards than are present in the criminal law context, oversight and accountability of prosecutorial discretion making in immigration matters are vital.

The influences and incentives that drive immigration prosecutorial discretion are also somewhat distinct from those that typically influence criminal prosecutorial discretion. Notably, immigration-related violations do not typically involve a "victim," so factors such as the credibility of the victim and the desire by the victim to move forward in a case do not play a major role (if any) in immigration cases. Immigration prosecutors have traditionally lacked incentives to forgo prosecution or remove an existing immigration case from the removal docket as a matter of prosecutorial discretion,[114] but the winds may be blowing in a different direction with the advent of guidance documents and more public fanfare by DHS about the importance of exercise prosecutorial discretion in appropriate cases.

4

Deferred Action

Examining the Jewel (or a Precious Form) of
Prosecutorial Discretion

In 2001, my Nanay (Mom in Tagalog) made the hardest
decision of her life—leaving my two siblings and me behind
in the Philippines in order to seek a better life and future
for our family. While we came a few months later, my parents had to work long hours just to put food on the table and
provide for our family's needs. Only after I'd grown up did I
realize they worked so hard not only to take care of our family but because they had something to prove to themselves,
to society, and to their children. They worked tirelessly to
prove that they made the right choice for our family to move
to the U.S. It was in the 10th grade that I found out about
my undocumented status. I really didn't know what it meant
and what to feel at that moment. When I started to apply for
college, I realized my life was limited by not having a social
security number but I was determined to succeed no matter what. In 2011, I graduated from University of California–
Irvine with a Bachelors of Art in Political Science. . . . My
dream is to draw on the law and public policy as a tool to
organize my community and I hope to earn a joint degree
in Law and a master's in Urban Planning in the near future.
Someday, I hope to pursue a PhD to teach Asian American
Studies in a University and empower my community.[1]

This quote comes from Anthony, an undocumented Filipino living in
the United States who qualified for a special form of deferred action
called Deferred Action for Childhood Arrivals (DACA).[2] This chapter educates the reader about deferred action, one of the most precious

forms of prosecutorial discretion. The chapter is broken into three parts: (1) general history of deferred action in immigration law, (2) the use of deferred action to protect victims of domestic violence, sexual assault, and other crimes, and (3) an analysis of deferred action data retrieved from INS and DHS. As recounted earlier, deferred action is one of many forms of prosecutorial discretion.[3]

General Background about Deferred Action

Deferred action is a form of prosecutorial discretion that has been applied to both individuals and groups meeting qualifying criteria. In theory, any person who is in the United States without authorization may apply for deferred action before any component of DHS. The outcome when someone applies for deferred action cases is perhaps obvious. An application may be granted, denied, or unresolved.[4] What is less obvious is the lack of transparency behind grants of deferred action. Historically, the agency took action on a deferred action request but applicants were not necessarily informed about the outcome. Part of the transparency problem is that deferred action—like most forms of prosecutorial discretion—has operated without a formal application form or a fee, or any process for appealing a denial. Once a person is granted deferred action, he or she is eligible to apply for work authorization and remain in the United States in legal limbo. The regulations that govern immigration law contain a specific subsection for individuals applying for work authorization on the basis of deferred action.[5] Yet if a person is denied deferred action, there is no mechanism for review by DHS or the immigration court.[6] Despite the fact that grave consequences attach when an agency fails to grant a person deferred action status, nonattorney DHS employees can make decisions about deferred action.[7] Nevertheless, deferred action is an important form of protection for undocumented persons seeking a way to live and work with dignity in the United States without the fear of deportation.

As described in chapter 2, INS first used the term "deferred action" in an internal memorandum known as an "Operations Instruction." The agency had dozens of Operations Instructions to guide INS officers on a variety of issues, but the Operations Instructions themselves lacked the force of law. Among the list of "instructions" was a specific one pertaining to the use of deferred action.[8] While the instruction was eventually removed from the public policy roster at INS, deferred action remained as internal guidance in the Meissner Memo issued in 2000. The Meissner Memo (named after former INS Commissioner Doris Meissner) read: "The 'favorable exercise of prosecutorial discretion' means a discretionary decision not to assert the full scope of the INS' enforcement authority as permitted under the law. Such decisions will take different forms, depending on the status of a particular matter, but include decisions such as not issuing an NTA . . . not detaining an alien placed in proceedings . . . and approving deferred action."[9]

The agency continued to recognize deferred action after INS was abolished and DHS was created in 2003. In 2005, Congress passed legislation containing specific language mentioning deferred action. This legislation described the necessary forms of evidence required to prove lawful status in the United States for a person seeking a federally recognized state driver's license or identification card, and stated that someone with "deferred action" could be granted such a license.[10] Likewise, DHS published several policy documents identifying "deferred action" as a form of prosecutorial discretion to use in compelling cases. For example, a memorandum issued by former ICE head John Morton identifies "granting deferred action" as an option for DHS to consider in deciding immigration cases.[11] Likewise, USCIS contemplated the use of deferred action in a draft memorandum prepared for the director in the midst of a congressional stalemate over immigration reform. The draft memo contemplated that USCIS could increase its use of deferred action and possibly require a separate fee or appropriation. Deferred action has also been identified as a remedy to keep immigrants who are the spouses, parents, and children of military members together.[12]

Deferred action programs can also be created for special groups of people. At least three public deferred action programs to benefit classes of individuals have been unleashed in the past decade. On November 25, 2005, USCIS announced certain foreign students and eligible dependents impacted by Hurricane Katrina would be granted deferred action. The USCIS press release stated the following: "A grant of deferred action in this context means that, during the period that the grant of deferred action remains in effect, DHS will not seek the removal of the foreign academic student or his or her qualified dependents based upon the fact that the failure to maintain status is directly due to Hurricane Katrina. Deferred action requests are decided on a case-by-case basis."[13] On June 9, 2009, former DHS Secretary Janet Napolitano granted deferred action to certain widows and widowers of U.S. citizens (and their minor children) residing inside the United States.[14] The most well-known deferred action program to benefit a specific class of persons came just before the 2012 presidential election. On June 15, 2012, the Department of Homeland Security issued a memorandum in tandem with an announcement from the White House that allows certain young people living in the United States without legal status to receive prosecutorial discretion in the form of "deferred action."[15] Formally known as Deferred Action for Childhood Arrivals, the program allows individuals to apply affirmatively for deferred action.[16] DACA is a form of deferred action permitting mostly students inside the United States who entered as children to apply for deferred action. The DACA program extends to individuals currently in school, those who have graduated or obtained the equivalent of a high school diploma, and certain honorably discharged veterans of the U.S. military. DACA-eligible individuals can apply as long as they are in good standing and can produce the necessary documentation required by USCIS. DHS used traditional humanitarian factors to outline the parameters for the DACA program, such as tender age and longtime residence in the United States. The program was intended to address a humanitarian crisis that formed after Congress entered a stalemate over a legislative solution to protect young people pursuing higher education and those in the U.S. military from deportation by creating a legal channel that would have allowed them to remain in the United States with a formal legal status and the opportunity to eventually apply for a green card. The politics of this congressional demise is explained in more detail in chapter 5.

Prosecutorial Discretion for Victims of Crime and Abuse

> Hernandez, who is originally from Mexico, said she lived with her abuser in the United States for ten years and was married for five. She said she never knew her husband was a citizen until the threats to report her to ICE became more frequent. He would say to her, she said, that ICE would deport her but they wouldn't deport him. Hernandez's two children

are also American citizens, by birth, which means Hernandez could be separated from them, if deported. Her fear of being deported to Mexico was overwhelming, she said. "Mucho terror" (so much terror), she said, explaining her panic. Except for work, Hernandez said, she was isolated. She had three jobs to support her husband and her two children—a daughter, who is now 9 years old and a son, 21. "I felt very controlled," she said, speaking through a translator. "I was a slave to work. I had to pay to maintain him and the kids and he would just take the checks from me. It was a very difficult situation, but it was normal for me. I didn't know how to leave," she said. Hernandez reported her husband to the police approximately ten times, she said, but each time the abuse got progressively worse. . . . "My biggest fear was being deported." But Hernandez said she got the courage to work through her fear because silence has always been her worse enemy. . . . "Sometimes I ask myself where I would be if I didn't have that visa. It's difficult to think about that. I'm very fortunate," she said. "My life has changed completely."[17]

This woman lived in fear in the United States until she was granted lawful status as a holder of a U visa, a status she gained by reporting abuse to law enforcement and assisting in the prosecution of her abuser. At one stage of the process, she was the beneficiary of prosecutorial discretion—rather than deporting her for being unlawfully present, U.S. government officials chose to refrain from enforcing the law against her and instead pursue her abuser. The use of prosecutorial discretion to protect victims of domestic violence, human trafficking, and other crimes enjoys a rich history. Formal protections by Congress highlight the unique barriers that noncitizens face when living in an abusive relationship with a spouse, partner, or trafficker. Common forms of prosecutorial discretion used by the agency to protect such victims include deferred action, parole, stays of removal, and dismissal or closure of a case that has already been docketed for removal.[18] While this chapter focuses largely on deferred action, I tuck in a description about general remedies available for victims.

As a first step to protecting immigrant victims, Congress in 1994 passed the Violence Against Women Act (VAWA), a portion of which was codified in the INA.[19] If an applicant for this kind of petition, commonly called a "VAWA Self-Petition," is approved for VAWA status before a visa is immediately available, he or she is given "deferred action" status.[20] The VAWA Self-Petition can protect (1) a spouse who is abused by a citizen or lawful permanent resident spouse, (2) children who are abused by a citizen or lawful permanent resident parent, and (3) parents who are abused by their adult citizen children.[21] While a person in a relationship with a qualifying U.S. citizen or green card holder might ordinarily rely upon his or her spouse, parent, or child to "sponsor" the person for a visa under the family immigration system, VAWA allows the victim to petition on his or her own behalf without having to rely on the abuser.

The significant role of deferred action in the VAWA Self-Petition context evolved through a series of memoranda published by INS.[22] In one memorandum, dated May 6, 1997, INS Acting Associate Commissioner Paul Virtue outlined the impact of the 1996 laws on a victim's ability to obtain protection and employment by highlighting deferred action as the preferred remedy for appropriate cases.[23] The memo instructed one USCIS unit, the Vermont Service Center (VSC), to place approved VAWA self-petitioners in deferred action status whenever possible so that immigrant victims could have the opportunity to work. Specifically, the Virtue Memo states, "[F]or many individuals, the ability to work is necessary in order to save the funds necessary to pay for the adjustment application and the penalty fee. As it has already been determined that these aliens face extreme hardship if returned to the home country and as removal of battered aliens is not an INS priority, the exercise of discretion to place these cases in deferred action status will almost always be appropriate."[24] On December 22, 1998, INS Acting Associate Commissioner for Programs Michael Cronin issued a more in-depth memorandum declaring the VSC responsible for deferred action determinations for all self-petitioners, their derivative children, and the children of abusive U.S. citizens and lawful permanent residents regardless of when and where their petitions were approved.[25] The Cronin Memo set time frames for the duration of deferred action status in individual cases. Data from USCIS through April 2003 indicate that 30 of the 499 deferred action cases processed listed VAWA as a reason for why deferred action was granted. The USCIS references the May 6, 1997, Virtue Memo in evaluating whether a victim would suffer "extreme hardship" upon deportation.[26] In one case that was granted, the paperwork from USCIS indicated "subject believes that if she returns to Mexico her husband will follow her and attempt to kill her."[27] VAWA was reauthorized by Congress in 2000, 2005, and March 2013.[28] Between 1997 and 2011, 98,192 VAWA petitions were filed with USCIS, of which 75 percent were approved.[29] One can predict that a good number of individuals approved for VAWA received "deferred action" as part of the process.

In addition to the VAWA Self-Petition, Congress later created the U and T visas to protect victims of crimes and human trafficking.[30] These visas were created by Congress in 2000 as part of the Victims of Trafficking and Violence Protection Act (VTVPA), which implemented several different protections for immigrant victims.[31] The U visa is intended to protect victims of crime, like the Hernandez.[32] Specifically, the U Visa is available to victims of a qualifying crime who suffer from substantial physical or mental abuse, have information about the criminal activity, and are being or are likely to be helpful to the investigation and/or prosecution of that qualifying criminal activity.[33] The INA caps the U visa category at ten thousand visas per year.[34] In contrast, the T visa extends to victims who have suffered severe forms of trafficking. To receive a T visa, victims must be physically present in the United States and meet specific requirements, like showing they have been a victim of trafficking as defined under the law and would suffer extreme hardship involving severe and unusual harm if removed from the United States.[35] The T visa category is capped at five thousand per year.[36] Although Congress created the U and T visa categories in 2000, INS and later DHS took several years to publish the agency regulations necessary to issue the visas. In the absence of regulations, the agency relied on prosecutorial discretion as a Band-Aid solution for qualifying victims. On August 30, 2001, Michael Cronin circulated a memo outlining interim procedures to help individuals who would otherwise qualify for a U or T visa.[37] The memo emphasized that these victims "should not be removed from the United States until they have had the opportunity to avail themselves of the [U and T visa]" and further advised "that it is better to err on the side of caution than to remove a possible victim to a country where he or she may be harmed by the trafficker or abuser, or by their associates."[38] The Cronin Memo revealed the agency's support for a wider range of prosecutorial discretion to protect victims of domestic abuse and crimes by identifying parole, deferred action, stays of removal, and motions to terminate or administratively close a case as possible tools.[39]

Two years later and in the absence of regulations on the U visa, DHS issued yet another memorandum to address U visa applications. On October 8, 2003, INS Associate Director of Operations William Yates declared that all U visa applications would be centrally processed at the VSC. The Yates Memo authorized the VSC to determine if an applicant was prima facie eligible for a U visa and to then place the noncitizen in deferred action status if appropriate. In fact, the Yates Memo advised that deferred action was usually appropriate: "By their nature, U nonimmigrant status cases generally possess factors that warrant consideration for deferred action."[40] Less than one year later, Yates issued another guidance document giving the VSC jurisdiction over all U visa cases, including those involving victims in removal proceedings. This policy was meaningful not only because it expanded the authority held by VSC to grant deferred action to victims who were prima facie eligible for a U visa, but also because it marked an agreement between USCIS and ICE whereby ICE would support the termination of a case after the VSC approved it for interim relief in the form of deferred action.[41] While it may seem obvious that ICE and USCIS should work collaboratively on cases in which both share a piece of the jurisdictional pie, the bureaucratic and cultural divide between USCIS and ICE has lingered in ways so that such collaboration has been rare.[42] Moreover, the flurry of guidance about how ICE should treat potential victims who are already in removal proceedings or with a removal order in hand demonstrates both the many enforcement stages in the immigration process where prosecutorial discretion should be considered and the variety of tools DHS employees have to exercise this discretion favorably.

After eight years of interim relief, USCIS finally began issuing U visas in 2008.[43] Today, both the U and T visa categories enjoy a lengthy set of regulations and reams of supplemental documents to guide victims and advocates. Deferred action remains an important protection, especially for individuals who are eligible for a U or T visa in a year when the statutory cap has already been reached. USCIS has stipulated that individuals who are prima facie eligible for a U visa will be added to a waiting list if their petitions exceed the quota.[44] These individuals will be granted deferred action or parole until a U visa becomes available. Likewise, guidance from ICE suggests that U and T visa applicants should not be prioritized for removal proceedings until a decision is made regarding their visa.[45] According to USCIS statistics, the number of U visas approved in 2010, 2011, and 2012 exceeded ten thousand. These individuals were possibly granted deferred action or parole and were added to the waiting list.[46] In December 2013, USCIS announced that the ten thousand statutory cap was reached again for 2013.[47] During a stakeholder conference call, USCIS indicated that U visa applicants and qualifying family members who are found eligible for a U visa but placed on a waiting list because of the cap would be granted deferred action and eligible to apply for work authorization.[48] Meanwhile, the number of principal T visas issued in each fiscal year has been less than one thousand (far lower than the statutory cap), meaning that very few if any eligible T visa applicants have required the deferred action remedy.[49]

Even with the new statutory protections, DHS continues to use prosecutorial discretion to assist victims who are eligible for formal protection but must wait for months or sometimes years for their immigration status to be processed. The wait time for these victims can be long if there are too few visa slots and too many victims. In addition, individuals who have clearly suffered abuse do not always qualify for a form of relief because they cannot meet all the corresponding statutory requirements. While a full discussion of the statutory remedies available for crime and trafficking victims is beyond the scope of this book,[50] the existence of various prosecutorial discretion tools used by DHS to protect victims until they can avail themselves of formal remedies or because they cannot do so is important to understanding the use of prosecutorial discretion in the immigration system. The use of "deferred action" as a tool to aid VAWA, T, and U visa applicants further illustrates a recurring theme in U.S. immigration law and policy. Prosecutorial discretion has long been used as a stopgap measure to benefit persons who otherwise would be deprived of immigration benefits to which Congress has said they should be entitled. Although deferred action has long been a feature of the immigration system, the public has not always had access to information on how this remedy is used and the sheer magnitude of cases.

Analyzing Deferred Action Cases Retrieved through the Freedom of Information Act (FOIA)

To gain information about the use of deferred action, I requested through the Freedom of Information Act data about deferred action cases from Department of Homeland Security units beginning in 2009. Before this time, Leon Wildes, the lawyer for music icon John Lennon, made similar requests to INS and DHS in the early 1970s and early 2000s, respectively. The final section of this chapter looks at the cases Wildes and I reviewed after requesting and sometimes suing the immigration agency for information under the Freedom of Information Act (FOIA).

In 1967, Congress enacted FOIA to prevent agencies from developing and applying "secret law."[51] For more than one year, Wildes, corresponded with INS to gain information about the INS's deferred action program. Wildes was eager to review the body of cases approved for deferred action (or nonpriority status) in order to argue that Lennon should be considered for the same. Wildes eventually filed an FOIA lawsuit against INS to obtain this information.[52]

As a result of the FOIA lawsuit, INS provided Wildes with the histories of 1,843 granted deferred action cases. These cases provided him with the basis for arguing that Lennon should be granted deferred action. After examining the cases, Wildes calculated that deferred action functions as an important remedy granted to people with specific equities. In reviewing the adverse factors contained in the body of cases, Wildes also concluded that INS decided cases based largely on humanitarian factors as opposed to a person's criminal history or actual deportation charge.[53] He identified five primary humanitarian factors that drove deferred action approvals: (1) tender age, (2) elderly age, (3) mental incompetency, (4) medical infirmity, and (5) family separation if deported.[54] The largest category of cases granted involved family separation.[55] Typical of the granted cases was this one: "A representative case is 1-12, in which the subject was a Mexican national, without an immigrant visa, who had a permanent resident husband and several United States citizen children. The report states the expulsion would '[r]esult in the separation of subject from her children in the United States. She has no means of support in Mexico.' Nonpriority status was granted despite her previous separation from her husband and the fact that she was on welfare."[56] A U.S. citizen or lawful permanent resident family member was involved in more than 80 percent of the cases granted.[57] These data indicate that the presence of a family member with long-term ties to the United States heavily influenced whether the agency granted deferred action in a particular case.

Wildes also learned several interesting aspects of cases involving the rationale of "tender age." He noticed that many individuals in tender age cases were teenagers or young adults when INS granted deferred action.[58] This trend continues today, as DHS remains generous regarding age under the agency's current DACA program. Under DACA, people are eligible to qualify for the program if they were under the age of thirty-one as of June 15, 2012.[59]

As to the 357 approved cases involving mental incompetency, Wildes astutely observed, "What is significant, if somewhat ironic, is that in most of these cases the grounds for deportability—e.g., mental defects, institutionalization after entry—are also grounds for nonpriority consideration because of the humanitarian factors involved. Thus the Immigration Service through its nonpriority program seems to be adding both flexibility and sensitivity to an otherwise indiscriminate and harsh law."[60] While mental illness is no longer a criterion for removal, it was still grounds for deportation at the time Wildes received his first body of cases. What he appropriately calls "ironic" supports the position that a person who is technically deportable for health problems or economic reasons may possess the very kinds of equities that are worthy of deferred action status.

Wildes also reviewed the "negative" factors present in the nearly two thousand approved deferred action cases. While he did not have access to the deferred action cases that were denied, the presence of negative factors in his data set is quite revealing as it shows that an adverse immigration history played a minor role in the granting of deferred action. Wildes deduced that "[n]onpriority has been granted to aliens who have committed serious crimes involving moral turpitude, [drugs], fraud, or prostitution. Moreover, nonpriority has been given to Communists, the insane, the feebleminded, and the medically infirm. In sum, nonpriority has been granted to those who have violated almost any provision of the Act."[61] To illustrate, Wildes offered the following case summary as "[t]he most convincing evidence of the relative unimportance of the ground of deportability—subject has a criminal record which includes convictions for auto theft, contributing to the delinquency of a minor, vagrancy (pimp), rape, burglary in the second degree, robbery, possession of narcotics, and numerous other arrests. Despite his lengthy criminal record and numerous grounds for deportability, he was granted nonpriority status based upon his subsequent good behavior, successful marriage, and the fact that deportation would result in the separation of a good family unit. Clearly this decision was reached through strict evaluation of humanitarian factors alone."[62] Because of Lennon's history, Wildes was curious about whether people with a drug conviction fared well with the agency when they requested deferred action. If such cases existed, Wildes could argue that Lennon should receive nonpriority status. Wildes's discovery and analysis of these first publicly revealed cases provided a body of precedent that could be cited by noncitizens desperate to remain in the United States for humanitarian reasons.

Deferred action continued to function as a form of relief after INS was abolished and DHS was created. However, the power to grant or deny deferred action was bestowed on three separate agencies within DHS. The decentralization of deferred action to three different agencies within DHS coupled with a post-9/11 culture of "no" may have impacted the transparency and volume of deferred action requests that were denied because of "bad timing" but in the "best of times" might have been approved. This is an unsupported assumption that I can base only on what I witnessed as a legislative lawyer in Washington, D.C., immediately after 9/11 and on the striking drop in deferred action cases and data available to the public, even with an FOIA request. The next section summarizes the data DHS has provided on deferred action and begins with a second quest by Leon Wildes. This time Wildes filed new FOIA requests to three USCIS regional offices for all records of cases in which deferred action was granted.[63] He received information from two of the three regions (Central and Eastern). In total, he received information about 499 deferred action cases.[64] Wildes found that roughly 89 percent of the cases were approved for deferred action.[65] As in his 1976 article, Wildes found that USCIS granted deferred action based on a strict set of criteria.[66] In most of the cases reviewed by Wildes, each decision took the form of a terse statement and omitted the overriding factors influencing the decision.[67] Nevertheless, grants of deferred action fell within seven specific categories: (1) separation of family, (2) medically infirm, (3) tender age, (4) mentally incompetent, (5) potential negative publicity, (6) victims of domestic violence, and (7) elderly age.[68] Possible separation from family continued to be an overriding factor in deferred action grants.[69] Nearly 30 percent of the cases involved family separation,[70] and more than 20 percent of the cases granted involved someone with a medical infirmity.[71] Cancer and HIV were common ailments listed in the medical cases.[72] The data once again confirm DHS's reliance on humanitarian criteria in granting deferred action.[73] Wildes observes, "In light of the fact that these cases involve alien spouses who are completely reliant on public assistance and receive state-funded medical care, it is striking that the government approved them for deferred action status. This fact exemplifies that the humanitarian goal of deferred action takes precedence over the usual concerns of the INS, which removes aliens who have become a burden upon United States resources and thus have become subject to the public charge provision, another distinct ground removal."[74]

Some of the cases analyzed by Wildes also included the factor of "potential negative publicity."[75] One report reads,

A nineteen-year-old Mexican [was] adopted at age three and then shuffled among several families from the age of six. . . . In fact, for one extended period as a young child he lived alone in an abandoned house next to a large family with fourteen children who gave him food but had no room for him to live with them. During another period of time he lived alone in a storage shed on a large ranch where he worked in the fields. . . . In the fifth grade his "foster" mother reclaimed him . . . she abandoned him shortly thereafter. . . . He has had several years of perfect school attendance, achieved outstanding grades, distinguished himself as an athlete and leader who inspires others, and acquired a craft at which he has become very proficient and by which he has supported himself for long periods of time. . . . Given the number and breadth of persons in our communities who support this young man's opportunity to remain in the U.S. and attend college, INS may be assured of SIGNIFICANT

ADVERSE PUBLICITY if some form of relief is not found. No other form of relief is known.[76]

INS chose to grant relief to this young man. The data reveal that separation from family and negative publicity coupled with other factors such as a medical condition influenced grants of deferred action.

To update the research conducted by Wildes, I sought deferred action records from USCIS beginning in 2009.[77] On June 17, 2011, I received a response to my FOIA request in the form of three compact discs,[78] which together contained a cover letter, a 270-page document containing data, and several spreadsheets listing statistical data.[79] More than 125 involved Haitian citizens who entered the United States after the 2010 earthquake.[80] Much of the data on these cases lack information about the facts and/or outcome. For example, one log read, "[T]hirteen-year old girl came to the U.S. with her seventeen-year old sister; house destroyed by earthquake; living with USC aunt and legal guardian in the U.S.; attending school in the U.S." Another log read, "Entered U.S. on B-2 visa with two daughters, one a USC; owned warehouse in Haiti that was destroyed by the earthquake; many customers killed in quake; living with brother in U.S."[81] I was not the only person to note the use of deferred action to benefit victims of Haiti's earthquake. As to the deferred action cases stemming from the earthquake in Haiti, the DHS ombudsman observed, "Over the past year, stakeholders expressed concerns to the Ombudsman's Office regarding the delayed processing of numerous deferred action requests submitted by Haitian nationals following the earthquake in January 2010."[82] In many instances, no other remedy existed to resolve these victims' dilemma, and so deferred action was the only tool available.

The remaining qualitative data I received from USCIS in 2011 included 118 identifiable deferred action cases, of which 107 were classified as approved, pending, or unknown.[83] Among these 107 cases, 50 involved a serious medical condition, 19 involved cases in which the applicant had U.S. citizen family members, 22 involved persons who had resided in the country for more than five years, and 32 involved persons with a tender or elder age. Many of these cases involved more than one "positive" factor. For example, many of the cases involved both a serious medical condition and U.S. citizen family members, or

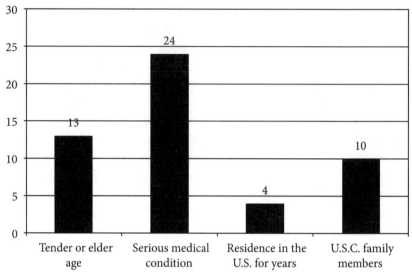

Fig. 4.1. Primary positive factors resulting in deferred action grant by USCIS, 2011.

involved both tender or elder age and a serious medical condition. The 48 granted cases fell in roughly four categories: (1) advanced or tender age, (2) serious medical condition, (3) residence in the United States for a number of years, and (4) U.S. citizen family members. Figure 4.1 provides a breakdown of noncitizens granted deferred action in these four categories. Many of these cases involved more than one positive factor. For example, deferred action was granted to a father of an eleven-year-old daughter who was a U.S. citizen and suffered from severe heart problems. Deferred action was granted to a forty-seven-year-old schizophrenic who overstayed his visa, was the son of a lawful permanent resident parent, and had siblings who were U.S. citizens.[84] The 2011 data from USCIS revealed that the immigration agency uses many of the same criteria as during the Lennon era in determining whether deferred action is appropriate and also the truly compelling nature of many of these claims given that some cases often involved more than one humanitarian factor.

In May 2013, I filed new and updated requests for deferred action records and cases with USCIS.[85] In September 2013, following a phone call from and supplemental letter to USCIS narrowing the scope of my

FOIA request, I received a spreadsheet of deferred actions for a four-month period.[86] The data contained information from four USCIS regions, with points such as the jurisdiction or USCIS office where the case was processed, basis for the request, manner of entry, nationality of the individual making the request, summary of the facts, and the outcome.[87] The "Basis" column indicated whether the individual was requesting deferred action for medical, family, or other reasons. The "Summary" column contained specific information about the case. For example, four cases involved individuals from Nigeria, presumably from the same family where one of the family members had cancer. The four individuals were granted deferred action for a period of two years. Another case involved a Mexican female who entered the United States without inspection and had two children who were U.S. citizens. One of her children had Down syndrome and other serious medical issues. This mother was also granted deferred action for a period of two years, as was the father. The data set included about 578 deferred action cases, 52 of which were "renewals," meaning that the individual had received deferred action in the past and was seeking an extension. Of note, 336 of the deferred action cases contained in this data set were based on a medical issue. Whereas most of the cases were labeled with one qualifier such as "family" or "medical," a few of the cases listed more than basis for the deferred action request such as "family/medical."[88]

Of these 578 cases, 233 (40 percent) were granted deferred action. The 233 granted cases fell into roughly three categories: (1) family, (2) medical, and (3) other. Of these 578 cases, 181 (31 percent) of these cases were denied deferred action.

More than eighty-four nationalities were represented in the sample size provided by USCIS. As Table 4.1 demonstrates, nationals from ten of these countries enjoyed 120 or 52 percent of the deferred action grants processed by USCIS during this four month time period.

As explained earlier, any person who is granted deferred action may be eligible to apply for work authorization with USCIS if he or she can show economic necessity.[89] Through FOIA, I received the data of work authorization applications processed by USCIS between June 17, 2011, and June 4, 2013, based on deferred action.[90] The data indicate that 17,040 work authorization applications processed by USCIS were made

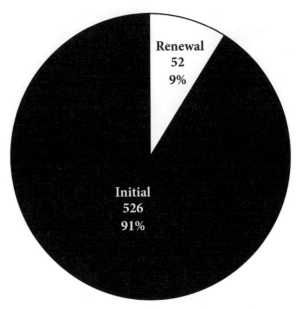

Fig. 4.2. Deferred action cases processed by USCIS during a four-month period, 2013.

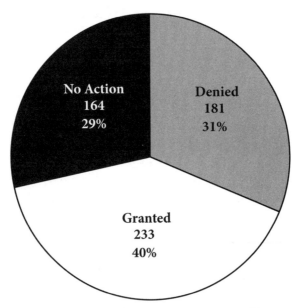

Fig. 4.3. Outcome in deferred action cases processed by USCIS during a four-month period, 2013.

Table 4.1. Outcome in Deferred Action Cases for Select Nationalities
Processed by USCIS during a Four-Month Period, 2013

Country	Approved	Denied	No action
Mexico	71	33	17
Columbia	7	12	11
Jamaica	2	6	22
Guatemala	11	12	4
Honduras	3	4	18
India	3	17	2
Haiti	8	10	3
Trinidad	0	8	11
Brazil	8	9	0
Dominican Republic	7	2	8

pursuant to a grant of deferred action. Of these, 13,135 were approved, meaning that more than three-quarters of deferred action grantees were provided work authorization by USCIS. Of the total cases, 6,751 applicants were represented by an attorney or representative. Another 6,384 of these approved cases involved an applicant but no attorney. Interestingly, this number might indicate that several applicants were requesting deferred action (or at least the work permit associated with a deferred action grant) on their own. Of the 13,135 approved cases, 8,058 were females and 5,072 were male applicants. Of the approved applicants, the gender was unknown in 5 cases. Also unknown was how many of these cases originated with ICE, meaning that ICE granted the actual deferred action request but the individual grantee submitted a work authorization request to USCIS. Also uncertain were the number of cases that involve U, T, and VAWA applicants eligible for an actual benefit based on their victim status but waiting out their period in deferred action until a visa becomes available. It is reasonable to conclude that the data set does not reflect DACA cases that were processed for work authorization as applicants have been advised by USCIS to apply for work authorization using a different code.[91] Notably, the data set does contain data points such as the duration of status, the applicant's country of citizenship, and the status of the deferred-action-based work authorization application. While deferred-action-based work authorization requests were made by citizens from over 150 countries, most requests

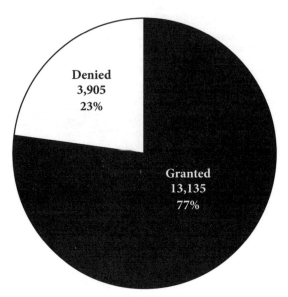

Fig. 4.4. Outcome in work authorization applications
adjudicated by USCIS pursuant to a deferred action
grant, June 17, 2011, to June 4, 2013.

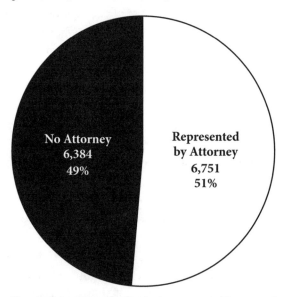

Fig. 4.5. Percentage of individuals represented by counsel
in work authorization applications adjudicated by USCIS
pursuant to a deferred action grant, June 17, 2011, to June
4, 2013.

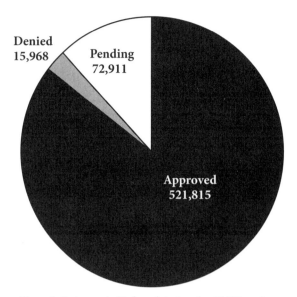

Fig. 4.6. Outcome in Deferred Action for Childhood
Arrivals requests processed by USCIS through the first
quarter of 2014. USCIS: http://www.uscis.gov/sites/
default/files/USCIS/Resources/Reports%20and%20
Studies/Immigration%20Forms%20Data/All%20Form%
20Types/DACA/DACA-06-02-14.pdf.

were made from citizens of Mexico, Colombia, Honduras, El Salvador,
and Guatemala.[92]

Beyond the individual deferred action data received through FOIA
requests, USCIS has published its data about the more publicized
DACA program on its own. Data processed through the first quarter
of 2014 reveal that USCIS received 638,054 applications for DACA, of
which more than 610,694 were accepted for review. During this time
period, 521,815 DACA applications were approved, 15,968 were denied,
and 72,911 are still pending.[93] The top five countries from which DACA
applicants hail are Mexico, El Salvador, Honduras, Guatemala, and
Peru.[94] The top five residences associated with DACA applications are
California, Texas, Illinois, New York, and Florida.[95] Public policy groups
like the Migration Policy Institute and the Center for American Progress have analyzed DACA data even further.[96] For example, one report
by the Center for American Progress, titled "Undocumented No More,"

distills information on 465,509 DACA applications obtained through two FOIA requests to DHS.[97] Below are some of the findings made by the center:

- The DACA implementation rate among the states varies significantly, from a low of 22 percent of eligible people in Florida to a high of 48.6 percent in Indiana. Note that because a portion of the DACA population will not be immediately eligible to apply, individual state implementation rates should not necessarily be viewed as low.
- Nationally, 53.1 percent of the DACA population is immediately eligible.
- Women represent 51.2 percent of the FOIA sample; men represent 48.7 percent.
- The average age of a DACA applicant in the FOIA sample is twenty years old, and older applicants are more likely than younger applicants to be denied.
- Mexican applicants are half as likely to be denied DACA as other groups. DACA applicants in the FOIA sample were born in 205 different countries, from the Democratic Republic of the Congo to Luxembourg and from Norway to North Korea.
- Mexicans make up 74.9 percent of the FOIA sample; Central Americans, 11.7 percent; and South Americans, 6.9 percent. Altogether, applicants from Latin America compose 93.5 percent of the total.[98]

Analyzing Deferred Action Cases at ICE

USCIS is not the only agency in DHS with the authority to grant deferred action. ICE also grants such cases, but their data were elusive until recently. I filed my first FOIA request to ICE in October 2009 asking for all records and policies involving prosecutorial discretion. However, ICE closed my request in December 2009. Nevertheless, I filed a new request in March 2010 requesting specific information about all deferred action cases. After corresponding with ICE about the status of my request on multiple occasions, I received a slim response in January 2011 in the form of a single chart listing a handful of active ICE grants of deferred action between 2003 and 2010. ICE provided no further detail.[99] The chart itself lacked any detail about the deferred action process, the factors used by ICE to grant or deny deferred action, and any

Table 4.2. Number of Active Cases Granted Deferred Action Status since 2003

CY	Detained	Not detained	Total
2003	0	117	117
2004	0	68	68
2005	0	62	62
2006	0	64	64
2007	0	71	71
2008	0	39	39
2009	2	34	36
2010	1	15	16
Total	3	470	473

Chart produced by ICE on the total number of active deferred action cases between CY 2003 and 2010.

explanation to demonstrate that the universe of deferred action cases presented in the chart was in fact accurate.[100]

Concerned in part that ICE did not make a complete search, I filed an appeal on March 29, 2011, hoping to receive more data.[101] ICE denied the appeal on September 27, 2011, concluding that, even after a further search, there were no records responsive to my request.[102]

After some deliberation, I filed an FOIA complaint in federal court, seeking all ICE records concerning prosecutorial discretion and deferred action.[103] Between June 2012 and September 2012, the DOJ and ICE attorneys assigned to my case and I discussed the nature of the records I was requesting and the limitation ICE had in providing records for deferred action cases prior to fiscal year 2011, or for producing entire case files for deferred action cases in any year.[104] Ultimately, we were able to settle the case without a trial, and the case was dismissed on October 1, 2012.[105]

Highlights from Data Collected between October 1, 2011, and June 30, 2012[106]

- ICE did not formally track deferred action case statistics prior to fiscal year 2012.
- ICE processed 4.5 times as many stays of removal as deferred action cases.[107]
- ICE processed 698 deferred action cases, of which 324 (46 percent) were granted between October 1, 2011, and June 30, 2012.

- The composition of deferred action cases among field offices varied significantly. More than one-half of the 698 deferred action cases granted were concentrated in the above five field offices.
- There were 78 nationalities (including "unknown") represented in the deferred action cases covered in this study. The single largest country of citizenship represented in deferred action cases was Mexico, followed by Guatemala, Honduras, El Salvador, and Jamaica. Mexico also had the highest number of deferred action grants.
- The five primary humanitarian factors (excluding "other") identified in granted deferred action cases were presence of a U.S. citizen dependent, presence in the United States since childhood, primary caregiver of an individual who suffers from a serious mental or physical illness, length of presence in the United States, and suffering from a serious mental or medical care condition.
- The single largest adverse factor contributing to a deferred action denial was "lack of compelling factors," which occurred 207 times (55 percent). Only 69 cases (18 percent) were denied because of a criminal history.
- Individuals from different age groups were considered for deferred action, and not limited to the age group that qualifies for DACA, the very young, or the elderly.

As part of the settlement, ICE provided me with deferred action data collected from all twenty-four of ICE's Enforcement and Removal Operations (ERO) field offices.[108] ICE Headquarters collected the data from each field office. The data included cases processed between October 1, 2011, and June 30, 2012. ICE also provided data on applications for "stays of removal" from all twenty-four ICE ERO field offices.[109] An administrative stay of removal is a form of prosecutorial discretion and, like its deferred action cousin, enables a noncitizen without legal status to apply for protection from removal and possible work authorization.[110] However, unlike deferred action, a stay of removal is available to the noncitizen only after a removal order has been entered and may be granted only by ICE.[111]

The data yielded a total of 3,837 cases,[112] 698 of which were deferred action cases while 3,139 were stay of removal cases. Of the 698 deferred action cases, 324 were granted. Of the 3,139 stay of removal cases, 1,957 were granted.

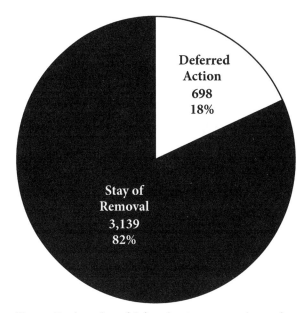

Fig. 4.7. Total number of deferred action cases and stay of removal cases processed by ICE, October 1, 2011, to June 30, 2012.

Humanitarian and Adverse Factors Identified in Deferred Action Cases

Many of the factors identified by DHS policy guidance like Morton Memo I were identified in the 698 cases granted deferred action. While the data provided by ICE contain a field titled "Reason for Grant/ Denial," each field contained only one factor for each entry. Therefore, the total number of reasons given (including "other") is exactly equal to the total number of cases reported. The five primary factors (excluding "other") identified in granted cases were the following:

- Presence of a U.S. citizen dependent
- Presence in the United States since childhood
- Primary caregiver of an individual who suffers from a serious mental or physical illness
- Length of presence in the United States
- Suffering from a serious mental or medical care condition[113]

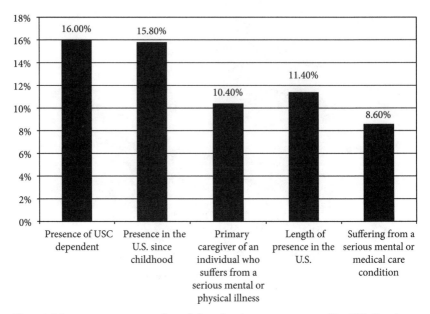

Fig. 4.8. Most common reasons for a deferred action grant processed by ICE, October 1, 2011, to June 30, 2012.

The data from ICE did not identify the factors leading to the greatest number of deferred action "grants" ("Other"), which raises procedural questions about whether ICE should be including additional fields in its data collection.[114] Thirty cases, or 9 percent, were identified as based on the individual's "serious mental or physical illness." While 9 percent appears low in contrast to the types of cases that have historically involved a serious medical infirmity of mental health condition, the overall reasons identified for deferred action in this data set were consistent with the categories of cases that have historically been granted deferred action.

The data provided by ICE confirm that field officers are required to identify a factor in denying deferred action, but the data fields themselves (e.g., "Lack of compelling factors") are not detailed enough to allow for a meaningful analysis of why a particular case was denied. As illustrated by the data, 69 among the 374 denials were based on a criminal history, while 207 cases were denied because of a "lack of compelling factors." The most common factors (excluding "other") for denials of deferred action were these:

1. Lack of compelling factors
2. Criminal history
3. Egregious record of immigration violations

Composition of Deferred Action Cases among Field Offices

There was significant variance in the number of deferred action and stay of removal cases processed among field offices, which processed anywhere from 38 to 720 of these cases during the period covered. For example, the data show that the Miami office processed a far greater number of deferred action and stay of removal cases in contrast to the other twenty-three field offices. The field offices with the highest number of such cases included the following: Miami (720 cases), Newark (341), New York City (276), Washington (253), and San Francisco (203).

An explanation for why ICE processed a far greater number of stays over deferred action cases is elusive at best but may be explained by the fact that stays of removal enjoy more predictability and accessibility for the ICE employee. Unlike deferred action, a stay of removal is grounded in the immigration regulations and furthermore includes a form and a fee; this likely makes it easier for ICE to track the case and for the employee to justify the decision. Likewise, a stay of removal is a form of relief granted only after a final order of removal is entered, whereas the deferred action remedy may be considered at any stage of the enforcement process and therefore may be viewed by ICE as a riskier decision, especially early in the enforcement process. Finally, a stay may be viewed as more "temporary" in nature than deferred action because "deferred action" is more politically controversial.

Looking just at deferred action cases, the composition of deferred action cases among field offices also varied significantly. The field offices with the highest number of deferred action cases were as follows: New York City (50 percent granted), New Orleans (23 percent granted), Washington (86 percent granted), Miami (52 percent granted), and Newark (40 percent granted). The Washington field office had the highest percentage of deferred action cases that were granted among the field offices that had more than fifteen cases.

The Washington field office had the highest number of grants for deferred action by a field office, granting it for 65 of the 76 cases. The

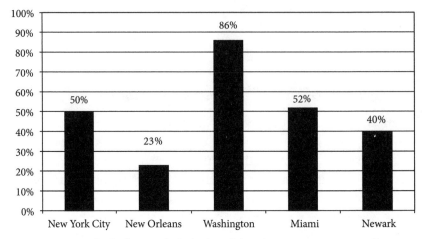

Fig. 4.9. Five ICE field offices with the highest deferred action grant rate, October 1, 2011, to June 30 2012.

most common factors identified for grants at the Washington field office were (1) primary caretaker of an individual who suffers from a serious mental or physical illness, (2) U.S. citizen dependent, and (3) individual present in the United States since childhood. The second highest volume of grants took place in the New York field office. Specifically, 52 of the 104 deferred action cases were granted in New York. The most common factors identified for New York were (1) other, (2) U.S. citizen dependent, and (3) the individual's length of presence in the United States. Notably, none of the deferred action cases granted in New York were identified as based on a serious mental or physical illness, which historically has driven many deferred action grants.

Certain field offices had a higher volume of deferred action applications as well as granted cases. The disparity in the distribution and outcomes might be explained by the fact that deferred action requests to ICE are normally made to the field office that lies within the jurisdiction of the applicant's residence and that potential applicants for deferred action are concentrated in specific locations. Notably, the jurisdictions covered by the Washington, New York, and Miami field offices have large unauthorized immigrant populations.[115] An additional explanation for the differences is that deferred action cases are more successful with ICE when the noncitizen is represented or assisted by an attorney. Also, there may be a higher rate of deferred action grants in areas where there are higher concentrations of immigration attorneys.

The findings outlined above improve transparency by providing potential applicants and attorneys who are working on deferred action cases with information such as "how an office handles cases involving a serious medical condition." These findings also reveal that ICE has limited ways in which the information about deferred action cases is sorted, as there is no explanation for which factors contribute to the "Other" category, which appears to be the largest basis for a deferred action grant. There is also no explanation for what constitutes a "lack of compelling factors," which appeared to be the single greatest basis for a denial in deferred action cases.

Perhaps more important, the findings do not include an analysis of how a negative factor interacts with a positive one. For example, how does ICE treat someone who has a criminal history and a U.S. citizen dependent? This kind of information is vital as it contributes to the public understanding about whether having a criminal history is fatal or just a factor behind a deferred action determination. Based on the information that we do have, the basis for a grant appears to rest more on the positive equities of the individual, many of which have served historically as the basis for deferred action. To recap, the most common reasons given for a deferred action grant in the 324 cases include having a U.S. citizen dependent, being an individual in the United States since childhood, being a primary caregiver of an individual who suffers from a serious mental or medical illness or has a longtime presence in the United States.

Distribution of Deferred Action Denials across Field Offices: Five Field Offices Had a Significantly Higher Number of Denials than the Average Denial Rate at Field Offices

The data provided by ICE show that the New Orleans field office had the highest number of cases denied deferred action—75 out of 97 cases. The most common factors identified in the New Orleans data were (1) lack of compelling factors and (2) criminal history. Though the New

York field office was identified as the location with the second highest number of deferred action grants, it also came in as yielding the second highest number of denials (52 out of 104 deferred action cases were denied). The most common reason for the cases denied in New York City was a lack of compelling factors. Notably, only one of the denials was identified as having been based on a criminal history.

Disparities in the Outcome of Deferred Actions by Field Office

I was interested to look at how field offices fared in contrast to the overall mean or average rate of denial and grant in deferred action cases. There was significant deviation from the mean at several field offices. Of the 649 deferred action cases at field offices with at least 15 cases, the mean grant rate was 44.5 percent, while the mean denial rate was 55.5 percent. While 15 cases is a rather small sample size, the disparity is notable. The data show that eight offices deviated from the mean by more than 20 percent.

The variance in deferred action cases among field offices signals disparity and challenges the quality of the program. Administrative law designs have been traditionally examined under values like efficiency,

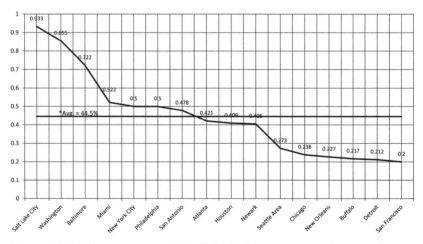

Fig. 4.10. Deferred action grant rate by ICE field office versus national average, October 1, 2011, to June 30, 2012.

Table 4.3. Outcome in Deferred Action Case by Select Nationalities

Country	Approved	Denied	Grant rate (%)
Mexico	70	107	39.54
Guatemala	23	26	46.93
Honduras	24	23	51.06
El Salvador	24	18	57.14
Peru	13	3	81

consistency, accuracy, and acceptability. When deferred action decisions are disparate, this leads to uncertainty about whether decisions are achieving these values.[116] In particular, when the agency makes different decisions about people who have similarly relevant facts, this can be viewed as unfair and an abuse of discretion. One complexity, and there are many, is to pin down whether such disparity reflects an abuse of discretion or whether the difference in outcome falls within the range of acceptable legal discretion. Likewise, there may be additional variables in each field office that are contributing to different outcomes. For example, it may be that the cases handled in the Washington office include those with stronger facts, greater compelling equities, and fewer negative points or more minimal criminal histories.[117]

Composition of Deferred Action Cases by Nationality

There were more than seventy nationalities represented in the deferred action cases collected between October 1, 2011, and June 30, 2012. Nationals from Mexico, Guatemala, Honduras, and El Salvador enjoyed the greatest number deferred action grants during this time period.

Age of the Individuals Processed for Deferred Action and Stays of Removal

The age of the individuals processed for deferred action and stays of removal was calculated by reviewing the birth date of the individual and the date of the decision. Figure 4.11 offers an overview of the age groups in the data collected by ICE. The age of applicants was distributed

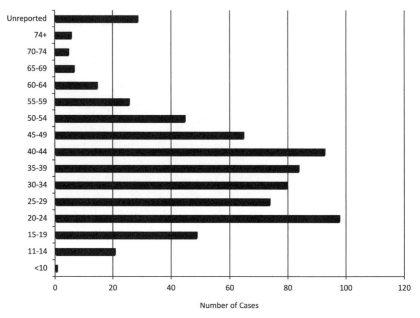

Fig. 4.11. Age of applicant for deferred action requests processed by ICE, October 1, 2011, to June 30, 2012.

almost in a bell-shaped curve, which is not entirely surprising given the sample size of 3,387.

Looking specifically at the age groups for deferred action cases, figure 4.11 shows that individuals between the ages of twenty and twenty-four (98 cases or 14 percent) were processed at a greater rate than any other age group. The data illustrate that individuals from different age groups are considered for deferred action, and that it is not limited to the age group that qualifies for DACA, the very young, or the elderly.

On the other hand, it may also be the case that the agency treats "tender age" with a broad lens, looking less at the age of the applicant at the time of the decision, for example, and instead at the age at the time of entry. The data provided by ICE do not contain a field for the date of entry or for the number of years the individual has resided in the United States. As such, it is not possible to determine whether there are more individuals of tender or advanced age at the time of entry in contrast to what is reflected in Figure 4.11. Also of note is the possibility that many of the cases were granted deferred action because of a U.S. citizen dependent who was a family member of tender or advanced age even if the recipient of deferred action was not labeled as such.

Looking at whether age played a role in the outcome of a deferred action case, the data reveal a diverse distribution of grants and denials among age groups, with two exceptions: individuals who were younger than nineteen or older than sixty-five at the time of the decision were granted at a higher rate (78 percent) than the average (58 percent). This suggests that in these extreme cases, individuals with a tender or advanced age actually were treated more favorably by the agency.

Making the Case for Notice and Comment Rule Making for Deferred Action

As I sought data on DHS records of deferred action, one aspect of the deferred action process jumped out at me: there was no administrative transparency connected with the process, and it was impossible to determine whether deferred action was being used wisely or widely. In large part, this was because deferred action was invisible to the normal procedures outlined in the Administrative Procedure Act. Administrative law icon Kenneth Culp Davis declared the notice and comment rule-making procedures of the Administrative Procedure Act "one of the greatest inventions of modern government" and advocated for greater rule making in order to increase public participation in and judicial review of agency decisions and policy.[118] This section analyzes the virtues for enacting a rule on deferred action. The concept of rule making comes from a bill enacted by Congress in 1946 known as the Administrative Procedure Act (APA).[119] The APA contains multiple sections related to the rule-making process. Under the APA, notice of proposed rule making by the agency must be published as a public document in the *Federal Register* or personally served on affected individuals not less than thirty days before the effective date of the rule.[120] The APA also requires that individuals be given an opportunity to comment on a proposed rule, after which the agency is required to consider relevant factors and include a statement of purpose in the newly minted rule.[121] Many of the immigration documents issued by DHS are subject to an "exception" of this rule-making requirement. Specifically, the APA contains the following exceptions to the substantive rule-making requirements:

(1) interpretative rules, general statements of policy, or rules of agency organization, procedure, or practice; or (2) when the agency shows that public procedures thereon are impracticable, unnecessary, or contrary to the public interest.[122] General statements of policy are issued by all levels of the agency, and can be created in a variety of formats such as a "policy letters," "press releases," "questions and answers," and "memoranda."[123] During its tenure, DHS has issued hundreds of policy statements bearing similar titles. Many of DHS's prosecutorial discretion policies have been published as a "memoranda" and treated by the agency as "general statements of policy," excepting them from the APA rule-making requirements. Thus, little transparency exists with regard to the process or the decision-making factors.

Whether a policy operates as a "rule" or a "general statement of policy" is not always guided by its label, but instead rests on the practical function and impact of such a policy. One notable case in which the court found that a policy of the Food and Drug Administration operated as a rule subject to notice and comment rule making is *Community Institute v. Young*.[124] Community Institute represented a group of organizations and private citizens challenging the Food and Drug Administration's regulation of contaminants (in particular, aflatoxin) in corn. While the statute at hand limited the amount of "poisonous or deleterious substances" in food, the FDA created a policy directed at food producers. The "policy" instructed that producers that contaminated above the action level would be subject to enforcement proceedings by the FDA. The court held that the FDA's policy for limiting the toxin levels in corn was a legislative rule because "FDA by virtue of its own course of conduct has chosen to limit its discretion and promulgated action levels which it gives a present, binding effect. Having accorded such substantive significance to action levels, FDA is compelled by the APA to utilize notice-and-comment procedures in promulgating them."[125] One critic of the outcome in *Young* has argued that the court created a disincentive for agencies to self-regulate.[126] While it may be true that a strongly administered internal rule can suffice to ensure that agencies follow the rule, I cast doubt on whether the DHS can achieve the same level of consistency and fairness in deferred action cases without notice and comment rule making.

Deferred action has not been subject to notice and comment rule making because deferred action was first implemented through an INS Operations Instruction, which the courts have generally held are internal guidelines or general statements of policy.[127] One exception is the Ninth Circuit case *Nicholas v. INS*, which found that the Operations Instruction operated like a substantive benefit: "It is obvious that this procedure exists out of consideration for the convenience of the petitioner, and not that of the INS. In this aspect, it far more closely resembles a substantive provision for relief than an internal procedural guideline. . . . Delay in deportation is expressly the remedy provided by the Instruction. It is the precise advantage to be gained by seeking non-priority status. Clearly, the Operations Instruction, in this way, confers a substantive benefit upon the alien, rather than setting up an administrative convenience."[128] This history is important to understanding the legitimacy of recognizing deferred action as a benefit and the moves INS made to modify the Operations Instruction to avoid such recognition.

As recounted earlier, the INS modified the Operations Instruction in 1981 to clarify that deferred action was a discretionary act as opposed to a formal benefit. Treating the Operations Instruction as a general statement of policy allowed the INS to amend and remove the once "mandatory" nature of the Operations Instruction without public notice or comment. Likewise, it permitted the courts to uphold decisions by the agency to deny deferred action status to particular individuals regardless of their equities. Finally, the court discussion as to whether the Operations Instruction constituted a substantive rule inspired the explicit language contained in current agency memoranda that prosecutorial acts are discretionary, immune from judicial review, and under no terms an "entitlement" to the noncitizen.

Courts have continued to interpret deferred action as a general statement of policy exempt from the APA's notice and comment requirements. And yet the cases analyzed in this chapter illustrate that the agency has long used specific criteria to both adjudicate deferred action cases and enable individuals to avoid removal and remain in the United States with dignity through grants of deferred action. Deferred action may officially walk like a "discretionary act," but to individuals who are granted this remedy it quacks like a substantive benefit.

5

Presidential Portrait

Prosecutorial Discretion during the Obama Administration

Barack Obama's presidency has been unique in that his administration has been very public about its use of prosecutorial discretion and has received much media attention and controversy. This chapter looks at the role of prosecutorial discretion in immigration matters during Obama's presidency. It reenacts the arguments from lawyers, policy pundits, select members of Congress and ICE's own union toward new prosecutorial discretion policies issued during the Obama administration. During this period, DHS issued no fewer than a dozen policy documents about the role of prosecutorial discretion in immigration law. This chapter summarizes some of the most salient of these documents and also analyzes the events that led to the administration's support and the public's divide around this topic. Finally, it examines the relationship between the failure of legislative reforms and the impulse for prosecutorial discretion to compensate for that failure.

President Obama took office in 2008 and early on made public announcements about the importance of reforming immigration holistically through "comprehensive immigration reform," a legislative scheme that in past years has included a statutory update to the family- and employment-based immigration system, a legal pathway for noncitizens to enter the United States in the future on the basis of work or a family relationship, and a registration program enabling individuals and other special populations such as high school students and migrant workers currently in the United States without authorization to come before the government and apply for legal status.[1] Even before President Obama was sworn in, he led a transition team that included a swath of immigration experts focused on creating immigration "blueprints" about his priorities as a president. In some ways, previous and unsuccessful cycles of "comprehensive" immigration reform during the preceding years provided President Obama with a rich narrative from which to build a platform for reform, but the support in Congress for such reform was insufficient.[2] Early on, Congress did appear poised to move forward on the Development, Relief, and Education for Alien Minors (DREAM) Act, a bill that would have provided legal status to eligible young residents who had been in the United States for an extended period, had finished high school, and had planned to enter college or serve in the military. The DREAM Act would have enabled young people who completed higher education or service in the military to achieve permanent residence in the United States after several years in "conditional" resident status.[3] The DREAM Act has been introduced in Congress on many occasions and in the past enjoyed strong support from both political parties. The Obama administration was sufficiently encouraged about the political posture of the DREAM Act that it issued a fact sheet before DREAM Act votes took place in Congress and reportedly made encouraging calls to influential members of political branches in the days prior to the vote.[4] Although the House successfully passed the DREAM Act in December 2010, the bill failed a Senate cloture by only five votes.[5] Senator Lindsay Graham (R-SC) remarked, "We're not going to pass the DREAM Act or any other legalization until we secure our borders. It will never be done stand-alone. It has to be part of comprehensive immigration reform."[6]

The 2010 failure of the DREAM Act was a blow to the administration and also to thousands of Dreamers who would have benefited from the bill. Coexisting with the loss on the DREAM Act were regular reports that the administration (through ICE) was deporting noncitizens at record levels.[7] According to ICE's own statistics, more than a million and a half people were removed from the United States between 2008 and 2012.[8] During this period, immigration policy was sometimes identified as "enforcement on steroids"; the administration was viewed as deporting noncitizens regardless of their equities, rather than implementing a robust prosecutorial discretion policy that placed compelling cases on the back burner. The lack of hope that immigration reform would move forward and anxiety about the record number of deportations during the first term of the Obama administration were well described by Roberto Suro in his segment for "Lost in Detention": "The possibilities of comprehensive reform have dropped so drastically.

I mean, no one thinks that it's likely to come anywhere close to getting enacted with the current configuration in Washington, so talking about it becomes kind of a meaningless exercise. In the meantime, however, [Obama] has continued the trajectory of aggressive enforcement."[9]

Even while the prospects of the DREAM Act were ripe, the Obama administration gave some thought to how the agency could exercise its prosecutorial discretion to protect humanitarian cases from removal. In August 2010, staff members of USCIS circulated an internal draft memorandum outlining potential ways in which the agency could reprieve individuals and certain classes of persons who are ineligible for legal immigration status but who nonetheless exhibit compelling qualities or equities.[10] The internal memo stated in part, "In the absence of comprehensive immigration reform, USCIS can extend benefits and/or protections to many individuals and groups by issuing new guidance and regulations, exercising discretion with regard to parole-in-place, deferred action and the issuance of Notices to Appear (NTA), and adopting significant process improvements."[11] In discussing deferred action, that memorandum acknowledged that it could be used as a tool to protect certain individuals or groups from the threat of removal.[12] With foresight that may have contributed to the agency's thinking about the future DACA program, the memo stated: "USCIS can increase the use of deferred action. Deferred action is an exercise of prosecutorial discretion not to pursue removal from the U.S. of a particular individual for a specific period of time. . . . Were USCIS to increase significantly the use of deferred action, the agency would either require a separate appropriation or independent funding stream. Alternatively, USCIS could design and seek expedited approval of a dedicated deferred action form and require a filing fee."[13] The leaked USCIS memo was met with criticism from advocates for immigration restrictions, conservative media pages, and select members of Congress. For example, the Center for Immigration Studies, a restrictionist organization, noted: "Since the administration apparently cannot pull off a congressional vote on a national legalization program, and since it apparently (and appropriately) does not want to rig up a 'you all come' near-total administrative amnesty, USCIS feels it must consider a third alternative, a multi-part series of bureaucratic adjustments that will legalize a significant portion of the currently illegal population."[14] The reaction from the *National Review Online* can be summed up by the title of the article, "The Amnesty Memo," which read in part, "According to an internal U.S. Citizenship and Immigration Services memo going the rounds of Capitol Hill and obtained by National Review, the agency is considering ways in which it could enact 'meaningful immigration reform absent legislative action'—that is, without the consent of the American people through a vote in Congress."[15] On the heels of the draft USCIS memo, some members of Congress also criticized the department for its modest exercise of prosecutorial discretion. Notably, in a congressional hearing dated March 9, 2011, Senator Charles Grassley (R-IA) interrogated DHS Secretary Janet Napolitano regarding the internal USCIS memo and the use of prosecutorial discretion.[16] The senator identified the document as an "internal amnesty memo" and was troubled by any thinking around administrative relief on a categorical basis. Secretary Napolitano acknowledged the memo but argued that "people in the Department come up with ideas and that is not a bad thing for people to be thinking."[17] The secretary further confirmed that the agency would not be giving deferred action to large groups of people and that such relief could be made only on a case-by-case basis. She also compared DHS's removal of 395,000 noncitizens in fiscal year 2010 and the fewer than 900 deferred action cases granted during the same period.[18] While the response by Secretary Napolitano may have pleased Senator Grassley, her response troubled immigration advocates and attorneys who supported a more expansive use of prosecutorial discretion. For example, the American Immigration Lawyers Association, a seminal private immigration bar, wrote to the secretary: "We are concerned that in your testimony on March 9 before the Senate Judiciary Committee regarding prosecutorial discretion, you highlighted that the number of cases where discretion was favorably exercised was very small, suggesting that your department is discouraging and limiting its exercise."[19] Similarly, the proreform group America's Voice issued a press statement quoting Frank Sharry, the group's executive director: "It's a sad day when the Obama Administration uses deportation statistics from the Bush years as a measure of success. It's also a sad day when policymakers in Washington, like Senator Grassley, try to bully government officials into being tough for tough's sake. DHS needs to exercise more discretion in its deportation practices, not less."[20]

Likewise, several members of Congress, attorneys, and public advocates took positions supporting the executive branch's exercise of prosecutorial discretion. For example, on April 13, 2011, twenty-two U.S. senators sent a letter to President Obama urging him to grant deferred action to qualifying DREAM Act students who were not a law enforcement priority to DHS.[21] The letter states: "We would support a grant of deferred action to all young people who meet the rigorous requirements necessary to be eligible . . . under the DREAM Act. . . . We strongly believe that DREAM Act students should not be removed from the United States, because they have great potential to contribute to our country and children should not be punished for their parents' mistakes."[22] The senators were critical of the department's lack of process for applying for deferred action and the fact that many DREAM Act students were unaware of this form of relief.[23] On the heels of this letter, Senator Charles Schumer, a Democrat from New York and chair of the Judiciary Committee, remarked in another letter to DHS:

> According to a March 2, 2011 memorandum of John Morton, Director of Immigration and Customs Enforcement, ICE only has the funding to remove 400,000 individuals per year. Given that this entire number can be filled by criminal aliens and others posing security threats, it makes eminent sense to focus ICE's enforcement efforts on these criminals and security threats, rather than non-criminal populations. On a daily basis, my office receives requests for assistance in many compelling immigration cases. These cases often involve non-criminal immigrants such as: (1) high-school valedictorians and honor students who did not enter the country through their own volition and yet are being deported solely for the illegal conduct of their parents; (2) bi-national same-sex married couples who are being discriminated against based on their sexual orientation who would otherwise be able to remain in the United States if they were in an opposite-sex marriage; (3) agricultural workers who perform back-breaking labor and are providing for their families; and (4) immigrant parents with U.S. citizen children, whose deportation will only lead to increased costs to the states in foster care and government benefits.[24]

Beyond the halls of Congress, bar associations, journalists, and advocacy groups highlighted the role of prosecutorial discretion. The

American Bar Association testified before the Senate Judiciary Committee on May 17, 2011:

> Prioritization, including the prudent use of prosecutorial discretion, is an essential function of any adjudication system. Unfortunately, it has not been widely utilized in the immigration context. There are numerous circumstances in which a respondent is not likely to be removed regardless of the outcome of the legal case. The most obvious cases are those where the respondent is terminally ill or is the parent or spouse of someone who is critically ill, but there are other examples where it is clear from the circumstances at the beginning of the process that the interests in removing the respondent will almost certainly be outweighed on humanitarian or other grounds.[25]

Similarly, the Migration Policy Institute (MPI) highlighted the importance of prosecutorial discretion in a 2011 report describing actions the executive branch could take in the absence of legislative reform.[26] Specifically, the MPI report recommended that the government develop a uniform set of enforcement priorities and, in cases of lesser priority, exercise prosecutorial discretion in the form of deferred action with work authorization.[27] Also, the ten-thousand-member organization NAFSA: Association of International Educators highlighted the importance of prosecutorial discretion in a May 2011 press release: "We urge President Obama to exercise his executive authority and act now to direct the Department of Homeland Security to implement such a deferred-action policy. This is a matter of humanitarian necessity, and it would represent the kind of national leadership that is needed to move the one-sided, enforcement-first debate about immigration that has so far poisoned prospects for what is ultimately needed—comprehensive reform—in a more fruitful direction."[28] Lawyers and advocates also created practical tools for noncitizens potentially eligible for deferred action. The American Immigration Lawyers Association created practice advisories and advocacy materials on the role of prosecutorial discretion in immigration law.[29] The law firms of Duane Morris, LLP and Maggio Kattar P.C. partnered with the immigration clinic at Penn State Law to publish a tool kit addressing private bills and deferred action to help thousands of advocates, Dreamers, and lawyers understand and approach these forms of relief armed with good information and legal strategies.[30] Finally, Asian Law Caucus, Educators for Fair Consideration, DreamActivist.org, and National Immigrant Youth Alliance published a resource manual titled *Education Not Deportation: A Guide for Undocumented Youth in Removal Proceedings* to assist undocumented students in removal proceedings.[31] These materials are not exhaustive but are revealing about the faith and investment advocates and attorneys in the immigrant rights movement placed in the remedy of prosecutorial discretion.

Cumulatively, the outpouring of support by members of Congress and stakeholders for prosecutorial discretion, the swelling number of humanitarian cases falling through the cracks, the record number of deportations, a continuing congressional stalemate, and a wave of Dreamers going public about their demands sparked a new emphasis on prosecutorial discretion policy from DHS. The paragraphs that follow summarize the copious guidance documents issued by DHS beginning in 2010 on the subject of prosecutorial discretion.

One memo was issued by ICE in June 2010 and focused primarily on the enforcement priorities of the DHS. Titled "Civil Immigration Enforcement: Priorities for the Apprehension, Detention, and Removal of Aliens," the Priorities Memo outlined three priorities. As discussed in chapter 1, prosecutorial discretion functions largely as a management tool for the agency to prioritize its resources effectively and also as a humanitarian one to protect cases involving compelling equities from removal. The economic basis of the Priorities Memo was established in the following prelude: "In light of the large number of administrative violations the agency is charged with addressing and the limited enforcement resources the agency has available, ICE must prioritize the use of its enforcement personnel, detention space, and removal resources to ensure that the removals the agency does conduct promote the agency's highest enforcement priorities, namely national security, public safety, and border security."[32] The Priorities Memo also included a striking statement that ICE had resources to remove only about four hundred thousand annually, less than 4 percent of the total unauthorized population.[33] The three priorities identified in this memo were individuals who (1) pose a public safety risk or danger to society, defined in part by a history of terrorist or criminal activity; (2) recently entered the United

States through means other than a valid port of entry or border checkpoint; and (3) have been identified by ICE as remaining in the United States with an outstanding order of removal "or otherwise obstruct immigration controls."[34] By identifying categories of people as priorities, ICE leadership was explaining that enforcement resources would be channeled to the highest priorities. Priority 1 includes "[a]liens who pose a danger to national security or a risk to public safety" and, according to the Priorities Memo, shall be ICE's "highest immigration enforcement priority" and also covers the following classes:

- Engaged in or suspected of terrorism or espionage, or who otherwise pose a danger to national security
- Convicted of crimes, with a particular emphasis on violent criminals, felons, and repeat offenders
- Not younger than sixteen years of age who participated in organized criminal gangs
- Subject to outstanding criminal warrants
- Otherwise pose a serious risk to public safety[35]

The Priorities Memo identified priority 2 as "[r]ecent illegal entrants" and noted, "In order to maintain control at the border and at ports of entry, and to avoid a return to the prior practice commonly and historically referred to as 'catch and release,' the removal of aliens who have recently violated immigration controls at the border, at ports of entry, or through the knowing abuse of the visa and visa waiver programs shall be a priority." Finally, priority 3 was identified as "[a]liens who are fugitives or otherwise obstruct immigration controls" and was described by ICE as follows: "In order to ensure the integrity of the removal and immigration adjudication processes, the removal of aliens who are subject to a final order of removal and abscond, fail to depart, or intentionally obstruct immigration controls, shall be a priority."[36]

While a detailed description of these priorities is beyond this chapter, it is worth noting that ICE's priorities themselves are broadly defined enough to reach individuals with a less serious criminal history, with no criminal history at all, or in some cases without actual knowledge that they are in violation of immigration law. The Priorities Memo included a note about the humanitarian side of prosecutorial discretion by referencing the previous guidance documents like the Meissner Memo and noting that "particular care should be given when dealing with lawful permanent residents, juveniles, and the immediate family members of U.S. citizens."[37] Interestingly, the Priorities Memo was reissued in March 2011 with a new paragraph clarifying that the document creates no right or benefit under law.[38] But the Priorities Memo and those that followed failed to explain how a case constituting an enforcement priority would fare if the individual also fell within a class that warrants "particular care and concern."

In June 2011, ICE issued a document that focused more specifically on the humanitarian reasons for prosecutorial discretion. Titled "Exercising Prosecutorial Discretion Consistent with the Civil Immigration Enforcement Priorities of the Agency for the Apprehension, Detention, and Removal of Aliens"[39] and nicknamed "Morton Memo" or "Morton Memo I," the document named nineteen factors ICE should consider in deciding whether prosecutorial discretion was warranted:

- The agency's civil immigration enforcement priorities
- The person's length of presence in the United States, with particular consideration given to presence while in lawful status
- The circumstances of the person's arrival in the United States and the manner of his or her entry, particularly if the alien came to the United States as a young child
- The person's pursuit of education in the United States, with particular consideration given to those who have graduated from a U.S. high school or have successfully pursued or are pursuing a college or advanced degrees at a legitimate institution of higher education in the United States
- Whether the person, or the person's immediate relative, has served in the U.S. military, reserves, or national guard, with particular consideration given to those who served in combat
- The person's criminal history, including arrests, prior convictions, or outstanding arrest warrants
- The person's immigration history, including any prior removal, outstanding order of removal, prior denial of status, or evidence of fraud
- Whether the person poses a national security or public safety concern
- The person's ties and contributions to the community, including family relationships

- The person's ties to the home country and condition in the country
- The person's age, with particular consideration given to minors and the elderly
- Whether the person has a U.S. citizen or permanent resident spouse, child, or parent
- Whether the person is the primary caretaker of a person with a mental or physical disability, minor, or seriously ill relative
- Whether the person or the person's spouse is pregnant or nursing
- Whether the person or the person's spouse suffers from severe mental or physical illness
- Whether the person's nationality renders removal unlikely
- Whether the person is likely to be granted legal status or other relief from removal, including as a relative of a U.S. citizen or permanent resident
- Whether the person is likely to be granted temporary or permanent status or other relief from removal, including as an asylum seeker, or a victim of domestic violence, human trafficking, or other crime
- Whether the person is currently cooperating or has cooperated with federal, state, or local law enforcement authorities, such as ICE, the U.S. attorneys or Department of Justice, the Department of Labor, or National Labor Relations Board, among others[40]

The Morton Memo also identified classes of citizens who warrant "particular care" when making prosecutorial decisions.[41] These groups were said to include these:

- Veterans and members of the U.S. Armed Forces
- Longtime lawful permanent residents
- Minors and elderly individuals
- Individuals present in the United States since childhood
- Pregnant or nursing women
- Victims of domestic violence, trafficking, or other serious crimes
- Individuals who suffer from a serious mental or physical disability
- Individuals with serious health conditions[42]

As in the prior memoranda issued by INS and DHS, the Morton Memo listed equities that the agency had long relied upon in determining whether prosecutorial discretion should be exercised favorably. Leon Wildes and I felt so much synergy among the old guidance, the Morton Memo, and our own research that we blogged about it.[43] As Wildes and I reflected:

> Our research of cases over several years also indicates that the favorable factors articulated in the 1975 Operations Instruction continue to be significant indicators for a favorable grant of prosecutorial discretion. . . . Building on the factors published as a result of the Lennon case, the Morton Memo lists several circumstances that should trigger a favorable exercise of prosecutorial discretion, noting that "particular care and consideration" should be given to long-time green card holders; minors and elderly individuals; those present in the U.S. since childhood; persons suffering a serious medical condition; and victims of domestic violence, trafficking, or other serious crimes; among others. . . . Like with previous memoranda, the Morton Memo highlights the relationship between prosecutorial discretion and ICE's limited monies to remove the entire unauthorized population, and further concludes that any exercise of prosecutorial discretion is tenuous at best and does not result in a right or benefit to the noncitizen.[44]

The Morton Memo also listed the adverse factors that should be given "particular care and consideration:"

- Individuals who pose a clear risk to national security
- Serious felons, repeat offenders, or individuals with a lengthy criminal record of any kind
- Known gang members or other individuals who pose a clear danger to public safety
- Individuals with an egregious record of immigration violations, including those with a record of illegal re-entry and those who have engaged in immigration fraud[45]

The Morton Memo represents the most comprehensive guidance on prosecutorial discretion by the agency in more than a decade and is a welcome addition to the binder of policy documents created by DHS.[46] One unresolved issue in the Morton Memo, however, is exactly how the agency should treat a person who both falls within one of ICE's "civil enforcement priorities" and at the same time brings equities that warrant a positive exercise of discretion. Back in 1976, Leon Wildes could comfortably conclude from his research of 1,843 cases that humanitarian equities drove deferred action grants, even in situations where the individual had a potentially serious criminal history. The same conclusion cannot be drawn from the language of the Morton Memo. DHS must engage the complexity when faced with an individual who both reflects a "civil enforcement priority" and yet possesses a strong equity or a group of compelling factors.

Restrictionists were quick to identify the Morton Memo as "amnesty."[47] The publication of the Morton Memo spurred a new wave of congressional criticism against the agency's use of prosecutorial discretion and deferred action in particular. On June 23, 2011, Congressman Lamar Smith (who ironically was the same man to take the lead in writing to Attorney General Reno in 1999 in support of prosecutorial discretion, the substance of which was showcased in chapter 2) announced his plans to introduce the HALT (Hinder the Administration's Legalization Temptation) Act and issued a related "Dear Colleague" letter.[48] The HALT Act was introduced in July 2011 in both the House of Representatives and the Senate and, among other provisions, was designed to prevent DHS from granting deferred action as a matter of prosecutorial discretion and "suspend" the handful of discretionary remedies available under the immigration laws for compelling cases.[49] The politics behind the HALT Act are plentiful and are illustrated in part by the fact that the bill was set to expire on January 21, 2013, at the end of President Obama's first term.[50] The HALT Act was the centerpiece of the congressional hearing,[51] featuring the president of ICE's Enforcement and Removal Operations union, Chris Crane.[52] The fanfare around a bill to "freeze" DHS authority to exercise discretion and opposition by ICE's own union to the Morton Memo and other agency acts of prosecutorial discretion speak volumes to the controversy that surrounded the Obama administration's prosecutorial discretion policies. Seventy-five Democratic members of the House of Representatives sent a letter to President Obama critical of Republican efforts to freeze executive branch authority by introducing legislation like the HALT Act.[53] At the HALT hearing, Representative Zoe Lofgren (D-CA) expressed her disbelief that Congress would waste so much time on a bill like the HALT Act and pointed to the unintended human consequences if the legislation were enacted.[54] Meanwhile, Representative John Conyers (D-MI) characterized the HALT Act as "not an attack on the Presidency but an attack on the President himself."[55]

In a series of related events, Senator John Cornyn (R-TX) accused DHS of having a secret policy to dismiss high-priority immigration cases as a matter of prosecutorial discretion after his staff reviewed a series of internal memoranda and emails retrieved by the *Houston Chronicle*.[56] The internal documents were obtained through an FOIA request and included guidance from the Houston Office of Chief Counsel to his attorneys to file motions to "dismiss" in cases that fell outside of ICE's three stated priorities.[57] The *Houston Chronicle* characterized the policy as a scandal or "secretive review process [that] resulted in the dismissal of hundreds of cases in Houston, most of them involving illegal immigrants who had lived in the United States for years without committing serious crimes."[58] The Houston policy was eventually rescinded under pressure from ICE Headquarters and critics.

On July 5, 2011, House Judiciary Committee Chairman Lamar Smith (R-TX) and Homeland Security Subcommittee Chairman Robert Aderholt (R-AL) sent a letter to Secretary Janet Napolitano chronicling the release of various draft and official agency memoranda on prosecutorial discretion and expressing concerns that these memos were being used to "circumvent Congress and use executive branch authority to allow illegal immigrants to remain in the U.S."[59] On July 13, 2011, and citing the Morton Memo, Orrin Hatch (R-UT), former chairman of the Senate Judiciary Committee, joined Senator Jeff Sessions (R-AL) and four more Republican colleagues in urging ICE to stop trying to "grant administrative amnesty to millions of illegal aliens" and to start enforcing immigration laws.[60]

Significantly, the administration worked around these politics and in August 2011 announced a plan for implementing the Morton Memo with regard to cases already in the removal system and those set to enter the system. The "announcement" came in August 2011—and was accompanied by an avalanche of documentation from DHS.[61] One recurring theme in this avalanche was the identification of the Morton Memo as the "cornerstone" guidance.

Around this time, USCIS issued new policy on how to handle Notices to Appear (NTAs).[62] The memo outlined the priorities USCIS would follow in deciding whether or not to issue an NTA or refer a case to ICE. The memo highlighted the significance of using prosecutorial discretion before deciding whether a noncitizen should be placed in the removal system. This new guidance also served as an important reminder that all of the components of DHS (not just ICE) are authorized to issue or file NTAs with the immigration court and in turn exercise prosecutorial discretion favorably at what may be the most important part of the enforcement process. Whereas the power of whether or not to bring civil immigration charges in the criminal context is cabined to the prosecutor as we saw in chapter 3, ICE, USCIS, and CBP literally all act as prosecutors when it comes to deciding whether or not to bring civil immigration charges against a noncitizen.

Notably and more than one year after the Morton Memo had been originally published, ICE issued yet another memo on prosecutorial discretion targeted at same-sex couples.[63] Referencing the category of "family relationships" identified in the Morton Memo, the Family Memo remarks,

Same-sex relationships that rise to the level of "family relationships" are long-term, same-sex relationships in which the individuals—

- are each other's sole domestic partner and intend to remain so indefinitely;
- are not in a marital or other domestic relationship with anyone else; and
- typically maintain a common residence and share financial obligations and assets.[64]

Even before the guidance, the White House had indicated that the Morton Memo encapsulates all family relationships, including same-sex ones. But the "family relationships" guidance is more explicit about the breadth of family under the Morton Memo.[65] Before the U.S. Supreme Court's decision in the *United States v. Windsor* in which the Defense of Marriage Act was found unconstitutional, many same-sex couples involving at least one noncitizen relied on prosecutorial discretion in order to stay together and avoid removal. The chronology that began with the absence of a statutory remedy for recognizing same-sex couples under immigration law and was followed by a specific prosecutorial discretion policy by the agency to address these cases fits squarely within the thesis of this book and the "third" theory of prosecutorial discretion, to act as a stop-gap measure while legislation is pending.

Reactions and Critiques to the Morton Memo

While the Obama administration was successful in producing more memoranda on prosecutorial discretion during its tenure than had previous administrations, immigration advocates were critical of the effectiveness with which these memoranda were implemented. For example, the proimmigration reform group America's Voice remarked, "For thousands of immigrant families throughout the nation, the policies outlined in the prosecutorial discretion memo are not merely words on a page—they are a lifeline for keeping families intact. The guidance in the memo includes the common-sense rationale that mothers and fathers whose sole violations are tied to their desire to be with their families should be treated differently than serious criminals. However, the unfortunate truth is that even under this new policy, loving families continue to be separated."[66] Similarly, the Fair Immigration Reform Movement published a report assessing the implementation of the Morton Memo one year later and found that noncitizens with compelling equities continued to be targets for deportation. In one story reported by the Fair Immigration Reform Movement,

> Marvin came to this country from Guatemala twelve years ago when he was still only a teenager. Marvin's life now revolves around his five-year old daughter Madelyn, a U.S. Citizen. Marvin and his wife, Leslie, have been married since 2009 and are active members of their church. In October 2011, Marvin was stopped by a police officer and detained because he didn't have a driver's license because it is illegal for him to obtain one. Marvin has now been in detention for seven months; his daughter and wife are suffering emotionally and financially without Marvin at home with them. With two U.S. Citizen sisters as well as his daughter, his strong ties to his community, and many years here, Marvin is also a clear example of the kind of person and family for whom the

prosecutorial discretion policy was supposed to provide relief. But ICE continues to keep him from his family and try to deport him.[67]

The public stories about how DHS failed to exercise prosecutorial discretion were compelling, and matched by striking statistics about the actual number of people benefiting from the new policies. According to one group of statistics ostensibly produced by DHS, ICE reviewed 219,554 pending removal cases as part of the August 2011 prosecutorial discretion plan, of which 6,544, or 7.5 percent, were identified as amenable for prosecutorial discretion as of April 16, 2012.[68] The DHS statistics also revealed that 20,608 out of the 232,181 nondetained cases reviewed by DHS had been "offered" prosecutorial discretion. Within this subset, 4,363 cases had been administratively closed or dismissed.[69] The DHS statistics also showed that ICE reviewed about 56,180 detained cases and identified less than 1 percent, or forty of these cases, as amenable to a grant of prosecutorial discretion, likely in the form of release from detention and/or support for a motion to administratively close or dismiss the case.[70] Curiously, and without specifying whether the individual was detained or not, the same data set revealed that nearly four thousand individuals had *declined* an offer of prosecutorial discretion.[71] Presumably these individuals rejected the offer based on advice from a lawyer and/or because they were eligible for formal relief before an immigration court such as defensive asylum or cancellation of removal.[72] This type of relief is typically available only before an immigration judge, so individuals would prefer *not* to have their immigration cases dropped or dismissed. Imagine an individual from Iran placed in removal proceedings following charges connected with a visa overstay but who exhibits strong facts in support of a claim for asylum based on political persecution. Offering such an individual an unopposed or joint motion to administratively close her case is misplaced to the extent that she potentially qualifies for the more secure remedy of asylum before an immigration judge.

The DHS statistics were met with strong criticism by immigration advocates and the media. The American Immigration Lawyers Association reported, "The prosecutorial discretion initiative has failed. . . . DHS has reviewed 288,000, a paltry 1.5 percent of the cases were actually granted discretion, and even those were granted only a temporary reprieve, keeping their lives completely in limbo. That's a very low rate—far less than the percentage that succeed in obtaining relief in court."[73] Similarly, the *New York Times* declared, "The numbers fall far short of expectations raised among immigrants, including many Latinos, when top administration officials announced they would comb through back-logged court dockets to close cases where the immigrants had strong family ties to this country and no criminal records."[74]

Beyond the potentially low number of cases considered for prosecu-torial discretion were concerns with the implementation of the Morton Memo.[75] DHS appeared to focus only on people in removal proceedings and outside detention. There was little to no information about people who lacked counsel.[76] DHS also documented a preference for admin-istrative closure as opposed to other forms such as deferred action, a stay of removal, cancellation of an NTA, and so on.[77] Administrative closure comes with limitations because it does not have an indepen-dent basis for work authorization, is limited only to people who are already in removal proceedings, and reflects a decision that is ultimately made by the immigration judge, not DHS.[78] These measures by DHS were viewed as piecemeal at best and inconsistent with the guidelines depicted by the administration when announcing the Morton Memo and related prosecutorial discretion policy.

Perhaps no other group felt the piecemeal (or perhaps in their view, pitiful) implementation of the Morton Memo than the Dreamers. With the same spirit used in pushing Congress unsuccessfully to pass the DREAM Act, Dreamers pushed the administration to implement a prosecutorial discretion policy to protect them. While the Morton Memo included "residence in the United States since a young age" as a category deserving "particular care and concern," Dreamers criticized its implementation. The sentiment felt by Dreamers post-Morton can be drawn from the following statement by Dreamer Mandeep Chahal: "While the memo seemed to be on the side of hardworking undocu-mented immigrants, deportations of young Dreamers and families have not stopped. In fact, DreamActivist, a website devoted to aiding undoc-umented youth, sends out emails almost daily about new deportation cases involving young immigrants. There has been no real change on the ground in terms of protecting immigrants who were brought to the U.S. as children."[79]

DACA: A Partial DREAM Come True

On the heels of the criticism about the implementation of the Morton Memo, public pressure from advocates of the DREAM Act, and an authoritative letter sent by ninety-six law professors about the administration's authority to exercise prosecutorial discretion on a group basis came President Obama's announcement of Deferred Action for Childhood Arrivals (DACA). Before going into the specifics of the DACA program, a short history about the law professor letter is in order. Eminent law professor and scholar Hiroshi Motomura was approached by DREAM Act activists about crafting a letter outlining the legal authority of the executive branch to exercise prosecutorial discretion favorably on a categorical basis, such as for Dreamers. Motomura drafted a letter that pointed to three specific programs used historically by the immigration agency to grant prosecutorial discretion on a group basis, namely Extended Voluntary Departure, Parole in Place, and deferred action (all three were detailed in chapter 2). The authorities outlined in the letter were obvious to any immigration scholar or historian but carried special weight in a political space where the DREAM Act had failed, the Morton Memo had failed Dreamers, and the administration had earlier stated that it could not exercise prosecutorial discretion on a group basis. Student leaders presented the letter to President Obama at a White House meeting and also held more minor sit-ins in various locations throughout the country to express their demand for a solution by the administration.[80] The letter went "viral" after it was delivered to the White House and headlined the *New York Times*, but perhaps the most important audience it swayed was the administration.

On June 15, 2012, the Department of Homeland Security issued a memorandum in tandem with an announcement from the White House that provides prosecutorial discretion in the form of "deferred action" to certain young people living in the United States without legal status.[81] To qualify for DACA individuals must demonstrate that they (1) came to the United States before the age of sixteen as of June 15, 2012; (2) were in the country on June 15, 2012, and had continuously resided in the United States for at least five years; (3) are currently in school, graduated from high school, obtained a general education development certificate, or were honorably discharged from the Coast Guard or

Armed Forces; (4) have not been convicted of a felony, significant misdemeanor, or three nonsignificant misdemeanors; (5) are not a threat to national security or public safety; and (6) were not older than thirty-one as of June 15, 2012.[82] Within two months, DHS assembled a process by which DACA applicants could submit their application to USCIS and issued guidance like a "Frequently Asked Questions" document for use by applicants and their attorneys. Chapter 7 provides a more expansive take on the transparency that came with the DACA program.

DACA was heralded by immigration advocates as an important (but temporary) remedy after young people turned out in the thousands to reveal their undocumented status and showcase their intellectual promise, and also pressured the White House and the administration to exercise prosecutorial discretion favorably toward them.[83] The private bar, law school clinics, and nonprofit organizations mobilized in dramatic ways to serve the potentially hundreds of thousands of individuals who may be eligible for DACA.[84] For example, the immigration clinic at the University of Texas School of Law served hundreds of potentially DACA-eligible individuals.[85] Likewise, an event organized by the Illinois Coalition for Immigrant and Refugee Rights drew more than two thousand people on the first day of the application period for DACA with a line "snaking through hallways in the Navy Pier event center and down the pier, past a charter yacht and a Ferris wheel and south along Lake Michigan."[86] Moreover, websites organized by Dreamers were replete with information and tools for DACA applicants.[87] Finally, organizations collaborated on written practice advisories and tools to complement the information posted by USCIS.[88] Through the first quarter of 2014, 638,054 individuals have applied for DACA and 521,815 applications have been approved.[89]

Despite its successes, DACA faced criticism by some members of Congress, ICE officials, and restrictionists.[90] In fact, ten ICE agents filed a lawsuit in federal district court in Texas challenging the legality of the Morton Memo and the DACA program.[91] *Crane v. Napolitano* was eventually dismissed because of a lack of standing,[92] but it spoke volumes to the divide even within DHS over the use of prosecutorial discretion. Building on this criticism is a constitutional challenge by law professors Robert Delahunty and John C. Yoo, who argue that the Obama administration has breached its constitutional duty to enforce the immigration laws against individuals eligible under DACA.[93] They made this argument not in a courtroom but rather in the *University of Texas Law Review*.[94] Yoo and Delahunty centered their argument on article II, section 3, of the U.S. Constitution (the "Take Care Clause"), which states in part that the president "shall take Care that the Laws be faithfully executed."[95] Specifically, they argue that the Obama administration's DACA program is a violation of the president's duties under the Take Care Clause because under DACA the president is failing to enforce the immigration statute. This argument is misplaced and based on a flawed understanding of immigration and constitutional law. Importantly, the president's faithful execution of the immigration laws is not just limited to bringing enforcement actions against individuals and ultimately deporting them but also includes prioritizing the deportable population in a cost-effective and conscientious manner and providing benefits to deportable noncitizens when they qualify for them.[96] Delahunty and Yoo fail to identify the numerous sources of authority for prosecutorial discretion in immigration law. The Supreme Court has reviewed the roles of prosecutorial discretion in the administrative, immigration, and criminal law contexts. Likewise, as we saw in chapter 4 the U.S. Congress has affirmed the role of prosecutorial discretion in immigration law. In language identifying the evidence that would be required for proving lawful status for purposes of a federally recognized state driver's license or identification card, Congress explicitly included "deferred action" as a valid lawful status in the REAL ID Act of 2005.[97]

Yoo and Delahunty also charge that by creating the DACA program, the Obama administration "effectively wrote into law 'the DREAM Act.'" While it is true that would-be Dreamers bear the equities and qualities that would be traditionally considered under a prosecutorial discretion policy, it is inaccurate to conclude that the DACA program is identical to the DREAM Act. Beneficiaries of the DREAM Act are provided with a secure lawful conditional permanent residence and eventually have the opportunity to apply for permanent status and citizenship. The DREAM Act contains a series of requirements relating to continuous physical presence, good moral character, and age at the time of entry into the United States.[98] Significantly, the DREAM Act requires noncitizens to show that they bear no significant criminal history and are "not inadmissible" under the INA. By contrast, DACA results in no lawful status, no path to permanent residency, and no means of qualifying for U.S. citizenship.[99]

The political dust of prosecutorial discretion briefly settled because of the debates on comprehensive immigration reform. For example, many of the immigration advocacy groups and attorneys who previously invested their time and resources to conduct workshops and legal clinics on DACA or engaged with agency officials to recommend generous interpretation of the ambiguous terminology used in the agency's DACA guidance, rechanneled some of this advocacy and education toward comprehensive immigration reform. Following the November 2012 presidential election and reality that 10 percent of voters were Hispanic, advocates believed they had greater leverage to demand a long-term legislative solution to immigration.[100] Indeed, a new legislative debate was sparked and in 2013 resulted in the passage of a thousand-plus-page bill in the Senate that would holistically repair the broken immigration system.[101] Meanwhile, Senator Marco Rubio (R-FL) inaccurately warned his colleagues that if Congress fails to act President Obama may attempt to legalize the entire undocumented population by executive order.[102] Furthermore, House Judiciary Chairman Bob Goodlatte (R-VA) has "gone off the rails" over DHS's sensible exercises of prosecutorial discretion and continued to advance an antireform legislative agenda.[103] The chatter about prosecutorial discretion appeared quieter as immigration reform legislation took center stage in 2013.

Pressure from immigration advocates and communities on the administration to expand its prosecutorial discretion policy was renewed in early 2014 when the prospects for immigration legislation in Congress again waned. Criticism against the administration was further sparked by the accumulated removal numbers during the Obama administration. In March 2014, in response to this criticism and during the completion of the manuscript for this book, President Obama indicated that he would review immigration enforcement policies.[104] As this manuscript goes to print and the window for comprehensive immigration reform in 2014 closes, there remains a possibility that the administration will announce a prosecutorial discretion policy aimed at undocumented people residing in the United States.

6

Going to Court

The Role of the Judiciary in Prosecutorial Discretion Decisions

Consider Sara Martinez, 47, whose daughter is an American citizen. Since arriving from Ecuador, Ms. Martinez has paid her taxes, learned English and never broken a law, according to the New York Immigration Coalition, which has taken up her case. In January 2011, she was on a bus in Rochester with her daughter when three border patrol agents asked her for identification. She could produce only her Ecuadorean passport, and was arrested. She has applied to Immigration and Customs Enforcement for prosecutorial discretion three times and been denied, without explanation, even though she meets new criteria for such discretion: she has close ties to the community and is not a threat to public safety. Ms. Martinez's six-year-old daughter has suffered from nightmares, had trouble sleeping and eating and expressed fear that the "police" will come again and take away her mother (who is not in detention while the case is pending) for good.[1]

For Sara, and an unknown number of other individuals, a prosecutorial discretion "denial" often leads to the noncitizen's deportation or "removal," which in turn has been equated to "banishment," "exile," and "punishment."[2] In addition to the hardships faced by a noncitizen removed from the United States are potential hardships on the family or community he or she leaves behind, and often the family is forced to move to the country of removal with him or her. Furthermore, absent a waiver, a removal order prevents the noncitizen from returning to the United States or applying for formal immigration benefits or relief from removal for a minimum of five years, and in some cases forever.[3] Prosecutorial discretion can alleviate such hardships. Prosecutorial discretion decisions, however, are made daily without publicly available information about the facts behind cases approved, data about cases denied, or concern for the human implications in a regime where such cases have no vehicle for review. The historic lack of transparency of prosecutorial discretion, reports of inconsistent application of discretion from one U.S. region to the next, and the lack of incentives for officers to exercise prosecutorial discretion judiciously cannot be ignored. Judicial review of such decisions has been discouraged, even though the very potential for such review can serve as an important incentive that strengthens the quality of a DHS officer's decision making and thereby reduces the need for judicial review.

The absence of judicial review can lead to absolute discretion, which Kenneth Culp Davis defines as "[w]hen no other authority can reverse the choice made, even if it is arbitrary and unreasonable."[4] Yet Davis himself concedes that some absolute discretion is inevitable and expresses this inevitability through examples such as an executive pardon and a police officer's decision to write a ticket.[5] Absolute discretion is also an accepted principle in immigration law. In 1889, the Supreme Court interpreted various portions of the U.S. Constitution to give the "political branches" the plenary power to regulate immigration without a check from the judiciary.[6] The plenary power doctrine continues to be used to uphold a variety of congressional and executive actions that might be deemed unconstitutional if applied to U.S. citizens. The acceptance of absolute discretion in immigration matters has also been recognized in administrative law through the Chevron doctrine, which basically requires the courts to "defer" to an agency's interpretation of a statute if the statute itself is ambiguous and the agency's interpretation is reasonable.[7] The theory behind agency deference is reasonable and rests on the idea that the agency (in this case DHS) has specialized knowledge about the rules they administer and enforce. A more detailed analysis about the philosophy of judicial review appears later in this chapter, but the goal here is to provide a context for thinking about the immigration agency's historical position against judicial review of immigration prosecutorial discretion decisions. The immigration agency's stance on judicial review has been tied to the legal conclusion that such decisions are committed to the agency's absolute "discretion" under the Administrative Procedure Act (APA), barred by the immigration statute, and therefore immune from judicial review. Judicial review authorizes courts to review both legislation and executive actions for compliance with the law.[8] Two important principles that emerge from the judicial review function are the "rule of law," or the extent that judges are charged with examining whether particular actions are in compliance with the law, and "separation of powers," which is recognized by the limits placed on the issues judges hear and the standard they apply even with such review. This chapter examines the role of the judiciary in prosecutorial discretion decisions and argues that as a normative (and possibly legal) matter, certain prosecutorial decisions by the DHS should be afforded judicial review under the standards promulgated under the APA. Over the past decade, the agency has published substantial guidance on prosecutorial discretion, which today contains "more than enough law" by which a federal court could review prosecutorial decisions that are contrary to the agency's own guidance.[9] While an exploration into whether and when selective enforcement of immigration laws can violate a constitutional right is beyond the scope of this book, it should be pointed out that prevailing on such a claim is difficult.[10]

Making the Case for Federal Court Review of Prosecutorial Discretion Decisions

For more than a decade, the immigration agency has relied on select provisions of the Immigration and Nationality Act, APA, and court opinions applying these provisions to support its position that prosecutorial discretion decisions in immigration matters are immune from judicial review. Specifically, the immigration agency has depended on the conclusions in two Supreme Court decisions, *Heckler v. Chaney* and *Reno v. ADC*, to (re)state that prosecutorial actions in immigration law are not susceptible to judicial review.[11] As an example, the 2000 Meissner Memo reads:

> Courts recognize that prosecutorial discretion applies in the civil, administrative arena just as it does in criminal law. Moreover the Supreme Court "has recognized on several occasions over many years that an agency's decision not to prosecute or enforce, whether through civil or criminal process, is a design generally committed to an agency's absolute

discretion." *Heckler v. Chaney*. Both Congress and the Supreme Court
have recently reaffirmed that the concept of prosecutorial discretion
applies to INS enforcement activities, such as whether to place an individual in deportation proceedings. INA section 242(g); *Reno v. American-
Arab Anti-Discrimination Committee*. The "discretion" in prosecutorial
discretion means that prosecutorial decisions are not subject to judicial
review or reversal, except in extremely narrow circumstances.[12]

But it remains uncertain whether every immigration prosecutorial
discretion decision is prohibited from federal court review. Once the
immigration agency decides to publish policy guidance and publicly
announces that it will not pursue particular kinds of enforcement
actions against certain individuals, judicial review may be appropriate
if the agency has abused its own standards. As documented in chapters 2 and 5, DHS has amassed a reading room of prosecutorial discretion decisions since *Reno*, which creates a highly meaningful standard
against which federal judges could review unlawful decisions.

As described in chapter 2, the Meissner Memo instructed that "[s]er-
vice officers are not only authorized by law but expected to exercise
discretion in a judicious manner at all stages of the enforcement process—from planning investigations to enforcing final orders—subject
to their chains of command and to the particular responsibilities and
authority applicable to their specific position."[13] The Meissner Memo
outlined a generous list of humanitarian factors that officers should
consider in making prosecutorial discretion decisions and made broad
references to criminal law to explain the legality of such discretion.[14]
Even after INS was abolished, DHS continued to issue guidance documents on prosecutorial discretion.[15] As described in chapter 5, ICE
published comprehensive guidance on prosecutorial discretion that
identified more than twenty different forms of prosecutorial discretion and several positive equities the agency should consider in making
discretionary determinations. Nearly every document created by DHS
identified Morton Memo I as the seminal guidance to be followed. Finally, DHS created the Deferred Action for Childhood Arrivals (DACA)
program for certain noncitizens who entered the United States before
the age of sixteen and were without lawful status on June 15, 2012. The
DACA program included specific eligibility criteria, a six-page form,

a ten-page set of written instructions about how to fill out the form, a mandatory fee, and reams of internal guidance and public information about how DACA requests would be processed. Together, these new policies coupled with robust procedures and instructions for the DACA program in particular require at least consideration about whether such policies are drawn in specific enough terms to permit judicial review.

The Administrative Procedure Act Provides Broad Review over Agency Actions

The APA is an important source of authority for review immigration prosecutorial discretion decisions that might otherwise be thought immune from judicial review. The APA is a federal statute that allows an individual to sue a federal agency based on an unlawful agency action. An APA lawsuit is normally filed in federal district court. The APA provides review to "[a] person suffering legal wrong because of agency action, or adversely affected or aggrieved by agency action within the meaning of a relevant statute."[16] Section 704 identifies the actions reviewable as "[a]gency action made reviewable by statute and final agency action for which there is no other adequate remedy in a court."[17] The APA was enacted by Congress in 1946 and had four central purposes: (1) to require agencies to keep the public informed of their organization, procedures, and rules; (2) to provide for public participation in the rule-making process; (3) to establish uniform standards for the conduct of formal rule making and adjudication; and (4) to define the scope of judicial review.[18]

The breadth of judicial review under the APA and a way that it could be used as a tool for immigration prosecutorial discretion review are illustrated by a case from the Supreme Court called *Abbott Laboratories v. Gardner*. *Abbott* involved thirty-seven individual drug manufacturers and one pharmaceutical association challenging regulations requiring that labels and advertisements for prescription drugs that bear proprietary names for the drugs or the ingredients carry the corresponding "established name" every time the name is used.[19] The petitioners argued that the regulations exceeded the Food and Drug Commissioner's authority under the statute and were subject to judicial resolution. The government argued that pursuant to the first APA exception, no review was available because the governing food and drug statute includes a special review procedure for some regulations and therefore excluded review of the others. Rejecting the government's argument, the Court held that judicial review was available under the APA, and that the impact of the food and drug regulations on the petitioners was "sufficiently direct and immediate."[20] The Court noted that "[t]he legislative material elucidating [the APA] manifests a congressional intention that it cover a broad spectrum of administrative actions, and this Court has echoed that theme by noting that the . . . 'generous review provisions' must be given a 'hospitable' interpretation."[21] This decision indicated that executive decisions thought to be immune from judicial review could in fact be reviewed if the impact was particular.

APA review has further received a "hospitable" interpretation in immigration cases involving a motion to "reopen." A motion to "reopen" a removal case is a discretionary decision ordinarily made by an immigration court or the Board of Immigration Appeals (BIA) in order to consider new facts or evidence in a removal case where a decision has already been rendered.[22] The details about motions to reopen are specified in the immigration regulations, and generally require the applicant to file a written motion and attach supporting documentation.[23] The BIA has rendered a number of decisions pertaining to the scope and jurisdiction of motions to reopen.[24] Despite the supposedly discretionary nature of such decisions, the Supreme Court has concluded that federal courts have jurisdiction to review denials of motions to reopen deportation proceedings and that such review will be based on an "abuse of discretion" standard.[25]

In 2010, in *Kucana v. Holder*, the Supreme Court unanimously held that motions to reopen decisions, made discretionary by the attorney general, remain subject to judicial review.[26] The petitioner, Agron Kucana, moved to reopen his removal proceedings based on new evidence in support of his asylum claim.[27] The BIA denied his motion to reopen and the Seventh Circuit Court of Appeals held that it lacked jurisdiction to review his case because the INA precludes such review.[28] The Supreme Court then granted certiorari to decide whether the preclusion language within INA § 242(a)(2)(B) applied only to determinations made by statute or also to decisions made discretionary through regulations.[29] In concluding that the regulation governing motions to reopen may be judicially reviewed, the Court relied upon the long-standing "presumption favoring interpretations of statutes [to] allow judicial review of administrative action,"[30] stating: "Any lingering doubt about the proper interpretation of 8 U.S.C. § 1252(a)(2)(B)(ii) would be dispelled by a familiar principle of statutory construction: the presumption favoring judicial review of administrative action. When a statute is 'reasonably susceptible to divergent interpretation, we adopt the reading that accords with traditional understandings and basic principles: that executive determinations generally are subject to judicial review.'"[31] While the *Kucana* decision is limited to the judicial review of discretionary decisions to deny or grant a motion to reopen, the principle expressed by this Court is broader and supports checks and balances over unfettered discretion by the executive branch.

Scope of APA Review over Agency Actions

Even if a federal court assumes jurisdiction over DHS prosecutorial discretion decisions, the scope and standard of review are pivotal to correct abuses. If review in a federal court is a means to a favorable outcome for the noncitizen, then it barely matters if courts identify certain prosecutorial discretion decisions within their scope of review but then apply too high of a standard of review. For example, if Maria has standing to file a challenge to a denial by DHS to "cancel" her Notice to Appear or charging document based on documentation that she entered the United States at the age of nine, has three U.S. citizen children, has long-term residence in the United States, and herself suffers from a medical condition that requires regular attention in the United States, a federal court judge may be sympathetic but unable to reverse to remand (send back) a decision to DHS for further review if the standard requires the judge to find that DHS's factual determination to not cancel the NTA was "clearly erroneous." The standard outlined in the APA is a bit more flexible than the preceding hypothetical. Section 706 of the APA instructs a reviewing court to set aside agency actions that are "arbitrary, capricious, an abuse of discretion or otherwise not in accordance with law."[32]

The APA standard for judicial review has been applied by numerous federal courts in immigration cases. For example, courts have reviewed whether an immigration adjudicator's denial of a "continuance" was arbitrary and capricious. A "continuance" is a request that is normally made in writing to an immigration judge with information about the time and date of a removal hearing, preferred dates that a party is available to reschedule such hearing, and reasons why a continuance is desired. The decision to grant or deny a continuance is discretionary and governed by a regulation that states, "The Immigration Judge may grant a motion for continuance for good cause shown."[33] There is no form for such motions, but the Department of Justice's Executive Office for Immigration Review (EOIR) has published information about continuances in its Immigration Court Practice Manual.[34] Similarly, the BIA has interpreted the "good cause" standard.[35] For example, a noncitizen defendant in removal proceedings might argue that he or she has just discovered (through a newly hired attorney) that he or she is potentially eligible to a form of relief that was not originally considered at this preliminary hearing. The defendant might request extra time to determine whether he or she meets the eligibility criteria. An immigration judge might determine that discovery of a new form of relief is "good cause" and then grant the motion to continue so the noncitizen can properly evaluate whether he or she is eligible for a new form of relief and then file the appropriate paperwork.

Although the grant of a continuance is within the discretion of the immigration judge, it is well established that the BIA and federal courts do have jurisdiction to review continuance decisions.[36] The BIA has further held that it will not reverse a decision to deny a motion to continue a case unless the respondent establishes that the denial materially affected the outcome of the case.[37] In *Hashmi v. Attorney General of the U.S.*, removal proceedings were continued several times for petitioner Ajmal Hussain Shah Hashmi while his marriage-based petition (I-130 application) was pending.[38] After eighteen months, the immigration judge (IJ) denied another continuance because the case had been pending far longer than the eight-month period suggested by the "case-completion goals" set by the Department of Justice.[39] The circuit court found that the IJ's denial of a motion for a continuance based on case-completion goals rather than on the facts and circumstances was arbitrary and an abuse of discretion.[40]

The foregoing cases illuminate how "arbitrary," "capricious," and "an abuse of discretion" might be applied to prosecutorial decisions in immigration matters. As many of the directives on immigration prosecutorial discretion list multiple factors that an immigration officer should consider in deciding whether or not prosecutorial discretion should be exercised favorably, it is unlikely that a noncitizen who is denied can always meet an "abuse of discretion" or similar standard by arguing that he or she met some of the "positive" factors listed in a particular directive. Even the directives themselves offer enough flexibility to the immigration officer to reject seemingly strong cases.[41] On the other hand, some directives like the Morton Memo caution that no one factor is determinative. To the extent that denials of prosecutorial discretion are based upon only one factor or fail to take into account those factors that warrant "particular care and concern" in Morton Memo I, federal court review may be appropriate. For example, if Maria (in the hypothetical case above) can document that DHS failed to take into account some of the humanitarian considerations that the Morton Memo has deemed worthy of "particular care and concern" such as being an individual with a serious medical condition and being present in the United States since she was a child, then she might be in a better position to meet the "abuse of discretion" standard by arguing that DHS failed to follow its own guidelines. Similarly, if Maria happens to have a relatively minor criminal history in the form of a misdemeanor shoplifting conviction from her teenage years and can show that DHS denied her request to cancel a Notice to Appear because of this conviction, she might be in a posture to argue that DHS abused its discretion by singling out one negative factor, ignoring her many positive attributes and denying her prosecutorial discretion.

Agency Actions That Are "Committed to Agency Discretion"

The preceding section revealed how courts have interpreted the APA to support judicial review of agency decisions. Despite the APA's strong presumption in favor of judicial review, the APA itself contains an exception to judicial review to the extent that "agency action is committed to agency discretion by law."[42] Below are some of the seminal decisions analyzing the APA's "committed to agency discretion" exception. In *Citizens to Preserve Overton Park v. Volpe*, the U.S. Supreme Court considered whether the petitioners had a right to judicial review under section 701 of the APA.[43] The petitioners, a group of private citizens and some local and national conservation organizations, argued that the Secretary of Transportation had violated two statutes, the Department of Transportation Act and Federal-Aid Highway Act, by approving the construction of a six-lane highway through a 342-acre city park in Memphis known as Overton Park.[44] The statutes prohibited the use of federal funds to build highways through public parks if a "feasible and prudent" alternative route existed.[45] The Court held that the secretary's action was subject to judicial review under the APA and reversed and remanded the case back to the district court to make a proper determination about whether the secretary's decision that no "feasible and prudent" alternative to a highway through a park was a meaningful determination or an abuse of discretion. Writing for the majority, Thurgood Marshall was clear in the Court's position that the secretary's determination about whether a feasible alternative existed was not a discretionary decision immune from court review and resolved that the "committed to agency discretion" limitation under the APA applies only in those rare instances where the particular statutes are so broad that "no law" can be found to apply.[46] "Law to apply" may include not only statutory language, but also regulations, policy statements, and memoranda.[47] In applying this new standard, the Court held that the "committed to agency discretion" exception did not apply. Following the language of the APA, the Court held that the proper standard of review was whether the action was " 'arbitrary, capricious, an abuse of discretion or otherwise not in accordance with law,' or if the action failed to meet statutory, procedural or constitutional requirements."[48]

Another case, *Heckler v. Chaney*, involved a group of death row inmates challenging the failure of the Food and Drug Administration (FDA) to take various enforcement actions in connection with drugs being used for human execution.[49] The Supreme Court construed the exception narrowly, suggesting that review is precluded "in those rare instances" where "the statute is drawn so that a court would have no meaningful standard against which to judge the agency's exercise of discretion."[50] The Court found that the FDA's decision not to prosecute violations under the Federal Food, Drug and Cosmetic Act was unreviewable because such exercises of prosecutorial discretion are "committed to the agency's discretion."[51] The Court found that an agency's "decision not to enforce often involves a complicated balancing of a number of factors which are peculiarly within its expertise."[52] The Court found that the agency's refusal to act is "only presumptively unreviewable; the presumption may be rebutted where the substantive statute has provided guidelines for the agency to follow in exercising its enforcement powers."[53] *Heckler* is distinguishable from the immigration cases that may be reviewable because it focused largely on the agency's refusal to take an enforcement action, as opposed to the implications of denying prosecutorial discretion and taking an enforcement action.[54] The Court took great care in pointing out this distinction when it stated: "In addition to these administrative concerns, we note that when an agency refuses to act it generally does not exercise its coercive power over an individual's liberty or property rights, and thus does not infringe upon areas that courts often are called upon to protect. Similarly, when an agency does act to enforce, that action itself provides a focus for judicial review, inasmuch as the agency must have exercised its power in some manner."[55] Notably, *Heckler* has been singled out by the immigration agency as the basis for shielding immigration decisions involving prosecutorial discretion from judicial review.[56] However, such a reading does not account for the agency's amassing of standards around prosecutorial discretion over the past decade, nor does it address situations where the agency diverges from these standards and acts to enforce the law. Today, the standards outlined in *Overton Park* and *Heckler* support the premise of this chapter that many of the guidelines identified in directives like Morton Memo I or DACA contain "more than enough law" by which a federal court could review prosecutorial decisions that are contrary to the agency's own guidance.[57]

The limitations of the outcome in *Heckler* are also illustrated by the body of decisions surrounding the review of "affirmances without opinions" by the BIA. The BIA is the highest administrative appellate body in the Department of Justice's EOIR.[58] In 1999, the DOJ issued regulations that enabled the BIA to issue truncated decisions in the form of an "affirmance without opinion" (AWO) for particular cases raised on appeal.[59] The BIA's authority to issue AWOs was expanded in 2002 by a regulation issued by former Attorney General John Ashcroft.[60]

Following the promulgation of the 2002 regulations, federal circuit courts were flooded with appeals from noncitizens who were given an AWO in lieu of a meaningful review by the BIA. The practical effect of the AWO practice was that federal circuit courts received thousands of appeals challenging the quality and legality of the decisions being made by the immigration courts.[61] At the same time, these courts grappled with whether judicial review was available for decisions in which an AWO was issued. In many of these cases, the government relied on *Heckler v. Chaney* to argue that the BIA's decision to streamline a particular case was committed to agency discretion and was not subject to judicial review.[62] Rejecting the government's position, the First, Third, and Ninth Circuits found that federal courts have jurisdiction to review AWO procedures in immigration cases.[63] To illustrate, in *Haoud v. Ashcroft*, the First Circuit held: "Here, the Board's own regulation provides more than enough 'law' by which a court could review the Board's decision to streamline. As 8 C.F.R. § 1003.1(e)(4) sets out supra, the Board cannot affirm an IJ's decision without opinion if the decision is incorrect, errors in the decision are not harmless or immaterial, the issues on appeal are not squarely controlled by Board or federal court precedent and involve the application of precedent to a novel fact situation, or the issues raised on appeal are so substantial that a full written opinion is necessary."[64] Federal courts have also considered the standards outlined in *Heckler* to analyze whether the decision to "administratively close" an immigration case is "committed to agency discretion by law."[65] As discussed in the previous chapter, administrative closure is a form of discretion not included in the INA or the governing regulations, but rather has historically been guided by the following passage from *Matter of Gutierrez*, a precedential decision by the BIA: "Administrative closure of a case is used to temporarily remove the case from an Immigration Judge's calendar or from the Board of Immigration Appeal's docket. A case may not be administratively closed if opposed by either of the parties."[66]

Significantly, *Matter of Gutierrez* confused the prosecutorial role of the DHS attorney and the independent discretion of the IJ by giving

DHS unilateral power over the administrative closure decisions. On January 31, 2012, the BIA issued an important decision, *Matter of Avetisyan*, to clarify the independent judgment and discretion of the IJ and posit that IJs may "administratively close [removal proceedings], even if a party opposes, if it is otherwise appropriate."[67] Specifically, the BIA held that

> [i]n determining whether administrative closure of proceedings is appropriate, an Immigration Judge or the BIA should weigh all relevant factors, including, but not limited to: (1) the reason administrative closure is sought; (2) the basis for any opposition to administrative closure; (3) the likelihood the respondent will succeed on any petition, application or other action he or she is pursuing outside of removal proceedings; (4) the anticipated duration of the closure; (5) the responsibility of either party, if any, in contributing to any current or anticipated delay; and (6) the ultimate outcome of removal proceedings (for example, termination of the proceedings or entry of a removal order) when the case is recalendared before the Immigration Judge or the appeal is reinstated before the BIA.[68]

In *Alcaraz v. Immigration and Naturalization Service*, the court considered whether the BIA erred by failing to administratively close a couple's removal proceedings because they were eligible for "repapering."[69] The petitioners were married, entered the United States without inspection in 1989, were both employed, and had a U.S. citizen daughter.[70] Although the directives governing repapering were subregulatory, in that they were issued in the form of memoranda by INS and EOIR, the court found that the petitioners were potentially eligible for repapering and remanded the cases for further consideration.[71] The court highlighted the legal position that agencies may be required by the courts to comply with internal memoranda.[72]

The court disagreed with the government's argument that the court lacked jurisdiction to review the case because the INS's repapering decision was either precluded by the statute under INA § 242(g) or "committed to the agency's discretion by law" under the exemption in the APA. As to the judicial exemption outlined in section 701(a)(2) of the APA, the court made a reference to *Heckler v. Chaney* to note that the jurisdictional bar "is applicable in those rare instances where statutes are drawn in such broad terms that in a given case there is no law to apply."[73] However, the court found that the discretion of the agency had been legally constrained by the repapering memoranda and guidance issued by INS, and for this reason the statute was not drawn in such broad terms that there is "no law to apply."[74] The court affirmed that the "law" in *Heckler*'s "no law to apply" corresponds not just to the statute but also to policy memoranda and guides from the agency.[75]

Distinguishable from this jurisprudence and the ample agency guidance on prosecutorial discretion are a few notable decisions by the Supreme Court that have found an action was "committed to agency discretion under law" and therefore immune to APA review. *Webster v. Doe* involved an employee terminated under a provision of the National Security Act of 1947 (NSA), which allowed the Central Intelligence Agency (CIA) director "in his discretion" to terminate any employee "whenever he shall deem such termination necessary or advisable in the interests of the United States."[76] The employee was a covert electronics technician and was terminated from his employment after voluntarily informing the CIA that he was a homosexual.[77] The employee filed a lawsuit in the federal district court seeking declaratory and injunctive relief alleging violations of the APA and the U.S. Constitution.[78] Deciding against the fired employee, the Court found that the decision by the CIA was "committed to agency discretion" because the NSA provision was drawn in such broad terms that it provided no meaningful standard for reviewing the termination reasons.[79] Contrast the language contained in the NSA statute allowing for termination of an employee "whenever he shall deem such termination necessary or advisable in the interests of the United States" with Morton Memo I or DACA guidance, which contain a wealth of language about the factors that should be considered when making prosecutorial discretion decisions.[80] Morton Memo I runs six pages and lists no fewer than nineteen factors that DHS employees should consider in deciding whether prosecutorial discretion should be exercised favorably while creating a short list of compelling humanitarian situations like "serious health conditions" and serious negative factors like "serious felons" worthy of "prompt particular" care. Moreover, the DACA policy is posted on the website of USCIS and includes an official form, written instructions on how to fill out the form, a processing fee, and a robust list of "Frequently Asked Questions" in five languages. The documents associated with DACA coupled with the specific eligibility criteria spelled out in the policy are so substantial and so obviously different from the single line in the NSA statute.

Indeed, the standards outlined in Morton Memo I and the DACA guidance are more developed than many of the documents that judges have previously concluded contain "more than enough law" to warrant APA review. Together, the intent of the APA to create a judicial review scheme by which agency actions may be "checked," the jurisprudence in support of judicial review over agency action, and the body of circuit case law reading "committed to agency discretion" narrowly all show that federal courts should have jurisdiction to review select immigration prosecutorial discretion decisions under the APA.[81] For example, if twenty-year-old Juanita qualifies for and is able to document the DACA core requirements of having entered the United States before the age of sixteen, graduated from a four-year college, and no having any criminal history or run-in with law enforcement, but then is denied without explanation, Juanita should be able to challenge the DACA denial under the APA because a judge has "more than enough law" in the form of a memorandum from the agency, a "Frequently Asked Questions and Answers" document on the agency website, a multipage form and form instructions, and a related regulation. The judge has ample guidance and information from which to draw a conclusion about whether Juanita's denial was arbitrary.

Examining Preclusions to Judicial Review within the Immigration and Nationality Act

The APA restricts judicial review not only for decisions that are "committed to the agency's discretion," but also in situations where "statutes preclude judicial review."[82] Accordingly, it is important to examine the Immigration and Nationality Act (INA) for indications that prosecutorial discretion decisions by the immigration agency are foreclosed from judicial review.

A plain reading of the APA would suggest that if a section of the INA specifically precludes judicial review for a particular action, then such actions are unreviewable under the APA as well. As described in chapter 2, Congress made significant changes to the immigration statutes in 1996.[83] One change narrowed judicial review in immigration matters and in this spirit included a provision governing judicial review over specific prosecutorial discretion decisions. INA § 242(g) expressly states that no court has "jurisdiction to hear any cause or claim by or on behalf of any alien arising from the decision . . . to commence proceedings, adjudicate cases or execute removal orders against any alien under this Act."[84]

In *Reno v. ADC*, the Supreme Court interpreted INA § 242(g) to mean that immigration prosecutorial discretion decisions are immune from judicial review.[85] Writing for the majority, Justice Scalia clarified that the bar to judicial review is limited to the three acts included in the statute "to commence proceedings, adjudicate cases or execute removal orders" and made a specific reference to the practice of granting "deferred action."[86] Even though Justice Scalia could have read INA § 242(g) in broad enough terms to capture any immigration prosecutorial discretion decision, he read the statute literally and left the door open for judicial review of decisions falling outside of these three acts "to commence proceedings, adjudicate cases or execute removal orders." The Court's narrow interpretation is so significant today because the public has a better understanding about immigration prosecutorial discretion and is better positioned to identify and pursue court review for a variety of immigration prosecutorial discretion decisions that fall outside INA § 242(g), such as (1) deciding to issue a Notice to Appear, (2) opposing a motion to dismiss or administratively close a Notice to Appear, (3) denying a stay of removal, and (4) denying a request for DACA. Similarly, the *Alcaraz* court (discussed above) considered the statutory prohibitions outlined in INA § 242(g) and clarified by *Reno* to conclude:

> Under [INA § 242(g)], we lack jurisdiction to consider "to hear any cause or claim by or on behalf of any alien arising from the decision or action by the Attorney General to *commence proceedings*, adjudicate cases, or execute removal orders." [INA § 242(g)] [emphasis added]. While the second step in the repapering process involves a decision to commence (or "reinitiate") proceedings, the first step, the administrative closure of proceedings, does not implicate [INA § 242(g)]. The Alcarazes' repapering

claim only raises the issue of administrative closure. Therefore, we are not barred from hearing this claim by [INA § 242(g)].[87]

In applying the narrow reading of section 242(g) to the full range of actions that encompass prosecutorial discretion, it becomes increasingly clear that decisions that lie outside the three acts listed in 242(g) may be subject to APA review. The analysis demonstrates that in spite of the statutory preclusions of review over a few discrete decisions involving prosecutorial discretion, there are a number of decisions that remain subject to APA review. The June 17 Morton Memo describes the following discretionary enforcement decisions to illustrate the scope of prosecutorial discretion, many of which fall outside the actions outlined in 242(g):

- Deciding to issue or cancel a notice of detainer
- Deciding to issue, reissue, serve, file, or cancel a Notice to Appear
- Focusing enforcement resources on particular administrative violations or conduct
- Deciding whom to stop, question, or arrest for an administrative violation
- Deciding whom to detain or to release on bond, supervision, personal recognizance, or other condition
- Seeking expedited removal or other forms of removal by means other than a formal removal proceeding in immigration court
- Settling or dismissing a proceeding
- Granting deferred action, granting parole, or staying a final order of removal
- Agreeing to voluntary departure, the withdrawal of an application for admission, or other action in lieu of obtaining a formal order of removal
- Pursuing an appeal
- Executing a removal order and
- Responding to or joining in a motion to reopen removal proceedings and to consider joining in a motion to grant relief or a benefit.[88]

Notable but not necessarily critical to the analysis is the fact that some of the examples furnished by Morton Memo I, such as the cancellation of an NTA and a motion to dismiss removal proceedings, are governed by regulations.[89] The BIA has further made a distinction between the DHS's scope of prosecutorial authority before the initiation of removal proceedings and similar decisions made after such proceedings.[90]

Congress has identified specific discretionary remedies as immune from judicial review as a matter of statute. Specifically, INA § 242(a)(2)(B) precludes judicial review over many of the formal immigration decisions involving a discretionary component such as the criminal waiver of inadmissibility, cancellation of removal, adjustment of status, and "any other decision or action . . . specified under this title to be in the discretion of the Attorney General or the Secretary of Homeland Security, other than the granting of relief under section 208(a)."[91] These decisions involve formal immigration remedies that include a discretionary component and are adjudicated by DHS or EOIR depending on the jurisdiction. For example, Francis is a mother of two U.S. children who has lived in the United States for the past twenty years and currently works as a manager at a local bank. If DHS places Francis in removal proceedings before an IJ after charging her with residing and working in the United States without permission, she might pursue a formal application for relief from removal called cancellation of removal. To be eligible for cancellation of removal, Francis would have to establish that she has been physically present in the United States for a continuous period of not less than ten years immediately preceding the date of such application, has been a person of good moral character during such period, has not been convicted of certain criminal offenses and that removal would result in exceptional and extremely unusual hardship to her U.S. citizen children.[92] Francis would also have to show that she qualifies for cancellation of removal as a matter of discretion. Cancellation of removal and other formal discretionary remedies specified in INA § 242(a)(2)(B) are different from immigration prosecutorial discretion because the eligibility criteria are typically spelled out in the immigration statute, confer a formal and lawful status for the applicant, and may in some cases result in permanent relief in the form of a green card. By contrast, the eligibility for immigration prosecutorial discretion is not spelled out in the statute, does not confer a lawful status, and cannot be granted by an IJ. Nevertheless, the humanitarian reasons for formal relief like cancellation and tenuous protection like prosecutorial discretion are similar and serve as a reminder for the reasons why judicial review even matters. The broad role of discretion in immigration law was articulated by the Supreme Court in *Arizona v. U.S.* when it stated, "Discretion in the enforcement of immigration law embraces immediate human concerns. Unauthorized workers trying to support their families, for example, likely pose less danger than alien smugglers or aliens who commit a serious crime. The equities of an individual case may turn on many factors, including whether the alien has children born in the United States, long ties to the community, or a record of distinguished military service."[93]

Even though some sections of the immigration statute like the one identified above appear to preclude judicial review, another section of the INA was amended in 2005 to give courts of appeal the jurisdiction to review constitutional claims or questions of law in cases related to a final order of removal.[94] While this amendment expanded review for certain claims previously barred from judicial review, such as crime-related removals, it is unlikely that INA § 242(a)(2)(D) created a new judicial review forum for prosecutorial discretion decisions. To illustrate, the language limits claims based on constitutional claims or questions of law raised upon a "petition for review," which is a document traditionally filed after the noncitizen has been ordered removed. By contrast, the actions barred by INA § 242(g) are broader than the review available upon a filing of a petition to review.

One normative question and counterargument to my proposal is whether Congress would have intended to support judicial review of decisions involving prosecutorial discretion when it went out of its way to preclude it for more formal discretionary forms of relief from removal. I am not particularly persuaded by the argument given the ordinary rules of statutory construction,[95] and the reasonable case that without APA review prosecutorial discretion decisions are immune from review before any administrative or judicial form. Contrast this with § 242(a)(2)(B), where the decisions themselves are legally reviewable by an IJ and the BIA.

Prosecutorial Discretion Review and Why It Matters

The literature on the role of judicial review over formal immigration decisions is illuminating, and also relevant to understanding the normative benefits of federal court review over prosecutorial discretion decisions.[96] These benefits of judicial review are well summarized by immigration scholar Stephen H. Legomsky: "The judicial attributes discussed up to this point, independence and generalist legal knowledge, effectively improve the quality of the decisions that actually are reviewed in court. But judicial review also serves another function, one that operates even in cases that never reach court. The mere possibility that an alien will seek judicial review of an asylum decision encourages the various administrative authorities to study the case carefully and to state their reasoning intelligibly. . . . As a final benefit, judicial review in federal court provides a structure for the gradual development of legal doctrine."[97] Perhaps recognition of judicial review over certain prosecutorial discretion decisions can also lead to higher quality decisions by DHS by creating the kind of internal accountability Professor Legomsky describes. In this way, success of a judicial review scheme that includes certain prosecutorial discretion decisions should not be measured simply by how many people challenge a denial on APA ground or succeed in having a prosecutorial discretion denial set aside and remanded to DHS. Success should also be measured by examining how prosecutorial discretion decisions are improved in the first instance and whether fewer prosecutorial discretion denials are even challenged or set aside in federal court precisely because the availability of judicial review has affected the self-check by a DHS.

Lenni Benson also argues that judicial review may have its "own efficiency value" to the extent that federal courts clarify the meaning of vague statutory terms such as the definition of "aggravated felony."[98] Moreover, Benson describes how federal circuit review over immigration cases provides greater clarity in the changing strategies of the agency prosecutors, the procedural behaviors of the IJs, and the institutional reforms of the administrative process. When courts refine the interpretive tools for applying statutes and implementing procedures, they provide guidance to the agency prosecutors and to the administrative officials. This conversation between the courts and the agencies can help answer the open questions and thus help the system operate more effectively.[99]

In distinguishing the journey "from here to there," Benson defines there as a "sound, effective, efficient and manageable method of judicial review."[100] But the here of judicial review cannot be ignored and, according to Benson, represents the "expensive, time-consuming and exponentially expanding reservoir of cases that is our current system."[101] Beyond the monetary costs associated with judicial review is the concern with empowering appointed federal judges with limited immigration expertise to override the decisions made by experts who specialize in immigration. On the other hand, Legomsky has argued that federal courts have the benefit of reviewing the evidence and decisions made by the "expert" immigration agent and have the training to provide legally sound opinions.[102] Moreover, there is a concern that noncitizens utilize judicial review in order to delay their deportation.[103] However, without specific data about the motivations by noncitizens, "intent to delay deportation" is speculative. It is plausible that most noncitizens choose judicial review in order to exercise a substantive or procedural right under the law. Arguably, cases that are reversed by the federal court or remanded to the BIA would indicate that review is a means to achieving justice or a fair result, not a delay tactic. Legomsky also points to uniformity as a cost to judicial review, meaning that judges can rule differently on cases that present similar facts and, as a consequence, create inequality.[104]

Judicial review can also have negative consequences on the administrator, especially when the challenge is based on an internal guidance or "subregulatory" guidance as opposed to a rule specified in the statute or regulations. Immigration scholar and former INS General Counsel David A. Martin argues that pushing for enhanced judicial review over subregulatory guidance in immigration matters may cause a reduction of such guidance. As described in an informal electronic communication by Martin:

> Judicial review will inevitably reduce transparency by discouraging the promulgation and publication of such guidance. From my perspective as a former central office government lawyer, it's usually good management and good administration to publish careful guidance. . . . But if the price (from the agency's perspective) of written guidance is immediate or at least expanded exposure to judicial review, then the agency will cut back on the issuance of written guidance. Much more will be left to case-by-case decisions by individual adjudicators, which can simply obscure

from view the important considerations or de facto policies. . . . We don't always have good administrators, of course, but then we don't always have good judges. It's important to structure reforms in a way that doesn't make life overly burdensome or inflexible (or impossible) for those who are good administrators and who try to change course or improve administration from the inside.[105]

Professor Martin raises a good point about the negative impact that exposure to judicial review can have on an agency's future policymaking. Indeed, most thoughtful people would be troubled by a situation where the fear of judicial review causes the agency to repeal its most substantial policies and replace them with something overbroad such as the statute in focus in *Webster v. Doe*. However, the agency should not be shielded from judicial review as it pertains to prosecutorial discretion decisions because of the possibility for less clear guidance in the future. It may also be the case that the prospect for court review can prompt the administrator to follow its own agency guidance more carefully. Moreover, the focus here is on the body of guidance the agency has actually produced to govern prosecutorial discretion and the possibility that judicial review is appropriate when such guidance is ignored or abused. Morton Memo I was released with great public fanfare, reaffirmed as the "cornerstone" guidance in subsequent policies issued by the agency, and raised in several public meetings with advocates and zorneys. Likewise, the DACA guidance was unleashed at a speech from the president's Rose Garden and thereafter accompanied by a flurry of memoranda and guidance for the public. Even if one accepts that "ordinary" internal guidance should be shielded from judicial review, Morton Memo I and DACA guidance were no ordinary policy.

Beyond judicial review, federal judges can contribute in meaningful ways to the immigration agency's use of prosecutorial discretion. Federal judges have weighed in about the immigration agency's prosecutorial discretion guidance in their opinions. Months following the publication of Morton Memo I and its progeny, Chief Judge Theodore A. McKee issued an important concurrence for the Third Circuit Court of Appeals about prosecutorial discretion.[106] The case involved a highly educated software engineer from India who was sponsored for a green card based on a petition from a U.S. employer but who nevertheless was deemed to be subject to the immigration law's ten-year unlawful presence bar because of a visa overstay.[107] While the case itself was rejected based on a classic Chevron deference to the BIA's earlier position (a position that has since been reversed by the BIA!)[108] that pending adjustment applicants who leave the United States and attempt to reenter on "advance parole" are nevertheless subject to the unlawful presence bars, Chief Judge McKee offered the following commentary:

> I can only hope that Cheruku will be afforded such review and that the result will be favorable to her. My optimism in that regard is buttressed by a memorandum issued by U.S. Immigration and Customs Enforcement proving guidance to "ICE" law enforcement personnel and attorneys for the exercise of discretion in removing aliens. . . . Some of the discretionary factors that ICE will consider include the person's criminal history or lack thereof, whether the person is otherwise likely to be granted temporary or permanent status or other relief from removal, and the person's length of presence in the United States. Although it is certainly not our place to tell an administrative agency how to apply its policies, I do note that it appears that Cheruku would qualify for a favorable exercise of discretion under the new policy given her lack of criminal background, her employer's desire that she continue working as a software engineer, and her residence in the United States for the last 16 years.[109]

Chief Judge McKee indeed had "enough law" by which to review how DHS had applied its prosecutorial policies to people like Cheruku, but, leaving that point aside, the case itself should inspire federal judges to take positions on DHS's use of prosecutorial discretion and question cases that are taking up federal resources by landing in court after a removal order is issued by the agency. Moreover, Chief Judge McKee's commentary should motivate the DHS to consider the importance of review and ensure that its officers follow the "should" directive embedded in its own prosecutorial discretion guidance.

Beyond the Third Circuit, on February 6, 2012, the U.S. Court of Appeals for the Ninth Circuit published five opinions that ordered DOJ to "advise the court by March 19, 2012, whether the government intends to exercise prosecutorial discretion in [these cases] and, if so, the effect, if any, of the exercise of such discretion on any action to be taken by this court with regard to [these cases]."[110] The petitioners in these cases presented strong equities, such as long-term presence in the United States, children who are U.S. citizens, and no criminal record.[111]

The orders by the Ninth Circuit were not exactly a "review" of prosecutorial discretion but instead a judicial request that the government review the cases in light of Morton Memo I and implementing guidance and return to the court with a decision on prosecutorial discretion. Notably, Judge Diarmuid O'Scannlain issued a dissent in all five cases concluding that the aforementioned memo was "internal guidance," the judicial branch had limited review over prosecutorial discretion, and the judiciary lacked authority to demand "a preemptive peek into whether and when (and no doubt, before long, why) the executive branch will exercise such discretion."[112] These five decisions raise important questions about the role of the judiciary in decisions involving prosecutorial discretion, because the court was able to encourage DHS to follow its own policy on prosecutorial discretion.[113] They also reveal the court's ability to examine whether or not prosecutorial discretion has been properly exercised and then remand it back to DHS if it feels that a favorable decision is consistent with policy memoranda. As an example, had the *Cheruku* case functioned as a review of the agency's prosecutorial discretion decision to place Cheruku in removal proceedings, Judge McKee may have reached a conclusion that this decision was arbitrary and inconsistent with Morton Memo I and consequently should have been set aside and remanded to DHS for further investigation.

Another valuable use of prosecutorial discretion is to reduce the burden on the circuit courts. Perhaps this is one reason why the federal circuit courts have discussed immigration prosecutorial discretion so plentifully and why some courts have taken creative steps to remove sympathetic immigration cases from their dockets. For example, in October 2012, the Second Circuit Court of Appeals announced that it would suspend pending petitions at the circuit for ninety days so that the government could determine whether or not the cases on the circuit's docket reflected high priorities to the administration or may be worthy of a favorable grant of prosecutorial discretion and removal from the docket. Said Judge Dennis Jacobs: "[I]t is wasteful to commit judicial resources to immigration cases when circumstances suggest that, if the Government prevails, it is unlikely to promptly effect the petitioner's removal."[114] Likewise, the First Circuit Court of Appeals delayed ruling in a case involving a couple whose son had applied for deferred action under DACA. Judge Michael Boudin detailed the list of equities that applied to the parents and further alluded to his desire that DHS grant prosecutorial discretion: "[B]ecause they are the parents of a young adult who appears to be a strong candidate for deferred action, the government may well wish to avoid splitting up the family by declining to remove them as well. To ensure that they are not removed before the government has time to consider the question, we also stay the mandate for 90 days."[115] In addition to the measures federal circuit courts have taken to motivate the immigration agency to remove "low priority" cases from their dockets, the recognition of APA review for certain prosecutorial discretion denials can reduce the number of cases that are filed with the federal circuit courts in the first place.

This chapter examined the normative arguments about judicial review over immigration decisions, described the standards outlined in the APA and INA for judicial review of agency actions, and applied these standards to a portion of federal circuit court decisions involving administrative discretion to conclude that noncitizens possibly do have a procedural right to challenge a prosecutorial discretion decision by the agency under the APA because there exists "more than enough law" against which a judge can determine whether a decision was rationally made. The implications of an arbitrary denial of prosecutorial discretion are real: "[I]t visits a great hardship on the individual and deprives him of the right to stay and live and work in this land of freedom. That deportation is a penalty—at times a most serious one—cannot be doubted. Meticulous care must be exercised lest the procedure by which he is deprived of that liberty not meet the essential standards of fairness."[116]

7

Open Government

Transparency in Prosecutorial Discretion and Why It Matters

Transparency is an instrument used by government to promote democracy and the government's own legitimacy.[1] Transparency is a challenge, however, because too much of it can reveal information that is sensitive to the national security or the individual; or transparency may prove too costly if it results in reams of regulation and public input during its development or even litigation that would not have taken place. The immigration system is by no means immune to the transparency challenge. This chapter defines transparency and explains why it matters. It also describes the agency's historical lack of transparency in immigration cases involving prosecutorial discretion.

While the agency has issued several guidance documents about prosecutorial discretion, they have never been treated as binding rules or been accompanied by published statistics or regulations on the method by which one should go about applying for such relief. It may be that the agency's dependence on memoranda and other guidance documents to set its policy on prosecutorial discretion has contributed to the opaqueness.[2] My quest for data on prosecutorial discretion from DHS sheds light on the lack of transparency and efficiency that has pervaded the agency for years. I filed multiple FOIA requests to the DHS subagencies (ICE, CBP, and USCIS) beginning in October 2009, first inquiring about all records and policies pertaining to prosecutorial discretion decisions and later narrowing the request to deferred action cases.[3] While the data I received from the agency are detailed in chapter 4, the paragraphs that follow focus on the procedural treasure hunt I undertook to receive data on deferred action, however incomplete. Importantly, many of the challenges I endured in obtaining from DHS linger, notwithstanding the welcome improvements that have taken place as a result of DACA and the policy changes described in chapter 5.

Transparency at USCIS

In the case of USCIS, the first data set I received in 2011 was a 270-page document in addition to statistical charts about deferred action.[4] The data were variable depending on the office and location, as USCIS did not formally track information about deferred action. It is not possible to conclude that the records I received were complete, nor is it possible to analyze the entirety of what I received because there was a disparity between how the data on deferred action were collected and recorded by each office, if at all. The legible data I received on deferred action came in one of three variations: (1) spreadsheet or chart, (2) Form G-312s Deferred Action Case Summaries, or (3) a written request or memorandum by the applicant or attorney seeking deferred action. Moreover, the data I received came more than one year after my initial FOIA request, and with assistance from the USCIS ombudsman, who agreed to help move my FOIA request along. The inchoate form of the data I received from USCIS and the method by which I received it are consistent with findings of the USCIS ombudsman with regard to transparency and the deferred action program in 2011:

- Stakeholders lack clear, consistent information regarding requirements for submitting a deferred action request and what to expect following submission of the request.
- There is no formal national procedure for handling deferred action requests.
- When experiencing a change in the type or number of submissions, local USCIS offices often lack the necessary standardized process to handle such requests in a timely and consistent manner. As a result, many offices permit deferred action requests to remain pending for extended periods.
- Stakeholders lack information regarding the number and nature of deferred action requests submitted each year; and they are not provided with any information on the number of cases approved and denied, or the reasons underlying USCIS's decisions.[5]

My subsequent efforts to obtain information from USCIS about the deferred action program through FOIA in 2013 were slightly more successful. While some of these data are analyzed in chapter 4, they are mentioned again here to highlight the increased transparency from USCIS and efforts made by the FOIA office to provide me with information in a timely manner. The first set of data was a spreadsheet detailing the outcome in 17,040 work permit applications among individuals granted deferred action between June 17, 2011, and June 4, 2013.[6] The second set of data was a spreadsheet containing information about the number of individual and renewal deferred action requests made during a four-month period. As described in chapter 4, the second data set profiled 578 deferred action cases with specific information about the person's nationality, a short reason for why deferred action was being granted or denied, and a few other data points. Absent from the data set were whether a person was represented and specific detail for why a case was granted or rejected. As an illustration, many of the "reasons" provided in the deferred action logs included a single word like "humanitarian" or a specific sentence like "Subject claims to be a victim of an immigration scam. No other extenuating circumstances provided."[7]

USCIS also provided a set of policy documents on its deferred action program following a request through FOIA.[8] The response included 2012 "Standard Operating Procedures" (SOP) for processing deferred action cases at USCIS field offices, clarification that deferred action is not an "adjudication," and confirmation that an individual who is denied deferred action will not automatically be placed into removal proceedings or removed from the United States.[9]

In reflecting on my quest for deferred action information by USCIS, I believe establishing a relationship with the FOIA office at USCIS improved my chances of receiving a response and also allowed for more flexibility at the agency because they would let me know offline whether they were able to practically pull data or whether the data even existed at all. My correspondence with USCIS in between my written FOIA requests allowed me to clarify my request by phone and, if necessary, reduce the scope of my request. Beyond having regular communication by email and telephone with USCIS about my FOIA requests, time and practice improved my requests. In comparing my initial deferred action request to USCIS in October 2009 to the ones I made in 2013, there is more specificity about the data I am requesting, more clarity about how far back I would like the agency to go in pulling certain records, and more disaggregation between a request for policy and a desire for "records" or cases involving deferred action. Finally and importantly, USCIS appears to have also improved its own tracking methodology for deferred action cases. They are able to pull information electronically about deferred action cases that was previously unavailable because the data were not captured.

Unfortunately, USCIS still lacks several tools necessary for making the deferred action program accessible and transparent. Outside of the DACA program, USCIS has not created any kind of form or instructions for the public on individual requests for deferred action. Likewise, there is no way for attorneys or individuals to assess whether a deferred action request has been accepted for processing or rejected because there is no requirement or language from USCIS about how it will handle a deferred action request once it is received or how long the processing will take. Finally, there is no stated list of criteria or body of cases by USCIS about the types of cases it will process for deferred action, nor is there a mechanism for appealing or asking for a reconsideration of a request when a request is denied. In fact, the promulgation of DACA may have only added to the public confusion about the non-DACA deferred action program. To date, the SOP I received through FOIA is the only document accessible to the public on the agency's policy for non-DACA deferred action. The public should not have to rely on an internal memorandum unearthed by an FOIA in order to access basic information like how or where to apply for deferred action.

Transparency at ICE

In the case of ICE, I initially received a single chart detailing active cases in which deferred action was granted, but the chart was thin on detail about the facts involved in each case, the process by which deferred action was considered, the evidence presented to meet the eligibility for deferred action, and the conditions under which each case was granted. It took a lawsuit and careful deliberation between myself and the opposing party to obtain information, years later, about deferred action cases and stays of removal at ICE.[10] ICE itself conceded that it has tracked its own deferred action cases only since fiscal year 2012.[11]

The data I eventually received from ICE also had some limitations. As described in chapter 4, it appears that the data field in which an ICE officer reports the primary "humanitarian" factor contributing to a grant of or a primary "adverse" factor contributing to a denial of deferred action is limited to one field, meaning that there may have been more than one positive or a combination of positive and negative factors that influenced the outcome of a deferred action cases. Therefore, it was impossible to conclude whether individuals with criminal histories were granted deferred action. Moreover, I was unable to obtain information about who initiated the case, the gender of the applicant, the number of family members, the level of education, whether or not work authorization was granted, whether or not the individual was detained, what stage of enforcement the individual was at when his or her deferred action case was processed (e.g., pre-removal, post-detention, post-removal, etc.), and the length of stay in the United States, among others. Moreover, the ICE data contained no information about the background of the individuals making decisions about the deferred action or stay of removal cases. Insight about adjudicators' background and experience has contributed to a rich analysis in other immigration studies, but it was utterly lacking in these deferred action cases.[12]

Likewise, the data appeared to be limited to cases that had been decided, as opposed to those that were still pending or were abandoned. Transparency in the number of cases pending or abandoned could be useful for determining the universe of cases on the agency's deferred action "docket" during a given period. Moreover, because the data provided by ICE lacked A-numbers or other identification markers, I could not verify if a single applicant submitted multiple applications for deferred action or submitted an application for both deferred action and a stay.

Finally, I was unable to conclude how many cases involved a pro se applicant. According to the data I received from ICE, only 30 of the 3,837 involved a pro se applicant. Out of these 30 pro se cases, 3 of 8 deferred action cases were granted, while 14 of 22 stay cases were granted. The sample size was too small to reach a conclusion about whether individuals proceeding without counsel are more or less likely to prevail in a deferred action case. The data were limited because the actual field ICE uses to record whether or not an applicant is pro se or proceeding without counsel is a nonmandatory field.[13] Therefore, it is possible that while only 8 (of 698) deferred action cases were marked as pro se in the data provided by ICE, the number could be much higher. By the same token, it is conceivable that the vast majority of individuals who are processed for deferred action are represented by counsel, seeing as deferred action has historically been an elusive remedy. Deferred action is available only to those individuals with compelling equities and attorneys familiar enough with how the agency handles such cases.[14] Another data point ICE was unable to provide was whether a stay or deferred action case was initiated by ICE or the applicant (or his or her attorney). I should also acknowledge that "at least I got something!" Without the information, I would not be in a position to specify what was missing and/or which additional data points would have been helpful.

ICE still faces several transparency challenges with regard to deferred action and its prosecutorial discretion program more generally. Notably, ICE has created several guidance documents about the humanitarian and other factors it will use to determine whether a favorable exercise of discretion is warranted.[15] However, there is no indication that the manner in which ICE collects information on deferred action has improved or changed. Moreover, ICE has not created any form for the attorneys or advocates to use in order to request deferred action or any other form of prosecutorial discretion, nor has it articulated the conditions under which one form of prosecutorial discretion may be favored over another. For example, an attorney could pursue deferred action, a stay of removal, or both, for a single case, but lack the tools necessary to know which form to try first. Likewise, there is no way for attorneys or individuals to assess whether a prosecutorial discretion request has been accepted for processing or rejected because there is no requirement about how ICE will handle prosecutorial discretion requests once they are received. Finally, there is a dearth of information by ICE about the guidelines they follow when they are representing the government in removal proceedings. Whereas the decisions by ICE to join or not oppose a motion to terminate, to continue a case, or to close a case all constitute forms of prosecutorial discretion, ICE has not produced any policy about the circumstances under which one motion might be favored over another, if at all. Likewise, there is little guidance from ICE about the situations where it will stipulate to relief or not appeal a case in which the immigration judge has granted the noncitizen relief from removal, two important forms of prosecutorial discretion.

Transparency at CBP

CBP earned the lowest transparency marks. In my earlier work, I specu-lated that CBP lacked a specific policy about how it executes prosecuto-rial discretion generally and deferred action in particular.[16] My FOIA experience also suggests that CBP lacks data about prosecutorial dis-cretion grants or denials.[17] The closest data resembling prosecutorial discretion relate to the number of Notices to Appear issued by CBP over a two-year period.[18] In response to an FOIA request made by the Penn State Law's Center for Immigrants' Rights to CBP about the rate and circumstances under which Notices to Appear are issued, cancelled, or filed, CBP turned over more than a thousand pages of information detailing the issuance of Notices to Appear during fiscal years 2011 and 2012.[19] The data included information about the country of citizen and entry date and time in the United States for each individual. The FOIA response also included a brief discussion about CBP's "policy" on NTAs and referenced its Border Patrol Training guidance. However, the response lacked any information about CBP's use of prosecutorial discretion when issuing or preparing NTAs or indication of how many NTAs were never issued or filed because of a prosecutorial discretion.

In addition, CBP provided documents to the American Immigra-tion Lawyers Association (AILA) in response to an FOIA request for CBP policies around the exercise of discretion. Specifically, CBP pro-vided AILA the following documents: clarification on a 2002 INS "Zero Tolerance Policy" memorandum, factors to consider when exercising discretion and a list of available forms of discretion, a memorandum on the exercise of discretionary authority, policy differences between the exercise of discretion and prosecutorial discretion, and a memorandum outlining CBP's civil immigration enforcement priorities.[20] In the sec-tion titled "Prosecutorial Discretion Options," the CBP memorandum on discretion identified (1) withdrawal of application for admission, (2) voluntary return, and (3) release from detention and issuance of a Notice to Appear as examples.[21] The documents provided to AILA were themselves redacted and in some cases outdated, but the receipt of any written information by CBP about its use of discretion was welcome. While CBP's policies about the use of prosecutorial discretion gener-ally have been largely elusive, some attorneys have come to understand these policies through personal experience. In the experience of one prominent attorney, "CBP exercises prosecutorial discretion by refraining from filing an NTA and admitting a person to the United States or by granting parole or deferred inspection such that the person later qualifies for admission."[22]

Even though advocates have been able to squeeze out a few items from CBP, a few dated and redacted policy documents and reams of charts identifying the NTAs do not translate to successful transparency. Attorneys and advocates remain uncertain about the role of CBP in immigration prosecutorial discretion and the guidelines it follows when making related decisions. Moreover, there is a lack of any public information or data from CBP about the forms of prosecutorial discretion it uses or statistics about the individuals who have been considered for such discretion.

Agency Improvements and the Future

Importantly, DHS has taken some important steps to improve transparency in a few areas. To illustrate, DHS has offered important and specific information about the requirements and statistics associated with Deferred Action for Childhood Arrivals (DACA).[23] As iterated in previous chapters, DACA is a program that enables certain people to apply for deferred action status and work authorization with the USCIS if they meet the following requirements: they entered the United States before their sixteenth birthday; have continuously resided in the United States since June 15, 2007; were in unlawful status and physically present in the United States on June 15, 2012, and at the time of application for DACA; are currently in school or have already graduated; and have not been convicted of a felony, significant misdemeanor, or three other crimes, and are not otherwise a threat to public safety or the national security.[24] As with traditional deferred action, a DACA grant provides an individual with protection from removal and a favorable grant of prosecutorial discretion.[25] USCIS has created a separate application and work authorization application form for DACA, and has published the processing times for DACA requests on a monthly basis.[26] In a never-before-seen format, USCIS has also hosted teleconferences to answer attorneys' and advocates' questions about the data or future of DACA,[27] and has created a separate webpage featuring "filing tips" for individual requesting DACA.[28] Notably, USCIS has been collecting and posting data about DACA applications on a monthly basis. The USCIS data also break down DACA applications by nationality, state residence, and case status.[29] The DACA data show that the most represented countries in the DACA program are Mexico, El Salvador, Honduras, and Guatemala.[30] Lacking from the publicly available DACA data provided by USCIS are the reasons why cases are approved or denied, and information about whether the individual has representation. USCIS has also shared its internal policy guidance on DACA following an FOIA request made in October 2012. The FOIA request was transferred to DHS and resulted in a response dated March 2013 and totaling 459 pages.[31] The document provided the internal training modules and policy guidance used by DHS to implement DACA and notably has served as a public reference for practitioners and potential applicants. While the data on DACA are by no means comprehensive, these efforts are groundbreaking in their transparency and provide an opening for considering the ways in which the agency can and should track data about deferred action more generally.

USCIS has also been more transparent about its policy about the circumstances under which it will exercise discretion during the NTA process. USCIS issued a robust memorandum on November 7, 2011, articulating the circumstances under which an NTA would be issued or referred to ICE for further consideration.[32] Titled "Revised Guidance for the Referral of Cases and Issuance of Notices to Appear (NTAs) in Cases Involving Inadmissible and Removable Aliens," the NTA policy was aimed at informing interested parties about the various categories for NTA issuance and achieving coordination and consistency with ICE's own prosecutorial discretion policy. Elaborating on this policy and in response to an FOIA request by Penn State Law's Center for Immigrants' Rights and the American Bar Association Commission on Immigration, USCIS produced its internal policy on the issuance of NTAs in addition to select charts containing data on the number of NTAs issued during fiscal years 2011 and 2012. The data set totaled 193 pages and illustrated more than twenty kinds of cases for which NTAs were issued by USCIS. In fiscal year 2012, 43,845 NTAs were issued, and many cases involved green card, asylum, and credible fear candidates.[33] Importantly, the documents provided by USCIS articulated a prosecutorial discretion policy for NTAs, noting that "USCIS has the prosecutorial discretion when deciding to issue, serve or file Form I-862, Notice to Appear."[34] Furthermore, the FOIA-produced guidance explains that people with a pending or approved USCIS application that may lead to permanent residence, those under the age of eighteen, and noncitizen spouses of those in the U.S. Armed Forces constitute "humanitarian factors" for which prosecutorial discretion should be exercised. The USCIS documents identify six steps that adjudicators must take if an NTA should not be issued, and also requires a prosecutorial discretion memorandum to be placed in the file of the affected individual.[35]

Beyond its efforts to improve transparency in a few discreet areas associated with prosecutorial discretion, DHS has created a new platform for requesting information through FOIA.[36] The new platform allows individuals to make requests electronically on a standardized form to various DHS components, including USCIS and ICE. The FOIA website for DHS also includes additional visual and text-based examples for how to check the status of an FOIA request and the kinds of information that are exempt from FOIA, among other items. DHS and USCIS in particular should be recognized for improving transparency about specific prosecutorial discretion topics such as DACA and NTAs. Likewise, the creation of a web-based platform for FOIA may increase the number of requests made by individuals for information about prosecutorial discretion at the immigration agency and lead to greater transparency. However, whether or not the information should be made available without having to go through FOIA is a worthwhile question. Moreover, the lack of transparency around the non-DACA deferred action program and the ongoing dearth of information or guidance from ICE or CBP about seeking prosecutorial discretion reveal that there is more to be done.

Transparency advances values that are crucial to the administration of government such as consistency in the outcome of cases that include similarly relevant facts, acceptability by the public, and efficiency in the actual administration of the program.[37] Without clear guidelines and transparency about the prosecutorial discretion program, individuals with identical factual circumstances will be treated differently. No agency should tolerate this kind of arbitrary outcome. This sentiment is illustrated in a statement by the CIS ombudsman about deferred action cases at USCIS: "[M]inimal measures, including tracking requests for deferred action and regular review by USCIS headquarters of the requests and the determinations made, would help to ensure that there is no geographic disparity in approvals or denials of deferred action requests and that like cases are decided in like manner. . . . If implemented, this recommendation would make USCIS more efficient by tracking requests for deferred action and helping to ensure consistency in adjudications."[38] "Acceptability" is not so much focused on whether a particular process is in fact fair or acceptable, but rather on whether the procedure is perceived to be fair by members of the public and parties to the process.[39] Open rules and procedures about prosecutorial discretion allow people to make reliable plans based on an articulated set of criteria proffered by the agency and over time will result in a body of case law to indicate how these criteria are applied to individual cases.[40]

"Efficiency" refers to the time and expense invested in a particular process. Professor Roger C. Cramton explains that efficiency "emphasizes the time, effort, and expense of elaborate procedures. The work of the world must go on, and endless nit-picking, while it may produce a more nearly ideal solution, imposes huge costs and impairs other important values."[41] One might think that by keeping the prosecutorial discretion process under wraps, DHS is being more efficient. After all, nearly every form of prosecutorial discretion lacks an official application form, processing fee, system for reviewing denials of prosecutorial discretion, and reporting or data collection requirements. But this secrecy has resulted in negative publicity about the "failure" of prosecutorial discretion, congressional hearings about prosecutorial discretion, and multiple FOIA requests to DHS seeking basic information about the prosecutorial discretion program.[42] These costs are significant to DHS and make the prosecutorial discretion program less efficient.

DHS can transcend the transparency challenge by enacting some of the reforms outlined in the final chapter, and recognizing why transparency matters in the long run. The Supreme Court has concluded that "[o]nce an alien enters the country, the legal circumstances change, for the Due Process Clause applies to all 'persons' within the United States, including aliens, whether their presence here is lawful, unlawful, temporary, or permanent"[43] and has furthermore compared deportation to "exile" or "banishment."[44] Transparency about prosecutorial discretion improves the possibility that justice will be served for people whose roots and presence are in the United States.

8

Reform

Improving Prosecutorial Discretion in the Immigration System

The human impact of U.S. immigration law cannot be overstated. Each person who faces deportation has a story that may include a spouse, children, and parents and deep roots inside the United States. She might be an undocumented mother who is a primary caregiver for a young U.S. citizen daughter who suffers from a life-threatening disease. He may be a teenager who aspires to work as a doctor and who was brought to the United States as a baby without any knowledge about his immigration status. He may be a middle-aged man who has faced hardship in his birthplace and a jail sentence in the United States but whose dream is to provide for his family in the United States and teach his own children about the value of hard work. Deportation can hand these people cruel and unusual fates, which can also damage the souls of those who are left behind. As this book demonstrates, prosecutorial discretion is a powerful sword because it empowers the government to decide this fate for thousands of people and their families.

The Department of Homeland Security should be commended for publicizing its position on immigration prosecutorial discretion under the Obama administration by issuing comprehensive guidance aimed at protecting people who present sympathetic equities. Notably, DHS has gone one step further with DACA by creating a program that is transparent and aimed at protecting young people who satisfy the program's core elements and in modern times reflect the humanitarian face of the long-standing deferred action program. The administration has also withstood the costs for showcasing its position on prosecutorial discretion and creating DACA, including congressional attempts to repeal its discretionary authority and critiques about the limits of its authority. This criticism lacks a foundation against a rich history of prosecutorial discretion in immigration law over several administrations, but the political risk taken by the Obama administration should be recognized. There is a gap, however, as one considers the impact of the administration's current prosecutorial discretion policy on the lives of people who remain in the shadows or alternatively are apprehended and eventually deported. Relying on the history and values explored in this book, this chapter identifies recommendations aimed at bridging this gap.

From my point of view, the principal flaw of the government's immigration prosecutorial discretion policy is a willingness to categorically label people who bear positive qualities, like being the parent of a U.S. citizen and a steadily employed construction worker, as an "enforcement priority" because of an infraction of immigration or criminal law and without regard to the nature of the violation or their equities. DHS must embrace the idea that a person with a criminal or immigration history may still be deserving of relief and explain in more detail how a person's positive attributes interact with his or her adverse ones. In a context where the criminal code has grown exponentially as illustrated by chapter 3, a congressional stalemate has emerged on immigration reform for yet another year, and the very premise of prosecutorial discretion is to intentionally take no action against people who have violated the law, it is infeasible for DHS to maintain a policy that uses a bright-line test to divide its "enforcement priorities" from those who are worthy of protection from removal. The challenge is that some people who deserve protection as a humanitarian matter are flawed and in some cases even forced to break the law when the immigration laws themselves are broken. While DHS has dutifully published "priorities" guidance describing the people who should be targeted for enforcement action by the agency, these documents fail to define priorities in a way that captures the whole person or prospects of a legislative solution. To illustrate, ICE "priorities" include a breadth of people—those with criminal histories, individuals who recently entered the United States unlawfully, and those who are inside the United States with removal orders.[1] Of the 368,644 noncitizens removed by ICE in fiscal year 2013, 151,834 had no criminal history and another 95,453 had criminal convictions involving a misdemeanor or crimes punishable by less than one year of imprisonment.[2] Possibly, these individuals had other qualities the agency never learned about or overlooked because they fell within one of the agency's priorities, which proved to be fatal to any favorable grant of prosecutorial discretion. In fact, some of the people identified as a "priority" for removal by ICE may affirmatively qualify for a legalization program passed by Congress in the future. While DHS memoranda on prosecutorial discretion specify that no one factor is dispositive to a prosecutorial discretion decision,[3] the profiles of those removed by ICE,[4] anecdotes from immigration advocates and members of Congress about the impact of these removals on families,[5] and the absence of any language in the current policy about how and if DHS will navigate the complexity involved in exercising prosecutorial discretion favorably toward people whose flaws are intermingled with otherwise humanitarian factors or equities suggest otherwise. The agency should modify its formula for "priorities" and design it in such a way that a person's equities are the primary feature of the calculus, and where no one factor is fatal to a prosecutorial discretion decision. This design is in keeping with the humanitarian purpose of immigration prosecutorial discretion and its history.

Prosecutorial Discretion Early in the Process

Historically, DHS has favored decisions for prosecutorial review as early as possible in the enforcement process.[6] Among the series of enforcement stages at which DHS may exercise discretion, the pre-removal stages of enforcement, such as whether to arrest a person, whether to issue, cancel, serve, or file an NTA, and whether or not to detain a person, are among the most important during which DHS can exercise prosecutorial discretion to ensure that resources are managed wisely and individuals with strong equities are not subject to isolation from the community, an unfair process, separation from family, or exile to another country. While the guidance from DHS on prosecutorial discretion accurately identifies these "early" enforcement forms of prosecutorial discretion, the guidance itself lacks information about the methods DHS officers can use to improve prosecutorial discretion before an NTA is filed with the immigration court or after removal proceedings have begun. As discovered in one study,[7] there appears to be little to no record keeping about the NTAs that are not prepared, perfected, served, or filed as a matter of prosecutorial discretion.[8] Echoing the recommendations of that report, which remain unrealized at least publicly,

DHS should stop issuing NTAs against lawful permanent residents with strong equities, individuals eligible for a benefit or relief at the USCIS (e.g., U visa applicants), and individuals who bear the qualities and equities outlined in DHS policy.[9] Likewise, NTAs should be filed with the immigration court only after a DHS attorney has reviewed and signed the NTA.[10] While some interpret stated DHS policy as embracing all of the above recommendations, the transparency challenges outlined in chapter 7 coupled with the anecdotes sprinkled in reports like "To File or Not to File"[11] suggest that these early-stage decisions are not being handled consistently or efficiently.

On the other hand, when DHS is presented with a person who qualifies for a type of relief that requires him or her to be in front of an immigration judge, such as cancellation of removal, or with an individual who technically could be issued a swift removal order, like a reinstatement removal order, which is aimed to remove people based on a previous removal order,[12] DHS must use the factors listed in existing and hopefully revised policy guidance to file the NTA and procedurally place the individual into a removal hearing. For the undocumented individual who is potentially eligible for cancellation of removal, filing an NTA opens the door for her to explain to an immigration judge how her longtime residence, good standing, and compelling hardship to a qualifying relative satisfy her burden for lasting relief.[13] For the person who might otherwise be deported rapidly through reinstatement, a filed NTA enables him to see an immigration judge and be afforded a fair hearing and the right to apply for relief like adjustment of status (green card) or asylum.[14] DHS must adopt a national policy that confirms through clear guidance and human examples how filing an NTA can serve as a favorable act of prosecutorial discretion.

After the NTA has been filed, DHS should adopt a clear policy for how it handles prosecutorial discretion in removal proceedings before the immigration judge. DHS should issue a policy that allows ICE attorneys to join noncitizens or affirmatively make motions to terminate, administratively close, or continue removal cases while any agency for DHS is processing a request for deferred action or other remedy. The policy should identify the menu of tools DHS may use to exercise prosecutorial discretion during removal proceedings and include not only the various types of motions identified above, but also other actions like a decision to not appeal a case where relief has been granted by the immigration judge. Likewise, if DHS chooses to appeal a decision in which the noncitizen was granted relief by the immigration judge and in custody, ICE must exercise its prosecutorial discretion to release the individual absent exigent circumstances. While EOIR has taken a positive step in issuing a policy about how immigration judges should adjudicate continuances, closures, and terminations in removal cases where DHS has decided to exercise prosecutorial discretion, the policy itself is incomplete because it is limited to cases where such discretion has already been granted, does not address detention, and was published only for EOIR so that it has no virtual or actual application to DHS.[15]

Improving the Policy and Procedures for Prosecutorial Discretion

Noncitizens must be notified about a prosecutorial discretion decision. Like the agency has done with the DACA program, DHS must notify any individual considered for prosecutorial discretion about the receipt and outcome of his or her case. Likewise, if the individual has filed for a specific type of prosecutorial discretion such as a stay of removal, cancellation of an NTA, joint motion to reopen, and so on, DHS must acknowledge the receipt of the request in writing and provide a written decision. The correspondence should also identify the existence and process for any related benefits, such as work authorization. Moreover, it should include an explanation about the limitations of prosecutorial discretion. Finally, a similar letter should be sent to the individual's attorney, when applicable.

Individuals who allege they have been denied as an abuse of prosecutorial discretion should have a right to review. In particular, judicial review should be available to certain decisions that are "arbitrary, capricious, and an abuse of discretion." The standard for review could be "abuse of discretion" and, echoing one judge, could be articulated as decisions "made without a rational explanation, inexplicably departed from established policies, or rested on an impermissible basis such as an invidious discrimination against a particular race or group."[16] In applying this standard to particular acts of prosecutorial discretion, the standard could be (1) whether the determination to deny prosecutorial discretion represented a change in policy and, if yes, (2) whether DHS had a rational explanation for altering its policy.

The importance of federal court review is not limited to a favorable outcome for the noncitizen; such review ensures that noncitizens denied prosecutorial discretion are given an appropriate "day in court." The investment DHS has made to ensure that prosecutorial discretion is exercised properly on the front end must be matched on the back end by a review process to protect individuals and families who present compelling equities. Moreover, the opportunity for federal court review may promote the agency's desire to follow its own guidance on prosecutorial discretion and (re)consider cases in which prosecutorial discretion was denied.[17]

As an alternative to a judicial review scheme, DHS should consider an administrative review process outside of USCIS, CBP, or ICE. The Office of the Secretary could create an office responsible for reviewing petitions by noncitizens denied prosecutorial discretion who present evidence that the various DHS memoranda on prosecutorial discretion were ignored or misapplied.[18] The review process could begin as a pilot, rely on electronic filings, and result in a body of published decisions. Published decisions can improve transparency about the prosecutorial discretion program and, among other benefits, enable noncitizens who proceed through the immigration process without counsel to understand the contours of prosecutorial discretion and the application process.

DHS or an entity outside of DHS should create a professional code of conduct about the prosecution function. The code should create a process whereby public and government employees may file complaints against officers who are alleged to have engaged in prosecutorial misconduct as well as language about the potential repercussions an officer may face for knowingly violating the code. DHS must have an instrument for holding officers accountable when DHS guidance on prosecutorial discretion is not followed. Possibly, this code of conduct should be published in the *Federal Register* by DHS or an outside government agency. Appropriate sanctions must be applied to officers who systemically deny prosecutorial discretion requests to individuals who fit within the humanitarian criteria outlined in DHS guidance, or who act in a manner that falls outside the newly created code of conduct.

Recommendations Specific to Deferred Action

DHS must publish deferred action as a regulation in the *Federal Register*.[19] The regulatory language must recognize both the humanitarian and economic bases for deferred action. The cases analyzed in chapter 4 illustrate how the agency has long used specific criteria to adjudicate deferred action cases, and to enable individuals to avoid removal and reside in a tenuous status within the United States with dignity. Deferred action is the kind of the program that should be subject to "notice and comment" rule making under the Administrative Procedure Act. As an alternative, DHS should consider codifying "best practices" for formulating policy guidance on deferred action.[20] DHS's failure to recognize deferred action as a rule has left noncitizen grantees vulnerable to removal at a future date while preventing a countless number of qualified noncitizens from having knowledge about deferred action.

Rule making would also assist with narrowing the various factors used by adjudicators to determine whether deferred action should be granted. The data on deferred action cases indicate that decisions are based on distinguishable criteria and that a single regulation would only bolster the application of these criteria in like cases, and stave the inevitable abuse of discretion that stems from a system where cases are decided by different officers and without accountability. The benefit of using rules to guide discretionary decisions is not a new argument and has been affirmed by scholars in various other immigration contexts.[21]

Rule making is also cost-effective. The costs associated with rule making could be recovered by enabling immigration adjudicators to follow a clear rule, since unclear rules foster a longer and more costly adjudications process. Clearer rules on deferred action could also remove the costs associated with documenting every rationale and factor in a particular A-file, or gaining approval from a supervisor before granting deferred action. Implementation of a regulation would not necessarily increase litigation costs but, to the contrary, infuse a level of internal quality control and incentive for immigration adjudicators to apply the rule faithfully.[22]

Any proposed rule should include information about the scope of deferred action, including the information that it is a temporary benefit available to eligible noncitizens who meet specific criteria and who warrant deferred action as a matter of discretion. Possibly, this rule might include the list of individuals identified in the Morton Memo as "warranting particular care and consideration:"

Veterans and members of the U.S. Armed Forces
Longtime lawful permanent residents
Minors and elderly individuals
Individuals present in the United States since childhood
Pregnant or nursing women
Victims of domestic violence trafficking, or other serious crimes
Individuals who suffer from a serious mental or physical disability
Individuals with serious health conditions[23]

Those who are successful in obtaining deferred action should be granted temporary residence for a renewable three-year period, work authorization, and permission to travel for good cause. A grant of deferred action should not lead directly to permanent residency, but neither should it prohibit a grantee from applying for a more permanent legal benefit if he or she is otherwise eligible. The period during which an individual is in deferred action status should be recognized as a lawful status.[24] If the regulation on deferred action requires alteration after it is published, DHS should make adjustments to the regulation, "relying on exceptions, time extensions, variances, and waivers."[25]

The proposed regulation should be modest in its scope and focus on a fragment of the undocumented population who present compelling equities consistent with the agency's historical criteria for deferred action. In this way, the goal would not be to create a regulation that grants deferred action to anyone. The political risk and inefficiencies of creating a regulation that broad are high and furthermore may undermine the integrity of the existing deferred action program. Moreover, the breadth of prosecutorial discretion forms analyzed in this book clarify that DHS has other countless tools outside of deferred action to protect people who are or should not be rubber-stamped as an enforcement priority.

The immigration agency has previously expressed reservations about promulgating rules under the Administrative Procedure Act. The best illustration of this was in 1979, when the INS proposed a rule that would have explained the various criteria utilized by officers in determining the discretionary component of "adjustment of status" and other immigration remedies involving a discretionary component.[26] Many of these provisions would have required a favorable exercise of discretion in the absence of adverse factors. This rule-making effort was abandoned in January 1981 because INS opined that it could not foresee the universe of discretionary factors that may be present and was concerned about losing its discretionary power.[27]

The tension described by INS between taking steps to limit arbitrary discretion on one hand and the difficulty of predicting the new or multiple relevant factors on the other is a difficult one, and may explain the reasons why the agency would today hold reservations about publishing a rule on deferred action. Nevertheless, the agency argument that regulatory language providing factors to assess discretionary adjudication would limit its flexibility is unpersuasive. The agency has the ability to craft a rule that both lists criteria and adopts a discretionary component. In fact, there are existing humanitarian-like remedies that operate in this way. For example, cancellation of removal is a remedy codified as a result of the 1996 laws that is available to eligible non-LPRs and LPRs who meet specific statutory requirements such as continuous physical presence and residence in the United States for a specified time period or hardship to a qualifying family member who is a green card holder or U.S. citizen, and cancellation furthermore requires showing that the individual qualifies for relief as a matter of discretion.[28]

While DHS has done a fine job in implementing the DACA program, there is much left to accomplish with the general deferred action program. DHS should centralize the processing of all deferred action cases at USCIS to promote consistency, uniformity, and efficiency. DHS should create a form for deferred action requests, and require a user fee for processing the form. Consistent with other benefits applications, an applicant who is unable to pay a filing fee should be eligible to fill out a fee-waiver form. The application should be filed at a regional service center. USCIS should provide a written notification of receipt and the outcome to each applicant or his or her attorney. Finally, DHS should specify that enforcement action would not generally be taken against an individual because of information provided in a deferred action application or a denial of such application. Centralizing deferred action processing will enable the agency to publish statistics and track cases more efficiently and consistently.

DHS should make available to the public statistics about all deferred action cases. DHS should provide information about the number of deferred action cases processed, the facts of sample cases, the gender and nationality of the individuals processed, whether or not such cases are initiated by the applicant or the agency, the number of cases granted and denied, descriptions about the reasons for the grant or denial in such cases, whether or not the individual is represented by counsel, and whether or not work authorization was granted. In some cases, this will require DHS to expand the number of data points it collects on deferred action cases. For example, if a case is denied because of a "lack of compelling factors," the agency should track what factors were lacking and/or provide a short summary of the facts so that supervisors and others reviewing the information can interpret the data in a meaningful way. Such statistics must be made part of the annual statistics published by DHS and also posted on the various websites. Likewise, DHS should consider collecting biographic information about the officers adjudicating deferred action cases. This kind of information would provide a window for the public and the agency about the background of its officers and the extent to which particular experiences influence how cases are handled or perceived. Finally, DHS must publish the training officers receive on deferred action. Cumulatively, collecting and publishing information about the deferred action program will advance transparency and provide the public with tools for measuring efficiency, accuracy, and consistency in deferred action cases.

Some of the proposals outlined above have been adopted by DHS for the DACA program, but they have by no means been expanded to cover non-DACA deferred action and individuals who fall within the new regulation. DHS must commit to using the "best practices" of the DACA program and the tools outlined in this chapter as a blueprint for overhauling and codifying its broad deferred action program.

* * *

As I was readying the final manuscript and about to review page proofs for this book (which was the result of years of laboring in obscurity), it turns out that President Barack Obama on November 20, 2014, shone an exciting, bright light on the issue, by enacting a generous deepening of deferred action and revised guidance on enforcement priorities and discretion. I quickly scrambled to write these two paragraphs in a vain hope that they would serve as a bookmark and placeholder, one to which I will return. But not now, and not in this book, which I have already put to bed. I know that my work is not the last word—not even my own last word—so I will be grateful to have a new chapter on prosecutorial discretion being written in life, as well as at my desk.

President Obama announced a series of executive actions on immigration that dramatically highlight the legal, policy, and political relevance of prosecutorial discretion. These actions include an expansion of the DACA program and the establishment of a new Deferred Action for Parental Accountability (DAPA) program for qualifying parents of U.S. citizens and lawful permanent residents in cases where the parents have resided in the United States since January 1, 2010. These actions also include a new priorities memorandum entitled "Policies for Apprehension, Detention, and Removal of Undocumented Immigrants," which sets forth refined priorities for immigration enforcement. Effective January 5, 2015, the memorandum also contains a prosecutorial discretion policy that supersedes many of the related memoranda published by former ICE Director John Morton in 2011.

These actions are significant, but they do not involve a concept that is new as a legal or historical matter. Rather, they are consistent with some of the values expressed in this book, especially those related to greater transparency, uniformity, and robust use of the deferred action program. For example, the administration has publicized its new prosecutorial discretion policy and expressed an intention to produce explanations, instructions, and forms as necessary. Likewise, the administration has centralized the expanded DACA and new DAPA program at USCIS and rested the qualifications on largely humanitarian-based factors, such as a close family relationship and long-term residence in the United States.

ABBREVIATIONS

AC—Administrative Closure
An order by the immigration court that removes the case from the court's calendar of hearings.

AFM—Adjudicator's Field Manual
A document, periodically updated bæy USCIS, that provides detailed guidance to immigration adjudicators as to the rules and procedures for the adjudication of applications and petitions. A redacted public version of the AFM is available on USCIS's website: http://www.uscis.gov/laws/afm.

BIA—Board of Immigration Appeals
The administrative unit within the Department of Justice that handles appeals made by DHS or noncitizens in response to a decision by the immigration judge.

CBP—Customs and Border Protection
The federal law enforcement component of DHS charged with regulating and monitoring the inspection of people and goods at borders and ports of entry.

DA—Deferred Action
One form of prosecutorial discretion in which DHS administratively decides not to prosecute or remove a noncitizen. The granting of DA may provide eligibility to apply for employment authorization.

DACA—Deferred Action for Childhood Arrivals
One form of deferred action in which eligible individuals can file an application and pay a related fee with USCIS in exchange for a deferred action and work authorization.

DHS—Department of Homeland Security
The federal agency charged with protecting the United States from domestic emergencies and with enforcing immigrations laws. DHS absorbed

many of the functions of the now defunct Immigration and Naturalization Service. The three primary immigration houses within DHS are U.S. Citizenship and Immigration Services (USCIS), Customs and Border Protection (CBP), and Immigration and Customs Enforcement (ICE).

ENFORCE—Enforcement Case Tracking System
The web-based case management system operated by ICE that provides DHS officers access to biometric data and information on investigations, apprehensions, detentions, removals, and returns.

EOIR—Executive Office for Immigration Review
The component of the Department of Justice, directed by the U.S. attorney general, charged with administratively adjudicating immigration cases. Two components within EOIR include the Office of the Chief Immigration Judge, including immigration judges, persons responsible for hearing and deciding whether a noncitizen, charged for violating immigration laws, should be removed or granted relief; and the Board of Immigration Appeals, the appellate body responsible for the administrative review of decisions made by immigration judges.

ERO—ICE Enforcement and Removal Operations
The subcomponent of U.S. Immigration and Customs Enforcement that identifies, apprehends, detains, transports, and removes noncitizens from the United States.

FOIA—Freedom of Information Act
The federal mandate that provides the public full or partial access to federal agency information.

GEMS—General Counsel Electronic Management System
The case management system that provides ICE attorneys with updated information regarding the ongoing litigation of immigration cases.

ICE—Immigration and Customs Enforcement
The federal law enforcement component of the Department of Homeland Security charged with enforcing immigration law within the United States rather than at the nation's borders.

INA—Immigration and Nationality Act
The collection of federal statutes that govern U.S. immigration law.

INS—Immigration and Naturalization Service
The former name of the agency within the Department of Justice charged
with enforcing and administering immigration law prior to the formation
of the DHS and its components.

Nonpriority Status
The original name of "deferred action" as expressed by the INS and published in a policy following a lawsuit by music legend John Lennon.

NTA—Notice to Appear
The charging document that informs a noncitizen the charges being used
as the basis for the removal and the time and place the removal proceedings will be held. Removal proceedings against a noncitizen commence
once the NTA has been filed with the immigration court.

OI—Operations Instructions
The now-defunct internal policy guidelines promulgated by the INS in the
1970s. One of these OI advised INS officers to consider deferred action for
noncitizens in appropriate cases.

Ombudsman—Citizenship and Immigration Services Ombudsman
The appointed position within the Department of Homeland Security
charged with providing individual case assistance and with providing recommendations to improve the administration of immigration benefits.

OPPM—Operating Policies and Procedures Memorandum
Guidance documents used by immigration judges and published by Executive Office for Immigration Review.

PD—Prosecutorial Discretion
The decision by the immigration agency about whether to enforce or not
enforce the full scope of the law against a person or group of persons.

PM—U.S. Citizenship and Immigration Services' Policy Manual
The USCIS Policy Manual is the agency's centralized online repository for
USCIS's immigration policies and will ultimately replace the Adjudicator's
Field Manual (AFM).

Pro Se
One who represents oneself in a court proceeding without the assistance of
a lawyer.

USCIS—U.S. Citizenship and Immigration Services
The component of DHS responsible for adjudicating benefits applications, such as applications for adjustment of status ("green card"), naturalization, and asylum.

AUTHORITIES

Statutes and Regulations

U.S. CONST. art. II, §3, cl. 5.
"[The President] shall take care that the laws be faithfully executed."

Immigration and Nationality Act of 1952, Pub. L. No. 82-414, 66 Stat. 163 (1952) (codified as amended in various sections of 8, 18, and 22 U.S.C.). Also known as the McCarran-Walter Act, the Immigration and Nationality Act of 1952 consolidated existing immigration provisions into one organized body of law, eliminated racial restrictions on immigration and naturalization, and revised the national origin quota system.

Homeland Security Act of 2002, Pub. L. No. 107-296, 116 Stat. 2135 (2002) (codified at 6 U.S.C. §101 (2002)).
In response to the September 11 attacks, Congress enacted the Homeland Security Act on November 25, 2002. The act abolished INS and moved most of its functions to the Department of Homeland Security, charged with protecting the United States from domestic emergencies and with enforcing immigration law and policies.

INA §103(a), 8 U.S.C. 1103 (2006).
The statutory sections governing the authority of the attorney general in administering and enforcing immigration laws.

INA §239, 8 U.S.C. §1229 (2006).
The statutory section governing Notices to Appear.

INA §240, 8 U.S.C. §1229a (2006).
The statutory section governing immigration removal proceedings.

8 C.F.R. §239 (2010).
The agency regulation governing Notices to Appear and cancellation of Notices to Appear.

8 C.F.R. § 1240 (2010).
The agency regulation governing removal proceedings.

8 C.F.R. § 287 (2010).
The agency regulation governing the powers and duties of immigration field officers.

Select Cases

Lennon v. Immigration and Naturalization Serv., 527 F.2d 187 (2d Cir. 1975).
In a footnote, the Second Circuit described the nonpriority program as an "informal administrative stay of deportation."

Nicholas v. Immigration and Naturalization Serv., 590 F.2d 802 (9th Cir. 1979).
The Ninth Circuit held that the Operations Instruction on deferred action conferred a substantive right for petitioners.

Heckler v. Chaney, 470 U.S. 821 (1985).
The Supreme Court held that the decision of an administrative agency to exercise its discretion to refuse to take certain enforcement actions is "presumptively unreviewable" under the Administrative Procedure Act.

U.S. v. Armstrong, 517 U.S. 456 (1996).
The Supreme Court held that in selective prosecution claims, defendants must show that the government declined to prosecute similarly situated suspects.

Reno v. American-Arab Anti-Discrimination Comm., 525 U.S. 471 (1999).
The Supreme Court held that the Illegal Immigration Reform and Immigrant Responsibility Act of 1996 precludes federal courts from reviewing the following discretionary actions: the decision to commence proceedings, to adjudicate cases, or to execute removal orders.

Government Memoranda on Prosecutorial Discretion and Related Analyses

(LEGACY) IMMIGRATION AND NATURALIZATION SERVICE, OPERATIONS INSTRUCTIONS, OI § 103.1(a)(1)(ii) (1975)
The now-defunct Operations Instruction on deferred action by the Immigration and Naturalization Service that remained private until the Lennon lawsuit.

Bernsen Memo (1976)
Memorandum from Sam Bernsen, General Counsel, Immigration and Naturalization Serv., on Opinion Regarding Service Exercise of Prosecutorial Discretion (July 15, 1976), available at http://www.ice.gov/doclib/foia/prosecutorial-discretion/service-exercise-pd.pdf.

Meissner Memo (2000)
Memorandum from Doris Meissner, Commissioner, Immigration and Naturalization Services, on Exercising Prosecutorial Discretion (November 17, 2000) (on file with author).

Forman Memo (2004)
Memorandum from Marcy M. Forman, Acting Director of Office of Investigations, U.S. Immigration and Customs Enforcement, on Issuance of Notices to Appear, Administrative Orders of Removal, or Reinstatement of a Final Removal Order on Aliens with United States Military Service (June 21, 2004), available at http://www.ice.gov/doclib/foia/prosecutorial-discretion/aliens-us-military-service.pdf.

Howard Memo (2005)
Memorandum from William J. Howard, Principal Legal Advisor, on Exercising Prosecutorial Discretion to Dismiss Adjustment Cases (October 6, 2005), available at http://www.ice.gov/doclib/foia/prosecutorial-discretion/pd-dismiss-adjustment-cases.pdf.

Howard Memo (2005)
Memorandum from William J. Howard, Principal Legal Advisor, on Prosecutorial Discretion (October 24, 2005) (on file with author)

Myers Memo (2007)
Memorandum from Julie L. Myers, Assistant Secretary, on Prosecutorial and Custody Discretion (November 7, 2007) (on file with author).

Vincent Memo (2009)
Memorandum from Peter S. Vincent, Principal Legal Advisor, U.S. Immigration and Customs Enforcement, on Guidance Regarding U Nonimmigrant Status (U visa) Applicants in Removal Proceedings or with Final Orders of Deportation or Removal (September 25, 2009), available at http://www.ice.gov/doclib/foia/prosecutorial-discretion/u-visa-applicants.pdf.

Morton Memo on Pending or Approved Applications or Petitions (2010)
Memorandum from John Morton, Assistant Secretary, U.S. Immigration and Customs Enforcement, on Guidance Regarding the Handling of
Removal Proceedings of Aliens with Pending or Approved Applications or
Petitions, to Peter S. Vincent and James Chaparro (August 20, 2010), available at http://www.ice.gov/doclib/foia/prosecutorial-discretion/handling
-removal-proceedings.pdf.

Morton Memo on Civil Immigration Enforcement (March 2011)
Memorandum from John Morton, Director, U.S. Immigration and Cus-
toms Enforcement, on Civil Immigration Enforcement: Priorities for the
Apprehension, Detention, and Removal of Aliens, to All ICE Employees
(March 2, 2011), available at http://www.ice.gov/doclib/foia/prosecutorial
-discretion/civil-imm-enforcement-priorities_app-detn-reml-aliens.pdf.

Morton Memo I (June 2011)
Memorandum from John Morton, Director, U.S. Immigration and Customs Enforcement, on Exercising Prosecutorial Discretion Consistent
with the Civil Immigration Enforcement Priorities of the Agency for the
Apprehension, Detention, and Removal of Aliens (June 17, 2011), available at http://www.ice.gov/doclib/secure-communities/pdf/prosecutorial
-discretion-memo.pdf.

Morton Memo II (June 2011)
Memorandum from John Morton, Director, U.S. Immigration and Customs Enforcement, on Prosecutorial Discretion: Certain Victims, Witnesses, and Plaintiffs (June 17, 2011), available at http://www.ice.gov/doclib/
secure-communities/pdf/domestic-violence.pdf.

USCIS Memo on NTAs (November 2011)
Policy Memorandum from U.S. Citizenship and Immigration Serv. on
Revised Guidance for the Referral of Cases and Issuance of Notices to
Appear (NTAs) in Cases Involving Inadmissible and Removable Aliens
(November 7, 2011), available at http://www.uscis.gov/USCIS/Laws/
Memoranda/Static_Files_Memoranda/NTA%20PM%20(Approved%20
as%20final%2011-7-11).pdf.

Vincent Memo on Case-by-Case Review (November 2011)
Memorandum from Peter S. Vincent, Principal Legal Advisor, U.S. Immigration and Customs Enforcement, on Case-by-Case Review of Incoming

and Certain Pending Cases, to All Chief Counsel and Office of Principal
Legal Advisor (November 17, 2011), available at http://www.ice.gov/doclib/
foia/prosecutorial-discretion/case-by-case-review-incoming-certain
-pending-cases-memorandum.pdf.

DACA Memo (2012)
Memorandum from Janet Napolitano, Secretary of Homeland Security,
on Exercising Prosecutorial Discretion with Respect to Individuals Who
Came to the United States as Children (June 15, 2012), available at http://
www.dhs.gov/xlibrary/assets/s1-exercising-prosecutorial-discretion
-individuals-who-came-to-us-as-children.pdf.

USCIS Parole Memo (2013)
Memorandum Parole of Spouses, Children and Parents of Active Duty
Members of the U.S. Armed Forces, the Selected Reserve of the Ready
Reserve, and Former Members of the U.S. Armed Forces or Selected
Reserve of the Ready Reserve and the Effect of Parole on Inadmissibility
under Immigration and Nationality Act § 212(a)(6)(A)(i) (November 15,
2013) (on file with author).

CRS on Prosecutorial Discretion (2013)
KATE M. MANUEL AND TODD GARVEY, CONG. RESEARCH SERV.,
R42924, PROSECUTORIAL DISCRETION IN IMMIGRATION ENFORCE-
MENT: LEGAL ISSUES (2013), available at http://www.fas.org/sgp/crs/
misc/R42924.pdf.

CRS Memo on DACA (2013)
Memorandum from Andorra Bruno, Todd Garvey, Kate M. Manuel, and
Ruth Ellen Wasem, on Analysis of June 15, 2012 DHS Memorandum, Exercising Prosecutorial Discretion with Respect to Individuals Who Came to
the United States as Children (July 13, 2012) (on file with author).

Legislative Documents

Hinder the Administration's Legalization Temptation Act (HALT Act), H.R.
2497, 112th Cong. (1st Sess. 2011), available at http://www.gpo.gov/fdsys/
pkg/BILLS-112hr2497ih/pdf/BILLS-112hr2497ih.pdf.

Hinder the Administration's Legalization Temptation Act (HALT Act), S. 1380, 112th Cong. (1st Sess. 2011), available at http://www.gpo.gov/fdsys/pkg/ BILLS-112s1380is/pdf/BILLS-112s1380is.pdf.

Law Reviews and Articles

Susan M. Akram and Kevin R. Johnson, Race, Civil Rights, and Immigration Law after September 11, 2001: The Targeting of Arabs and Muslims, 58 N.Y.U. ANN. SURV. AM. L. 295 (2002).

Celesta A. Albonetti, Prosecutorial Discretion: The Effects of Uncertainty, 21 LAW & SOC'Y REV. 291 (1987).

Rachel E. Barkow, Institutional Design and the Policing of Prosecutors: Lessons from Administrative Law, 61 STAN. L. REV. 869 (2009).

Angela J. Davis, The American Prosecutor: Independence, Power, and the Threat of Tyranny, 86 IOWA L. REV. 393 (2001).

Bruce A. Green and Fred C. Zacharias, Prosecutorial Neutrality, 2004 WIS. L. REV. 837 (2004).

Stephen H. Legomsky, The New Path of Immigration Law: Asymmetric Incorporation of Criminal Justice Norms, 64 WASH. & LEE L. REV. 469 (2007).

David A. Martin, On Counterintuitive Consequences and Choosing the Right Control Group: A Defense of Reno v. AADC, 14 GEO. IMMIGR. L.J. 363 (2000).

Nancy Morawetz, Understanding the Impact of the 1996 Deportation Laws and the Limited Scope of Proposed Reforms, 113 HARV. L. REV. 1936 (2000).

Michael A. Olivas, Dreams Deferred: Deferred Action, Prosecutorial Discretion, and the Vexing Case(s) of DREAM Act Students, 21 WM. & MARY BILL RTS. J. 463 (2012).

Jaya Ramji-Nogales, Andrew I. Schoenholtz, and Phillip G. Schrag, Refugee Roulette: Disparities in Asylum Adjudication, 60 STAN. L. REV. 295 (2007).

Carolyn B. Ramsey, The Discretionary Power of "Public" Prosecutors in Historical Perspective, 39 AM. CRIM. L. REV. 1309 (2002).

Shoba Sivaprasad Wadhia, Business as Usual: Immigration and the National Security Exception, 114 PENN ST. L. REV. 1485 (2010).

Shoba Sivaprasad Wadhia, The Immigration Prosecutor and the Judge: Examining the Role of the Judiciary in Prosecutorial Discretion Decisions, 16 HARV. LATINO L. REV. 39 (2013).

Shoba Sivaprasad Wadhia, My Great FOIA Adventure and Discoveries of Deferred Action Cases at ICE, 27 GEO. IMMIG. L.J. 345 (2013).

Shoba Sivaprasad Wadhia, The Policy and Politics of Immigrant Rights, 16 TEMP. POL. & CIV. RTS. L. REV. 387 (2007).

Shoba Sivaprasad Wadhia, Reflections on Prosecutorial Discretion One Year after the Morton Memo, 2012 EMERGING ISSUES 6417 (June 2012).

Shoba Sivaprasad Wadhia, Response to the Obama Administration, the DREAM Act and the Take Care Clause, 91 TEXAS L. REV. 59 (2013).

Shoba Sivaprasad Wadhia, The Role of Prosecutorial Discretion in Immigration Law, 9 CONN. PUB. INT. L.J. 243 (2010).

Shoba Sivaprasad Wadhia, Sharing Secrets: Examining Deferred Action and Transparency in Immigration Law, 10 U.N.H. L. REV. 1, 34–38 (2011).

Leon Wildes, The Deferred Action Program of the Bureau of Citizenship and Immigration Services: A Possible Remedy for Impossible Cases, 41 SAN DIEGO L. REV. 819, 830 (2004).

Leon Wildes, The Nonpriority Program of the Immigration and Naturalization Service Goes Public: The Litigative Use of the Freedom of Information Act, 14 SAN DIEGO L. REV. 42 (1976).

Leon Wildes, The Operations Instructions of the Immigration Service: Internal Guides or Binding Rules?, 17 SAN DIEGO L. REV. 99 (1979).

Books

ANGELA J. DAVIS, ARBITRARY JUSTICE: THE POWER OF THE AMERICAN PROSECUTOR (2007).

KENNETH CULP DAVIS, DISCRETIONARY JUSTICE: A PRELIMINARY INQUIRY (1969).

DANIEL KANSTROOM, AFTERMATH: DEPORTATION LAW AND THE NEW AMERICAN DIASPORA (2012).

DANIEL KANSTROOM, DEPORTATION NATION: OUTSIDERS IN AMERICAN HISTORY (2007).

DAVID M. REIMERS, STILL THE GOLDEN DOOR: THE THIRD WORLD COMES TO AMERICA (2d ed. 1992).

NOTES

INTRODUCTION

1. The Alien Act of June 25, 1798, ch. 58, §1, 1 Stat. 570, 571 (expired 1800) ("[I]t shall be lawful for the President of the United States at any time during the continuance of this act, to order all such aliens as he shall judge dangerous to the peace and safety of the United States . . . to depart out of the territory of the United States."); *see also* STEPHEN H. LEGOMSKY AND CRISTINA M. RODRÍGUEZ, IMMIGRATION AND REFUGEE LAW AND POLICY (2009).

2. *Deferred Action for Childhood Arrivals*, U.S. DEPARTMENT OF HOMELAND SECURITY, http://www.dhs.gov/deferred-action-childhood-arrivals (last visited Dec. 20, 2013).

3. *See* USCIS OFFICE OF PERFORMANCE AND QUALITY, DEFERRED ACTION FOR CHILDHOOD ARRIVALS (February 6, 2014), http://www.uscis.gov/sites/default/files/USCIS/Resources/Reports%20and%20Studies/Immigration%20Forms%20Data/All%20Form%20Types/DACA/DACA-06-02-14.pdf.

4. *See, e.g.*, Stephen H. Legomsky, *Restructuring Immigration Adjudication*, 59 DUKE L.J. 1635 (201); Jill E. Family, *A Broader View of the Immigration Adjudication Problem*, 23 GEO. IMMIGR. L.J. 595 (2009); Dana Leigh Marks, *An Urgent Priority: Why Congress Should Establish an Article I Immigration Court*, 13 BENDER'S IMMIGR. BULL. 3 (2008).

5. For related articles and analyses on this topic, *see* Shoba Sivaprasad Wadhia, *Immigration: Mind over Matter*, 5 U. MD. L.J. RACE, RELIG., GENDER & CLASS 201 (2005); *Comprehensive Reform of Our Immigration Laws*, BACKGROUNDER (National Immigration Forum) (Sept. 2008).

CHAPTER 1. PRIMER

1. Arizona v. United States, 132 S. Ct. 2492, 2499 (2012).

2. *See, e.g.*, Memorandum from John Morton, Director, U.S. Immigration and Customs Enforcement, on Exercising Prosecutorial Discretion Consistent with the Civil Immigration Enforcement Priorities of the Agency for the Apprehension, Detention, and Removal of Aliens (June 17, 2011), *available at* http://www.ice.gov/doclib/secure-communities/pdf/prosecutorial-discretion-memo.pdf. *See also* Memorandum from Doris Meissner, Commissioner, Immigration and Naturalization Service, on Exercising Prosecutorial Discretion (Nov. 17, 2000) (on file with author) [hereinafter Meissner Memo]. This book is limited to an analysis of prosecutorial discretion by immigration personnel employed by DHS, including but not limited to officers, attorneys, and

supervisors. Beyond the scope of this book is a scrutiny of the discretion exercised by administrative judges under the Department of Justice's Executive Office for Immigration Review in the context of formal applications for relief from removal. Similarly, this book does not address the discretion exercised by immigration officers as part of the formal adjudicatory process.

3. *See, e.g.*, Shoba Sivaprasad Wadhia, *The Role of Prosecutorial Discretion in Immigration Law*, 9 CONN. PUB. INT. L.J. 243 (2010); Memorandum from the Congressional Research Service to Multiple Congressional Requesters, on Analysis of June 15, 2012 DHS Memorandum, Exercising Prosecutorial Discretion with Respect to Individuals Who Came to the United States as Children (July 13, 2012), *available at* http://www.ilw.com/immigrationdaily/news/2012,0720-crs.pdf.

4. Memorandum from John Morton, Assistant Secretary, U.S. Immigration and Customs Enforcement, on Civil Immigration Enforcement: Priorities for the Apprehension, Detention, and Removal of Aliens (June 30, 2010), *available at* http://www.ice.gov/doclib/news/releases/2010/civil-enforcement-priorities.pdf [hereinafter Priorities Memo].

5. As described by the late Maurice Roberts more than thirty years ago: "In the fiscal year ending June 30, 1974, the Service apprehended a record 788,000 deportable aliens and it has estimated that the total number of illegal aliens 'is possibly as great as 10 or 12 million.' While the accuracy of these high estimates has been questioned, it is clear that the Service has identified many more aliens here unlawfully than it has proceeded against. In determining which illegal aliens should be singled out for the initiation of deportation proceedings and which should be permitted to remain unmolested, for how long they should be permitted to remain and under what conditions, the Service exercises what is tantamount to prosecutorial discretion." Maurice A. Roberts, *The Exercise of Administrative Discretion under Immigration Laws*, 13 SAN DIEGO L. REV. 144, 146 (1975–76).

6. *See, e.g.*, Homeland Security Act of 2002, Pub. L. No. 107-296, 116 Stat. 2135 (2002).

7. *See, e.g., id.*

8. U.S. CITIZENSHIP AND IMMIGRATION SERVICES, http://www.uscis.gov (last visited Dec. 20, 2013).

9. *See generally* U.S. CITIZENSHIP AND IMMIGRATION SERVICES, http://www.uscis.gov (last visited Dec. 20, 2013).

10. U.S. CUSTOMS AND BORDER PROTECTION, http://www.cbp.gov (last visited Dec. 20, 2013); U.S. IMMIGRATION AND CUSTOMS ENFORCEMENT, http://www.ice.gov (last visited Dec. 20, 2013).

11. *See generally*, U.S. CUSTOMS AND BORDER PROTECTION, http://www.cbp.gov (last visited Dec. 20, 2013).

12. *See generally* U.S. IMMIGRATION AND CUSTOMS ENFORCEMENT, http://www.ice.gov (last visited Dec. 20, 2013).

13. U.S. IMMIGRATION AND CUSTOMS ENFORCEMENT, Office of the Principal Legal Advisor (OPLA), http://www.ice.gov/about/offices/leadership/opla/ (last visited July 20, 2014).

14. *See generally Executive Office for Immigration Review*, U.S. DEPARTMENT OF JUSTICE, http://www.usdoj.gov/eoir (last visited Dec. 20, 2013); *Visas*, U.S. DEPARTMENT OF STATE, http://travel.state.gov/content/visas/english.html (last visited July 18, 2014).

15. *Administration for Children & Families*, U.S. DEPARTMENT OF HEALTH AND HUMAN SERVICES, http://www.acf.hhs.gov (last visited Dec. 20, 2013); *About the Office for Civil Rights and Civil Liberties*, U.S. DEPARTMENT OF HOMELAND SECURITY, http://www.dhs.gov/xabout/structure/editorial_0371.shtm (last visited Dec. 20, 2013); *Executive Office for Immigration Review*, U.S. DEPARTMENT OF JUSTICE, http://www.usdoj.gov/eoir (last visited Dec. 20, 2013).

16. *See* David A. Martin, *Immigration Policy and the Homeland Security Act Reorganization: An Early Agenda for Practical Improvements*, MIGRATION POLICY INSTITUTE INSIGHT (April 2003), *available at* http://www.migrationpolicy.org/insight/insight_4-2003.pdf.

17. INA § 103(a), 8 U.S.C. § 1103(a) (2010).

18. *See, e.g.*, Homeland Security Act of 2002, Pub. L. No. 107-296, 116 Stat. 2135 (2002); Memorandum from William J. Howard, Principal Legal Advisor, U.S. Immigration and Customs Enforcement, on Prosecutorial Discretion (Oct. 24, 2005) (on file with author) [hereinafter Howard Memo]; Meissner Memo.

19. *See, e.g.*, Morton Memo on Prosecutorial Discretion; Meissner Memo; Howard Memo.

20. *See, e.g.*, Morton Memo on Prosecutorial Discretion; Meissner Memo; Howard Memo.

21. *See* INA § 239, 8 U.S.C. § 1229 (2006). Some noncitizens are administratively removed from the United States without formal removal proceedings. For example, under the INA § 235, arriving noncitizens who enter an airport without proper documents or false documents can be summarily be removed by the DHS, and do not have a legal right to review by an immigration judge. Similarly, under the INA § 217, individuals who enter the United States under the Visa Waiver Program (VWP) are required to "waive" their right to appeal or review in a court as a condition of their admission under the VWP. An interesting point is how prosecutorial discretion impacts individuals like the VWP entrant or the individual subject to expedited removal, especially if such persons possess the kinds of equities and qualities that are worthy of a favorable grant of prosecutorial discretion.

22. *See* 8 C.F.R. § 1003.14 ("Jurisdiction and commencement of proceedings. (a) Jurisdiction vests, and proceedings before an Immigration Judge commence, when a charging document is filed with the Immigration Court by the Service. The charging document must include a certificate showing service on the opposing party pursuant to § 1003.32 which indicates the Immigration Court in which the charging document is filed."). It should be noted that DHS also may exercise prosecutorial discretion by canceling an NTA even before it is filed with the immigration court.

23. *FY 2012 Statistical Yearbook*, EXECUTIVE OFFICE FOR IMMIGRATION REVIEW, http://www.justice.gov/eoir/statspub/fy12syb.pdf (last updated Mar. 2013).

24. *See* INA §§ 245, 8 U.S.C. § 1255 (2006); 240A, 8 U.S.C. § 1229b (2006); 208, 8 U.S.C. § 1158 (2006).

25. Outside of the removal context, a DHS officer may engage in a similar exercise of "adjudicatory discretion" when considering a waiver of inadmissibility or application for immigration benefit.

26. *See Office of the Chief Immigration Judge,* U.S. DEPARTMENT OF JUSTICE, http://www.justice.gov/eoir/ocijinfo.htm (last visited Dec. 20, 2013). *See also* INA § 240; 8 C.F.R. § 1240.1 (2013).

27. *See, e.g.,* 8 C.F.R. § 1003.23; 8 C.F.R. § 1239.2; *Matter of Gutierrez,* 21 I. & N. Dec. 479 (BIA 1996); *Matter of G-N-C,* 22 I. & N. Dec. 281 (BIA 1998). 21 I. & N. Dec. 479 (BIA 1996).

28. *See, e.g.,* Morton Memo on Prosecutorial Discretion; American Bar Association Commission on Immigration, *Reforming the Immigration System: Proposals to Promote Independence, Fairness, Efficiency, and Professionalism in the Adjudication of Removal Cases* (2010), *available at* http://www.americanbar.org/content/dam/aba/publications/ commission_on_immigration/coi_complete_full_report.pdf. In some cases, a person who faces a truncated removal from ICE in lieu of a removal proceeding or wishes to seek a type of relief from removal that requires him or her to be in removal proceedings may affirmatively seek an NTA from the government.

29. *See* INA § 242(a)(2)(A-C), 8 U.S.C. § 1252 (2006).

30. Defined simply to illustrate the Congress and the executive branch's "plenary" authority over immigration law. For a broader explanation, *see* Stephen H. Legomsky, *Fear and Loathing in Congress and the Courts: Immigration and Judicial Review,* 78 TEX. L. REV. 1615, 1615–16 (2000).

31. *See, e.g.,* Daniel Kanstroom, *Surrounding the Hole in the Doughnut: Discretion and Deference in U.S. Immigration Law,* 18 IMMIGR. AND NAT'LITY L. REV. 137 (1997); Daniel Kanstroom, *The Better Part of Valor: The REAL ID Act, Discretion, and the "Rule" of Immigration Law,* 51 N.Y.L. SCH. L. REV. 161, 163 (2006); Stephen H. Legomsky, *Political Asylum and the Theory of Judicial Review,* 73 MINN. L. REV. 1208 (1989); Jill E. Family, *A Broader View of the Immigration Adjudication Problem,* 23 GEO. IMMIGR. L.J. 595, 608–9 (2009); Lenni B. Benson, *Making Paper Dolls: How Restrictions on Judicial Review and the Administrative Process Increase Immigration Cases in the Federal Courts,* 51 N.Y.L. SCH. L. REV. 37, 39 (2006); Legomsky, *Fear and Loathing in Congress and the Courts.*

32. Adam B. Cox and Cristina M. Rodríguez, *The President and Immigration Law,* 119 YALE L.J. 458, 518–19 (2009) ("[T]his effort to insulate decisions regarding relief from the prosecutorial arm of the immigration agencies has been undermined by the recent changes to the relief provisions. These changes have had the effect of shifting more aspects of the deportation decision back to [ICE]. Far from eliminating discretion, then, the statutory restrictions on discretionary relief have simply consolidated this discretion in the agency officials responsible for charging decisions. Prosecutorial discretion has thus overtaken the exercise of discretion by immigration judges when it comes to questions of relief.").

CHAPTER 2. THE EARLY YEARS

1. Lennon v. INS, 527 F.2d 187, 195 (2d Cir. 1975).

2. Leon Wildes, *The Nonpriority Program of the Immigration and Naturalization Service Goes Public: The Litigative Use of the Freedom of Information Act*, 14 SAN DIEGO L. REV. 42 (1976); Leon Wildes, *The Operations Instructions of the Immigration Service: Internal Guides or Binding Rules?*, 17 SAN DIEGO L. REV. 99, 101 (1979); *see also* Lennon v. Richardson, 378 F. Supp. 39 (S.D.N.Y. 1974); *see also* Leon Wildes, *The United States Immigration Service v. John Lennon: The Cultural Lag*, 40 BROOK. L. REV. 279 (1975).

3. Interview with Leon Wildes, Senior Partner, Wildes and Weinberg P.C. (May 20, 2013) [hereinafter Interview with Leon Wildes].

4. Leon Wildes, *Not Just Any Immigration Case*, CARDOZO LIFE (Spring 1998), *available at* http://www.cardozo.yu.edu/life/spring1998/john.lennon.

5. Pam Zimmerman, *The Ballad of John Lennon and Leon Wildes*, JWEEKLY.COM, Dec. 9, 2010, http://www.jweekly.com/article/full/60161/the-ballad-of-john-lennon -and-leon-wildes/.

6. Wildes, *The Nonpriority Program of the Immigration and Naturalization Service*, at 44 n.5, 45 n.6; *see also* Lennon v. INS, 527 F.2d 187, 189 (2d Cir. 1975).

7. Wildes, *The Nonpriority Program of the Immigration and Naturalization Service*, at 45 n.6.

8. Lennon v. INS, 527 F.2d 187, 189 (2d Cir. 1975).

9. Interview with Leon Wildes.

10. *See, e.g.*, Zimmerman, *Ballad of John Lennon*.

11. Interview with Leon Wildes. *See generally* JON WIENER, GIMME SOME TRUTH: THE JOHN LENNON FBI FILES (1999).

12. Interview with Leon Wildes.

13. Wildes, *Not Just Any Immigration Case*.

14. *Id.*

15. Interview with Leon Wildes.

16. At the time of Lennon's case, the statute at Immigration and Nationality Act (INA) 212(a)(23) read: "(T)he following classes of aliens shall be ineligible to receive visas and shall be excluded from admission into the United States. . . . (23) Any alien who has been convicted of a violation of, or conspiracy to violate, any law or regulation relating to the illicit possession of or traffic in narcotic drugs or marihuana. . . ."

17. Wildes eventually won on the point that Lennon had no *mens rea* that he possessed an illicit substance. He was able to do this by showing that one year after Lennon's conviction, the British statute under which he was convicted had added the word "knowing" as an element. Interview with Leon Wildes; *see also* Wildes, *The United States Immigration Service v. John Lennon*, at 287 n.43.

18. Interview with Leon Wildes.

19. *Id. See also* Wildes, *Not Just Any Immigration Case*; Lennon v. INS, 527 F.2d 187, 195 (2d Cir. 1975).

20. Throughout this book, "nonpriority" and "deferred action" are used inter-changeably.

21. Interview with Leon Wildes.

22. Lennon v. INS, 527 F. 2d 187 (2d Cir. 1975).

23. Interview with Leon Wildes; *see also* Wildes, *The Nonpriority Program of the Immigration and Naturalization Service*, at 45 n.7.

24. Wildes, *The Nonpriority Program of the Immigration and Naturalization Service*, at 50 n.32.

25. Interview with Leon Wildes.

26. *Id.; see also* Wildes, *The Nonpriority Program of the Immigration and Naturaliza-tion Service*, at 75 n.96; Lennon v. INS, 527 F.2d 187, 191 (2d Cir. 1975).

27. Wildes, *The Nonpriority Program of the Immigration and Naturalization Service*, at 46 n.17; *see also* Wildes, *The Deferred Action Program of the Bureau of Citizenship and Immigration Services: A Possible Remedy for Impossible Immigration Cases*, 41 SAN DIEGO L. REV 819, *n*, at 824 n.28.

28. (LEGACY) IMMIGRATION AND NATURALIZATION SERVICE, OPERA-TIONS INSTRUCTIONS, OI § 103.1(a)(1)(ii) (1975).

29 *Id.*

30. Memorandum from Sam Bernsen, General Counsel, Immigration and Natural-ization Service, Legal Opinion Regarding Service Exercise of Prosecutorial Discretion 2 (July 15, 1976), *available at* http://www.ice.gov/doclib/foia/prosecutorial-discretion/ service-exercise-pd.pdf [hereinafter Bernsen Memo].

31. "One of the earliest manifestations of prosecutorial discretion in an immigration-related field is Department of Justice Circular Letter Number 107, dated September 20, 1909 dealing with the institution of proceedings to cancel naturalization. That letter states: 'In the opinion of the department, as a general rule, good cause is not shown for the institution of proceedings to cancel certificates for naturalization alleged to have been fraudulently or illegally procured unless some substantial results are to be achieved thereby in the way of betterment of the citizenship of the country.'" Bernsen Memo, at 4.

32. *Id.*, at 4.

33. Lennon v. INS, 527 F.2d 187, 191 n.7 (2d Cir. 1975). Of note, John Lennon was approved for nonpriority status before the circuit decision, on Sept. 23, 1975. Wildes, *The Operations Instructions*, at 101 n.7, 102 n.10; *see also* Wildes, *Deferred Action*, at 821 nn.7, 10.

34. Soon Bok Yoon v. INS, 538 F.2d 1211, 1211 (5th Cir. 1976). *See also* Wildes, *The Operations Instructions*, at 102 n.7.

35. Soon Bok Yoon v. INS, 538 F.2d 1211, 1211 (5th Cir. 1976).

36. *See* Vergel v. INS, 536 F.2d 755 (8th Cir. 1976).

37. *Id.*

38. *See* David v. INS, 548 F.2d 219 (8th Cir. 1977).

39. *See id.*

40. *See id.*

41. David v. INS, 548 F.2d 219 (8th Cir. 1977).

42. *See* Vergel, 536 F.2d 755; David, 548 F.2d 219.

43. Wildes, *The Operations Instructions*, at 103–4 n.7.

44. Nicholas v. INS, 590 F.2d 802 (9th Cir. 1979).

45. *Id.*

46. *Id.*

47. *Id.* at 807.

48. *Id.* at 806–7.

49. OI § 103.1(a)(1)(ii). The spirit of *Nicholas* was impaired by the alteration of the Operations Instructions and viewed by the courts as bestowing no substantive benefit on aliens seeking inclusion in the deferred action category. *See* Wan Chung Wen v. Ferro, 543 F. Supp. 1016, 1017–18 (W.D.N.Y. 1982); Pasquini v. Morris, 700 F.2d 658, 661 (11th Cir. 1983); Velasco-Gutierrez v. Crossland, 732 F.2d 792, 798 (10th Cir. 1984); Siverts v. Craig, 602 F. Supp. 50, 53 (D. Haw. 1985); De Romiero v. Smith, 773 F.2d 1021 (9th Cir. 1985).

50. Email from Stephen H. Legomsky, John S. Lehmann University Professor, Washington University School of Law in St. Louis, to author (Aug. 1, 2009) (on file with author).

51. Memorandum from Doris Meissner, Commissioner, Immigration and Naturalization Service, on Exercising Prosecutorial Discretion 4–5 (Nov. 17, 2000) (referencing the Standard Operating Procedures that pertain to deferred action cases: "[S]tandards and procedures for placing an alien in deferred action status are provided in the Standard Operating Procedures for Enforcement Officers: Arrest, Detention, Processing, and Removal (Standard Operating Procedures), Part X.)."

52. Memorandum from Paul W. Virtue, Acting Executive Associate Commissioner, Immigration and Naturalization Service, on INS Cancellation of Operations Instructions (June 27, 1997).

53. *Id.*

54. Interview with Paul Virtue, former Executive Associate Commissioner, Immigration and Naturalization Service, in Washington, D.C. (July 23, 2009).

55. *Id.* It was Virtue's vision that the Standard Operating Procedures manual would be made publicly available and be operated with subregulatory authority like the Department of State's Foreign Affairs Manual.

56. CHARLES GORDON, STANLEY MAILMAN, AND STEPHEN YALE-LOEHR, IMMIGRATION LAW AND PROCEDURE § 72.03(2)(h) (2009).

57. *See* Illegal Immigration Reform and Immigrant Responsibility Act of 1996 (IIRAIRA), 8 U.S.C.S. § 1103 (2008); Antiterrorism and Effective Death Penalty Act of 1996 (AEDPA), 8 U.S.C.C. § 1105 (2006). The term "1996 immigration laws" will be used to refer to amendments made to the Immigration and Nationality Act in 1996, and specifically, IIRAIRA and AEDPA.

58. *See* IIRAIRA, 8 U.S.C.S. § 1103 (2008); INA §§ 235(b), 236(c), 8 U.S.C. §§ 1324(a), 1185 (2006).

59. *See* IIRAIRA, 8 U.S.C.S. § 1103 (2008); INA §§ 235(b), 236(c), 8 U.S.C. §§ 1324(a), 1185 (2006).

60. *See* IIRAIRA, 8 U.S.C.S. § 1103 (2008); AEDPA, 8 U.S.C.C. § 1105 (2006).

61. Arguably, one provision created by IIRAIRA that corresponds to judicial review was partially improved by Congress years later with the passage of the REAL ID Act of 2005, 8 U.S.C.S. § 1101 (2008). Congress created subsection 242(a)(2)(D), titled "Judicial Review of Certain Legal Claims," which now reads: "Nothing in subparagraph (B) or (C), or in any other provision of this Act (other than this section) which limits or eliminates judicial review, shall be construed as precluding review of constitutional claims or questions of law raised upon a petition for review filed with an appropriate court of appeals in accordance with this section." *See* INA § 242(a)(2)(D), 8 U.S.C. § 1252(a)(2)(D)(2006). While this change opened the door for certain decisions previously barred under IIRAIRA to be reviewed in federal court if the decision raised a legal question, the majority of restrictions created by IIRAIRA remain.

62. *See, e.g.,* Daniel Kanstroom, *Deportation, Social Control, and Punishment: Some Thoughts about Why Hard Laws Make Bad Cases*, 113 HARV. L. REV. 1890 (2000); Nancy Morawetz, *Understanding the Impact of the 1996 Deportation Laws and the Limited Scope of Proposed Reforms*, 113 HARV. L. REV. 1936 (2000); Shoba Sivaprasad Wadhia, *The Policy and Politics of Immigrant Rights*, 16 TEMP. POL. AND CIV. RTS. L. REV. 387 (2007).

63. Letter from Members of Congress to Janet Reno, Attorney General, Department of Justice, on Guidelines for Use of Prosecutorial Discretion in Removal Proceedings (Nov. 4, 1999), *available at* http://www.ice.gov/doclib/foia/prosecutorial-discretion/991104congress-letter.pdf.

64. *Id.*

65. Letter from Robert Raben, Assistant Attorney General, Department of Justice, to Barney Frank, Representative, U.S. House of Representatives, on Use of Prosecutorial Discretion to Avoid Harsh Consequences of IIRAIRA (Jan. 19, 2000), *available at* http://www.ice.gov/doclib/foia/prosecutorial-discretion/000119frank.pdf.

66. *Id.*

67. *See* Memorandum from Bo Cooper, General Counsel, Immigration and Naturalization Service, on INS Exercise of Prosecutorial Discretion (July 11, 2000) (on file with author).

68. *See id.*

69. *See id.*

70. *See id.*

71. *See* Memorandum from Doris Meissner, Commissioner, Immigration and Naturalization Service, on Exercising Prosecutorial Discretion (Nov. 17, 2000) (on file with author).

72. *See id.* at 7–8.

73. *See id.* at 4–5.

74. *See id.* at 7–8.

75. *See id.* at 8.

76. *See id.* at 7–8.

77. *See id.* at 1.

78. OI § 103.1(a)(1)(ii) (1975). "In every case where the district director determines that adverse action would be unconscionable because of the existence of appealing humanitarian factors, he *shall recommend* consideration for deferred action category" (emphasis added). *See also* Wildes, *Deferred Action*, at 821 n.7.

79. Symposium, *Immigration and Criminal Law*, 4 N.Y. CITY L. REV. 9 (2001).

80. *Id.* at 28.

81. *Id.* at 30.

82. *Id.* at 50.

83. *See* Adam B. Cox and Cristina M. Rodríguez, *The President and Immigration Law*, 119 YALE L.J. 458 (2009).

84. *Id.* at 517–18.

85. INA § 103(a), 8 U.S.C. § 1103(a) (2006).

86. Memorandum from Johnny N. Williams, Executive Associate Commissioner of the Office of Field Operations, U.S. Immigration and Naturalization Service, on Family Unity Benefits and Unlawful Presence (Jan. 27, 2003) (on file with author).

87. *Id.*

88. *Id.*

89. Memorandum from William R. Yates, Associate Director for Operations. U.S. Citizenship and Immigration Services, on Service Center Issuance of Notice to Appear (Form I-862) (Sept. 12, 2003) ("Lastly, it is important to remind officers that each decision to issue an NTA must be made in accordance with the attached memorandum entitled: *Exercising Prosecutorial Discretion*, dated November 17, 2000. Although that memorandum was issued prior to September 11, 2001 and the implementation of enhanced security checks on all applications and petitions, it established the guiding principles for determinations regarding prosecutorial discretion and remains in force.").

90. Memorandum from William J. Howard, Principal Legal Advisor, U.S. Immigration and Customs Enforcement, on Prosecutorial Discretion 2 (Oct. 24, 2005) (on file with author).

91. *Id.* at 3–4.

92. *Id.* at 5–6.

93. *Id.* at 8.

94. Memorandum from John P. Torres, Director, U.S. Immigration and Custom Enforcement, on Discretion in Cases of Extreme or Severe Medical Concern 2 (Dec. 11, 2006), *available at* http://www.ice.gov/doclib/foia/dro_policy_memos/discretionin casesofextremeorseveremedicalconcerndec112006.pdf.

95. Memorandum from Julie L. Myers, Assistant Secretary, U.S. Immigration and Customs Enforcement, on Prosecutorial and Custody Discretion (Nov. 7, 2007) (on file with author).

178 | NOTES

96. Julia Preston, *Immigration Quandary: A Mother Torn from Her Baby*, N.Y. TIMES, Nov. 17, 2007, http://www.nytimes.com/2007/11/17/us/17citizen.html? pagewanted=all&_r=0.

97. Memorandum from Julie L. Myers, Assistant Secretary, U.S. Immigration and Customs Enforcement, on Prosecutorial and Custody Discretion (Nov. 7, 2007) (on file with author).

98. *See generally*, Letter from a Group of Law Professors to President Obama on Executive Authority to Grant Administrative Relief for DREAM Act Beneficiaries (May 28, 2012), *available at* http://lawprofessors.typepad.com/files/executiveauthori-tyfordreamrelief28may2012withsignatures.pdf; Shoba Sivaprasad Wadhia, *The Role of Prosecutorial Discretion in Immigration Law*, 9 CONN. PUB. INT. L.J. 243, 246–47 n.3 (2010); JANUARY CONTRERAS, U.S. CITIZENSHIP AND IMMIGRATION SERVICES OMBUDSMAN, DEFERRED ACTION: RECOMMENDATIONS TO IMPROVE TRANS-PARENCY AND CONSISTENCY IN THE USCIS PROCESS (July 11, 2011), *available at* http://www.dhs.gov/xlibrary/assets/cisomb-combined-dar.pdf.

99. Lynda J. Oswald, *Extended Voluntary Departure: Limiting the Attorney General's Discretion in Immigration Matters*, 85 MICH. L. REV. 152, 158 (1986). *See also* KATE M. MANUEL AND TODD GARVEY, CONG. RESEARCH SERV., R42924, PROSECUTO-RIAL DISCRETION IN IMMIGRATION ENFORCEMENT: LEGAL ISSUES (2013), *available at* http://www.fas.org/sgp/crs/misc/R42924.pdf.

100. Oswald, *Extended Voluntary Departure*, at 158 n.40. *See* U.S. CITIZENSHIP AND IMMIGRATION SERVICES, ADJUDICATOR'S FIELD MANUAL §38.2, *available at* http://www.uscis.gov/ilink/docView/AFM/HTML/AFM/0-0-0-1/0-0-0-16606/ 0-0-0-16764.html; *see also* Hotel and Restaurant Employees Union, Local 25 v. Attor-ney Gen. of United States, 804 F.2d 1256, 1261 (D.C. Cir. 1986).

101. Oswald, *Extended Voluntary Departure*, at 158–59.

102. RUTH ELLEN WASEM AND KARMA ESTER, CONG. RESEARCH SERV., RS20844, TEMPORARY PROTECTED STATUS: CURRENT IMMIGRATION POLICY AND ISSUES (Jan. 27, 2006), *available at* http://pards.org/tps/tps2006,0207 -CRS.pdf.

103. INA, Pub. L. No. 82-414, 66 Stat. 163 (codified as amended at 8 U.S.C. §§1101 *et seq.*).

104. *See, e.g.*, INA §212(d)(5), 8 U.S.C. §1182(d)(5) (2006).

105. INA §212(d)(5)(A), 8 U.S.C. §1182(d)(5) (2006).

106. DAVID M. REIMERS, STILL THE GOLDEN DOOR: THE THIRD WORLD COMES TO AMERICA 25, 157 (2d ed. 1992).

107. *Id.* at 157–58.

108. President Dwight D. Eisenhower, Statement by the President Concerning Hun-garian Refugees (Jan. 1, 1957).

109. *See* Refugee Act of 1980, Pub. L. No. 96-212, 94 Stat. 102 (1980) (codified as amended in scattered sections of 8 U.S.C.).

110. *See* INA §101(a)(42), 8 U.S.C. §1101(a)(42) (2006).

111. One example is illustrated by the more than 100,000 "Mariel" refugees who came from Cuba under the Carter administration. REIMERS, STILL THE GOLDEN DOOR, at 170–75.

112. David A. Martin, *A Defense of Immigration-Enforcement Discretion: The Legal and Policy Flaws in Kris Kobach's Latest Crusade*, 122 YALE L.J. 167, 179 (2012), *available at* http://www.law.yale.edu/documents/pdf/conference/ILR13_CCDavidMartin.pdf.

113. For an excellent primer on PIP, *see* MARGARET D. STOCK, *A Path to Citizenship for Undocumented Military Family Members*, WESTLAW IMMIGRATION BRIEFINGS (July 2012).

114. *Id.*

115. Policy Memorandum PM-602-0091, U.S. Citizenship and Immigration Services, on Parole of Spouses, Children and Parents of Active Duty Members of the U.S. Armed Forces, the Selected Reserve of the Ready Reserve, and Former Members of the U.S. Armed Forces or Selected Reserve of the Ready Reserve and the Effect of Parole on Inadmissibility under Immigration and Nationality Act § 212(a)(6)(A)(i) (Nov. 15, 2013), *available at* http://www.uscis.gov/sites/default/files/USCIS/Laws/Memoranda/2013/2013-1115_Parole_in_Place_Memo_.pdf.

116. *See* Press Release, U.S. Citizenship and Immigration Services, USCIS Announces Interim Relief for Foreign Students Adversely Impacted by Hurricane Katrina (Nov. 25, 2005) (on file with author).

117. *See* Press Release, U.S. Department of Homeland Security, DHS Establishes Interim Relief for Widows of U.S. Citizens (June 9, 2009), *available at* http://www.dhs.gov/news/2009/06/09/dhs-establishes-interim-relief-widows-us-citizens.

118. *Id.*

119. Violent Crime Control and Law Enforcement Act of 1994, Pub. L. No. 103-322, 108 Stat. 1796 (1994).

120. *See* WILLIAM A. KANDEL, CONG. RESEARCH SERV., RL42477, IMMIGRATION PROVISIONS OF THE VIOLENCE AGAINST WOMEN ACT (VAWA) (May 15, 2012), *available at* http://www.fas.org/sgp/crs/misc/R42477.pdf.

CHAPTER 3. LESSONS FROM CRIMINAL LAW

1 Robert H. Jackson, *The Federal Prosecutor*, 24 J. AM. JUD. SOC'Y 18 (1940), *available at* http://www.roberthjackson.org/the-man/speeches-articles/speeches/speeches-by-robert-h-jackson/the-federal-prosecutor.

2. *See, e.g.*, ANGELA J. DAVIS, ARBITRARY JUSTICE: THE POWER OF THE AMERICAN PROSECUTOR (2007); Angela J. Davis, *They Must Answer for What They've Done*, LEGAL TIMES, Aug. 2007, at 1–3; Bruce A. Green and Fred C. Zacharias, *Prosecutorial Neutrality*, 2004 WIS. L. REV. 837 (2004); Carolyn B. Ramsey, *The Discretionary Power of "Public" Prosecutors in Historical Perspective*, 39 AM. CRIM. L. REV. 1309 (2002); Celesta A. Albonetti, *Prosecutorial Discretion: The Effects of Uncertainty*, 21 LAW AND SOC'Y REV. 291 (1987); Rachel E. Barkow, *Institutional Design and the Policing of Prosecutors: Lessons from Administrative Law*, 61 STAN. L. REV. 869 (2009).

3. *See generally* Juan Cardenas, *The Crime Victim in the Prosecutorial Process*, 9 HARV. J.L. AND PUB. POL'Y 357 (1986); John D. Bessler, *The Public Interest and the Unconstitutionality of Private Prosecutors*, 47 ARK. L. REV. 511 (1994); Comment, *The Private Prosecution: A Remedy for District Attorneys' Unwarranted Inaction*, 65 YALE L.J. 209 (1955); Matthew S. Nichols, *No One Can Serve Two Masters: Arguments Against Private Prosecutors*, 13 CAP. DEF. J. 279 (2001). *See also* KATE M. MANUEL AND TODD GARVEY, CONG. RESEARCH SERV., R42924, PROSECUTORIAL DISCRETION IN IMMIGRATION ENFORCEMENT: LEGAL ISSUES (2013), *available at* http://www.fas.org/sgp/crs/misc/R42924.pdf.

4. *See* Cardenas, *The Crime Victim*, at 361.

5. *See id.* at 366.

6. *See id.* at 366.

7. *See id.* at 368–69.

8. *See id.* at 369. *See also* DAVIS, ARBITRARY JUSTICE.

9. DAVIS, ARBITRARY JUSTICE, at 11. *See also* Angela J. Davis, *The American Prosecutor: Independence, Power and the Threat of Tyranny*, 86 IOWA L. REV. 393 (2001).

10. *About DOJ*, U.S. DEPARTMENT OF JUSTICE, http://www.justice.gov/about/about.html (last updated Mar. 2012).

11. *See, e.g.*, Roger A. Fairfax, Jr., *Delegation of the Criminal Prosecution Function to Private Actors*, 43 U.C. DAVIS L. REV. 411 (2009).

12. *See, e.g.*, John L. Worrall, *Prosecution in America: A Historical and Comparative Account*, in THE CHANGING ROLE OF THE AMERICAN PROSECUTOR 3 (2008), *available at* http://www.sunypress.edu/pdf/61690.pdf.

13 DAVIS, ARBITRARY JUSTICE, at 11 n.2. *But see* Worrall, *Prosecution in America*, at 11, who identifies the following crime commissions: "The Cleveland Survey of Criminal Justice (1922); the Wickersham Commission (National Commission, 1931b); and early 20th-century commission reports (e.g., Illinois Association for Criminal Justice, 1929; Missouri Crime Survey, 1926 . . .)." Thereafter, Worrall criticizes such commissions for lacking insight about the practical challenges faced by the prosecutor.

14. DAVIS, ARBITRARY JUSTICE, at 12 n.2.

15. JOAN E. JACOBY, THE MINNESOTA COUNTY ATTORNEY'S ASSOCIATION, THE AMERICAN PROSECUTOR IN HISTORICAL CONTEXT 6, *available at* http://mcaa-mn.org/docs/2005/AmerProsecutorHistoricalContext252705.pdf.

16. *Id.* at 6.

17. *Id.* at 8 (quoting NATIONAL COMMISSION ON LAW OBSERVANCE AND ENFORCEMENT, REPORT ON PROSECUTION (1931)).

18. *See, e.g.*, United States v. Armstrong, 517 U.S. 456 (1996), which has been cited over 1,300 times in other cases, and nearly 1,000 more in law reviews and other secondary sources; Reno v. Am.-Arab Anti-Discrimination Comm., 525 U.S. 471, 492 (1999).

19. *See, e.g.*, U.S. DEPARTMENT OF JUSTICE, U.S. ATTORNEYS' MANUAL (1997), *available at* http://www.justice.gov/usao/eousa/foia_reading_room/usam (last visited Dec. 20, 2013); the Take Care Clause, U.S. Const. art. II, § 3, cl. 5.

20. Armstrong, 517 U.S. at 464 (citations omitted).

21. Jackson, *The Federal Prosecutor*, at 19.

22. DAVIS, ARBITRARY JUSTICE, at 13 n.2.

23. Defining the Problem and Scope of Over-criminalization and Over-federalization: Hearing Before H. Comm. on the Judiciary Over-criminalization Task Force (2013) (statement of John G. Malcolm, Rule of Law Programs Policy Director and Senior Legal Fellow, The Heritage Foundation), *available at* http://www.heritage.org/research/testimony/2013/06/defining-the-problem-and-scope-of-overcriminalization -and-overfederalization. Beyond the Immigration and Nationality Act, the United States Code contains immigration-related violations that may be prosecuted in the criminal justice system. While these violations are not strictly part of the immigration system, they do reveal the extent to which the number of immigration violations has exploded. Beyond the scope of this chapter but worth noting is the increased number of criminal immigration charges that prosecutors have filed against noncitizens. For example, according to Human Rights Watch, more than 80,000 criminal prosecutions in 2012 involved illegal entry and reentry, surpassing drug, firearms, and white-collar crime offenses.

24. DAVIS, ARBITRARY JUSTICE, at 76 n.2.

25. U.S. DEPARTMENT OF JUSTICE, U.S. ATTORNEYS' MANUAL § 9-27.230(B) (1997).

26. Matthew Ygelsias, *Amnesty for David Vitter*, THINKPROGRESS, July 27, 2011, http://thinkprogress.org/yglesias/2011/07/27/280949/amnesty-for-david-vitter.

27. U.S. DEPARTMENT OF JUSTICE, U.S. ATTORNEYS' MANUAL (1997).

28. *Id.* § 9-27.230(A).

29. *Id.* § 9-27.230(B).

30. *Id.* § 9-27.230(B).

31. DAVIS, ARBITRARY JUSTICE, at 6 n.2.

32. *Id.* at 6 n.2.

33. *Id.* at 6 n.2.

34. KENNETH CULP DAVIS, DISCRETIONARY JUSTICE: A PRELIMINARY INQUIRY 222 (1969).

35. BESIKI KUTATELADZE, VANESSA LYNN, AND EDWARD LIANG, DO RACE AND ETHNICITY MATTER IN PROSECUTION? A REVIEW OF EMPIRICAL STUDIES (2012), *available at* http://www.vera.org/sites/default/files/resources/downloads/race-and-ethnicity-in-prosecution-first-edition.pdf.

36. DAVIS, ARBITRARY JUSTICE, at 23 n.2.

37. Kenneth J. Melilli, *Prosecutorial Discretion in an Adversary System*, 1992 BYU L. REV. 669, 671 (1992), *available at* http://lawreview.byu.edu/archives/1992/3/mel.pdf (citing David M. Nissman and Ed Hagen, The Prosecution Function 2 (1982); Jackson, *The Federal Prosecutor*; James Vorenberg, *Decent Restraint of Prosecutorial Power*, 94 HARV. L. REV. 1521, 1522, 1525–26 (1981)).

38. Melilli, *Prosecutorial Discretion*, at 672 (citing FRANK W. MILLER, PROSECUTION: THE DECISION TO CHARGE A SUSPECT WITH A CRIME 3 (1969);

Stanley Z. Fisher, *In Search of the Virtuous Prosecutor: A Conceptual Framework*, 15 AM. J. CRIM. L. 197, 232 n.152 (1988); MONROE H. FREEDMAN, LAWYERS' ETHICS IN AN ADVERSARY SYSTEM 84 (1975); MONROE H. FREEDMAN, UNDERSTAND- ING LAWYERS' ETHICS 218, 218 (1990); DAVIS, DISCRETIONARY JUSTICE, at 190; Vorenberg, *Decent Restraint of Prosecutorial Power*, at 1525).

39. PROSECUTION FUNCTION, AMERICAN BAR ASSOCIATION (1992) (empha- sis added), *available at* http://www.americanbar.org/publications/criminal_justice_ section_archive/crimjust_standards_pfunc_blkold.html.

40. Abbe Smith, *Can You Be a Good Person and a Good Prosecutor?*, 14 GEO. J. LEGAL ETHICS 355, 387 (2001).

41. *Id.* at 387 n.205.

42. DAVIS, ARBITRARY JUSTICE, at 25.

43. Kevin K. Washburn, *Restoring the Grand Jury*, 76 FORDHAM L. REV. 2333, 2336 n.4 (2008) ("grand jury review represents, at best, 'a modest screening power, a fact recognized by the familiar courthouse saying that a grand jury would indict a ham sandwich if the prosecutor asked it do so' ") (quoting Ronald Wright and Marc Miller, *The Screening/Bargaining Tradeoff*, 55 STAN. L. REV. 29, 51 n.70 (2002)); Melilli, *Prosecutorial Discretion*, at 673 n.22. *See also* DAVIS, ARBITRARY JUSTICE, at 26. *See also* Peter J. Henning, *Prosecutorial Misconduct in Grand Jury Investigations*, 51 S.C. L. REV. 3 (1999); Susan W. Brenner, *The Voice of the Community: A Case for Grand Jury Independence*, 3 VA. J. SOC. POL'Y & L. 122 (1995).

44. Washburn, *Restoring the Grand Jury*, at 2352.

45. Davis, ARBITRARY JUSTICE, at 26. *See also* Jeffrey Standen, *Plea Bargaining in the Shadow of the Guidelines*, 81 CAL. L. REV. 1471 (1993) (discussing the exercise of discretion in plea bargaining); Leslie C. Griffin, *The Prudent Prosecutor*, 14 GEO. J. LEGAL ETHICS 259, 268–75 (2001) (discussing discretion in the plea bargaining and charging stages).

46. DAVIS, ARBITRARY JUSTICE, at 45.

47. James Vorenberg, *Decent Restraint of Prosecutorial Power*, 94 HARV. L. REV. 1521, 1532–33 (1981).

48. DAVIS, ARBITRARY JUSTICE, at 45–46.

49. Lafler v. Cooper, 132 S.Ct. 1376, 1388 (2012).

50. Missouri v. Frye, 132 S.Ct. 1399, 1407 (2012).

51. Lafler, 132 S.Ct. at 1384 (citing Frye, 132 S.Ct. at 1386–87); *see also* Padilla v. Kentucky, 130 S.Ct. 1473, 1486 (2010); Hill v. Lockhart, 474 U.S. 52, 57 (1985). The Court in *Lafler* went on to add that "[d]uring plea negotiations defendants are 'entitled to the effective assistance of competent counsel.' In *Hill*, the Court held 'the two-part *Strickland v. Washington* test applies to challenges to guilty pleas based on ineffective assistance of counsel.' The performance prong of *Strickland* requires a defendant to show 'that counsel's fell below an objective standard of reasonableness.' In this case all parties agree the performance of respondent's counsel was deficient when he advised respondent to reject the plea offer on the grounds he could not be convicted at trial.

In light of this concession, it is unnecessary for this Court to explore the issue." *Lafler*, 132 S.Ct. at 1384 (citations omitted).

52. SMART ON CRIME: REFORMING THE CRIMINAL JUSTICE SYSTEM IN THE 21ST CENTURY, DEPARTMENT OF JUSTICE 2 (Aug. 2013), *available at* http://www.justice.gov/ag/smart-on-crime.pdf.

53. DAVIS, ARBITRARY JUSTICE, at 56.

54. Attorney General Eric Holder, Remarks at the Annual Meeting of the American Bar Association's House of Delegates (Aug. 12, 2013), *available at* http://www.justice.gov/iso/opa/ag/speeches/2013/ag-speech-130812.html; *see* SMART ON CRIME.

55. Holder, Remarks at the Annual Meeting.

56. *Id.* In a blueprint titled "Smart on Crime" Holder remarked, "As a start, the Attorney General is announcing a change in Department of Justice charging policies so that certain people who have committed low-level, nonviolent drug offenses, who have no ties to large scale organizations, gangs or cartels will no longer be charged with offenses that impose draconian mandatory minimum sentences." SMART ON CRIME.

57. BRUCE FREDERICK AND DON STEMEN, THE ANATOMY OF DISCRETION: AN ANALYSIS OF PROSECUTORIAL DECISION MAKING, SUMMARY REPORT TO THE NATIONAL INSTITUTE OF JUSTICE, VERA INSTITUTE OF JUSTICE (2012), *available at* http://www.vera.org/sites/default/files/resources/downloads/anatomy-of-discretion-summary-report.pdf.

58. *Id.*

59. *Id.*

60. *See generally* Albonetti, *Prosecutorial Discretion.*

61. *Id.* at 311.

62. *Id.* at 298–303.

63. *Id.* at 295.

64. Smith, *Can You Be a Good Person and a Good Prosecutor?*, at 390.

65. PROSECUTION FUNCTION.

66. *See generally* DAVIS, ARBITRARY JUSTICE; Smith, *Can You Be a Good Person and a Good Prosecutor?*; MICHELLE ALEXANDER, THE NEW JIM CROW: MASS INCARCERATION IN THE AGE OF COLORBLINDNESS (2012).

67. Holder, Remarks at the Annual Meeting.

68. *See* Arizona v. United States, 132 S. Ct. 2492, 2506–7 (2012).

69. *Id.* at 2499 (internal citations omitted).

70. *See, e.g.*, Memorandum from Sam Bernsen, Gen. Counsel, Immigration and Naturalization Service, on Legal Opinion Regarding Service Exercise of Prosecutorial Discretion (July 15, 1976) [hereinafter Memorandum from Bernsen], *available at* http://www.ice.gov/doclib/foia/prosecutorial-discretion/service-exercise-pd.pdf; Memorandum from Doris Meissner, Commissioner of Immigration and Naturalization Service, on Exercising Prosecutorial Discretion (Nov. 17, 2000) [hereinafter Memorandum from Meissner] (on file with author); Memorandum from William J. Howard,

Principal Legal Advisor, U.S. Immigration and Customs Enforcement, on Prosecutorial Discretion (Oct. 24, 2005) [hereinafter Memorandum from Howard] (on file with author); Memorandum from Julie L. Myers, Assistant Sec'y of Homeland Security (Nov. 7, 2007) [hereinafter Memorandum from Myers] (on file with author).

71. Memorandum from Bernsen.

72. *See* Memorandum from Bo Cooper, Gen. Counsel, Immigration and Naturalization Service, on INS Exercise of Prosecutorial Discretion 2 (citing WAYNE R. LAFAVE AND JEROLD H. ISRAEL, CRIMINAL PROCEDURE §13.2 (1992)) [hereinafter Memorandum from Cooper] (on file with author).

73. *See, e.g.*, Memorandum from Bernsen; Memorandum from Cooper; Memorandum from Meissner.

74. Memorandum from Meissner, at 2.

75. U.S. DEPARTMENT OF JUSTICE, U.S. ATTORNEYS' MANUAL §9-27.220 (1997).

76. Memorandum from Meissner, at 5 n.3.

77. *Id.* at 2.

78. *See, e.g.*, Memorandum from Bernsen, at 72; Memorandum from Meissner; Memorandum from Howard; Memorandum from Myers; Memorandum from John Morton, U.S. Immigration and Customs Enforcement, on Exercising Prosecutorial Discretion Consistent with the Civil Immigration Enforcement Priorities of the Agency for the Apprehension, Detention, and Removal of Aliens (June 17, 2011), *available at* http://www.ice.gov/doclib/secure-communities/pdf/prosecutorial-discretion-memo.pdf; Memorandum from John Morton, on Civil Immigration Enforcement Priorities for the Apprehension, Detention, and Removal of Aliens (Mar. 2, 2011), *available at* http://www.ice.gov/doclib/news/releases/2011/110302washingtondc.pdf; Memorandum from John Morton, on Civil Enforcement Priorities (Jun. 30, 2010), *available at* http://www.ice.gov/doclib/news/releases/2010/civil-enforcement-priorities.pdf.

79. INA §265, 237, 8 U.S.C. §§1305, 1227 (2006).

80. INA §212(a)(2)(A)(i)(I), 8 U.S.C. §1182(a)(2)(A) (2006).

81. INA §212(a)(6)(A)(i), 8 U.S.C. §1182(a)(6)(A) (2006).

82. INA §212 (a)(9)(B)(i), 8 U.S.C. §1251(a)(9)(B) (2006).

83. 8 C.F.R. §287.3(d) (2009).

84. 8 C.F.R. §239.1 (2013) ("Any immigration officer, or supervisor thereof, performing an inspection of an arriving alien at a port-of-entry may issue a notice to appear to such alien.").

85. 8 C.F.R. §§1003.14, 239.1 (2013).

86. INA §239(a)(1)(D), 8 U.S.C. §1229 (2006).

87. Memorandum from John Morton, on Exercising Prosecutorial Discretion Consistent with the Civil Immigration Enforcement Priorities of the Agency for the Apprehension, Detention, and Removal of Aliens (June 17, 2011), *available at* http://www.ice.gov/doclib/secure-communities/pdf/prosecutorial-discretion-memo.pdf.

88. Chart data from PENNSYLVANIA STATE UNIVERSITY DICKINSON SCHOOL OF LAW'S CENTER FOR IMMIGRANTS' RIGHTS, TO FILE OR NOT TO FILE A

NOTICE TO APPEAR: IMPROVING THE GOVERNMENT'S USE OF PROSECU-
TORIAL DISCRETION 12 (Oct. 2013) (prepared for the American Bar Association
Commission on Immigration), *available at* https://law.psu.edu/sites/default/files/
documents/pdfs/NTAReportFinal.pdf.

89. *See* Department of Homeland Security, Immigration Enforcement Actions:
2012, John Simanski and Lesley M. Sapp (December 2013), *available at* https://www
.dhs.gov/sites/default/files/publications/ois_enforcement_ar_2012_1.pdf.

90. *See* Letter from Martha Terry, U.S. Customs and Border Protection FOIA Division, to Shoba Sivaprasad Wadhia (July 10, 2013), *available at* http://law.psu.edu/_file/
Immigrants/FOIA-CBP-NTA.pdf.

91. *See* Letter from Jill A. Eggleston, Freedom of Info. Act Dir., U.S. Citizenship
and Immigration Services, to Shoba Sivaprasad Wadhia 175 (May 30, 2013), *available at*
http://law.psu.edu/_file/Wadhia/FOIA_Letter_May_30_2013.pdf.

92. *See, e.g.,* PENNSYLVANIA STATE UNIVERSITY DICKINSON SCHOOL OF
LAW'S CENTER FOR IMMIGRANTS' RIGHTS, TO FILE OR NOT TO FILE, at 51.

93. *See, e.g.,* INA § 238, 8 U.S.C. § 1228 (2006); INA § 241(a)(1)(5), 8 U.S.C. § 1231(a)
(5), (2006).

94. INA § 240A, 8 U.S.C. § 1229b (2006).

95. INA § 240B, 8 U.S.C. § 1229c (2006).

96. INA § 240B, 8 U.S.C. § 1229c (2006); 8 C.F.R. § 1240.26 (2009).

97. INA § 240(d), 8 U.S.C. § 1229a(d) (2006); 8 C.F.R. 1003.25(b) (2013).

98. *See, e.g.,* Jennifer Lee Koh, *Waiving Due Process Goodbye: Stipulated Orders of
Removal and the Crisis in Immigration Adjudication*, 91 N.C. L. REV. 475 (2013); *see also*
DAN KANSTROOM, AFTERMATH, DEPORTATION LAW AND THE NEW AMERI-
CAN DIASPORA (2012).

99. *See, e.g.,* INA §§ 235(b), 236, and 241, 8 U.S.C. §§ 1324(a), 1185, and 1231 (2009).

100. *But see* Zadvydas v. Davis, 533 U.S. 678 (2001) (finding that indefinite civil
immigration detention raises serious constitutional concerns and holding that the
post-removal-period detention statute limits detention to a "period reasonably necessary to bring about that alien's removal from the United States.").

101. *See, e.g.,* Memorandum from John Morton, Director, U.S. Immigration and
Customs Enforcement, on Civil Immigration Enforcement: Priorities for the Apprehension, Detention, and Removal of Aliens (Mar. 2, 2011), *available at* http://www.ice
.gov/doclib/news/releases/2011/110302washingtondc.pdf.

102. *See* ICE Policy Directive 11064.1 from John Sandweg, Acting Director,
U.S. Immigration and Customs Enforcement, on Facilitating Parental Interests in
the Course of Civil Immigration Enforcement Activities (Aug. 23, 2013), *available at*
http://www.ice.gov/doclib/detention-reform/pdf/parental_interest_directive_signed
.pdf.

103. Ted Hesson, *New Obama Immigration Policy Goes Easier on Parents*, ABC-
NEWS, Aug. 23, 2013, http://abcnews.go.com/ABC_Univision/Politics/obama
-immigration-policy-easier-parents/story?id=20054169.

104. *See, e.g.,* INA § 236(c), 8 U.S.C. § 1226 (2006).

105. *See* Zadvydas v. Davis, 533 U.S. 678 (2001); Diop v. ICE/Homeland Security, 656 F.3d 221 (3d Cir. 2011); Rodriguez v. Robbins, No. 12-56734 (9th Cir. Apr. 16, 2013), *available at* http://cdn.ca9.uscourts.gov/datastore/opinions/2013/04/16/12-56734.pdf.

106. *See* SMART ON CRIME.

107. Angie Junck, *Mandatory Minimums: Unjust for Immigrants Too*, HUFFPOST CRIME BLOG, Aug. 19, 2013, http://www.huffingtonpost.com/angie-junck/mandatory -minimums_b_3777738.html.

108. 8 C.F.R. § 287.3(d) (2009).

109. U.S. CONST. amend. VI ("In all criminal prosecutions, the accused shall enjoy the right to a speedy and public trial, by an impartial jury of the State and district wherein the crime shall have been committed, which district shall have been previously ascertained by law, and to be informed of the nature and cause of the accusation; to be confronted with the witnesses against him; to have compulsory process for obtaining witnesses in his favor, and to have the Assistance of Counsel for his defense.").

110. ACCESSING JUSTICE: THE AVAILABILITY AND ADEQUACY OF COUNSEL IN IMMIGRATION PROCEEDINGS, NEW YORK IMMIGRANT REPRESENTATION STUDY 1 (Dec. 2011), *available at* http://www.cardozolawreview.com/content/denovo/ NYIRS_Report.pdf.

111. INA § 292, 8 U.S.C. § 1362 (2006). *See also* RESOLUTION, AMERICAN BAR ASSOCIATION HOUSE OF DELEGATES, ABA POLICIES ON ISSUES AFFECTING IMMIGRANTS AND REFUGEES (2006), *available at* http://www.abanet.org/intlaw/ policy/humanrights/immigration2.06107A.pdf (citing to INA § 292). Related stud-ies and analyses include Andrew I. Shoenholtz and Hamutal Bernstein, *Improving Immigration Adjudications Through Competent Counsel*, 21 GEO. J. LEGAL ETHICS 55 (2008); Jaya Ramji-Nogales, Andrew I. Schoenholtz, and Philip G. Schrag, *Refugee Roulette: Disparities in Asylum Adjudication*, 60 STAN. L. REV. 295 (2007); Andrew I. Schoenholtz and Jonathan Jacobs, *The State of Asylum Representation: Ideas for Change*, 16 GEO. IMMIGR. L.J. 739, 746 n.53 (2002); Donald Kerwin, *Revisiting the Need for Appointed Counsel*, MIGRATION POLICY INSTITUTE INSIGHT (Apr. 2005), *available at* http://www.migrationpolicy.org/insight/Insight_Kerwin.pdf.

112. INA § 240(c)(2)(A), 8 U.S.C. § 1229a(c)(2)(A) (2006).

113. INA § 240(c)(3)(A), 8 U.S.C. § 1229a(c)(3)(A) (2006).

114. As described by immigration scholar Nancy Morawetz in an interview I conducted in 2009: "I think there is a false analogy with the criminal cases. In criminal cases the criminal prosecutor has to think about the strength of the evidence, the difficulty of proceeding with the case, and the prosecutorial priorities of the office. In contrast in immigration, it tends to be little work to have the case proceed in court. As a result, there are no institutional disincentives to having the immigration court dispose of the case. As a practical matter, once someone is in [removal] proceedings, it is easier for the ICE trial attorney to prove removal than it is to write a memo to get superiors to agree to exercise discretion." Telephone interview with Nancy Morawetz, Immigration Scholar and Professor, New York University (July 15, 2009).

CHAPTER 4. DEFERRED ACTION

1. *Undocumented and Unafraid: Anthony's Story*, UNITED WE DREAM, http://
unitedwedream.org/dreamer-narratives/undocumented-unafraid-anthonys-story (last
visited Dec. 1, 2013).

2. *See Consideration of Deferred Action for Childhood Arrivals Process*, U.S. CITI-
ZENSHIP AND IMMIGRATION SERVICES, http://www.uscis.gov/humanitarian/
consideration-deferred-action-childhood-arrivals-process (last updated July 2, 2013).

3. *See, e.g.*, Memorandum from John Morton, Director, U.S. Immigration and Customs Enforcement, on Exercising Prosecutorial Discretion Consistent with the Civil
Immigration Enforcement Priorities of the Agency for the Apprehension, Detention,
and Removal of Aliens (June 17, 2011), *available at* http://www.ice.gov/doclib/secure
-communities/pdf/prosecutorial-discretion-memo.pdf [hereinafter Morton Memo I].

4. *See, e.g.*, U.S. DEPARTMENT OF HOMELAND SECURITY, CITIZENSHIP AND
IMMIGRATION SERVICES OMBUDSMAN, DEFERRED ACTION: RECOMMEN-
DATIONS TO IMPROVE TRANSPARENCY AND CONSISTENCY IN THE USCIS
PROCESS (July 11, 2011), *available at* http://www.dhs.gov/xlibrary/assets/cisomb
-combined-dar.pdf.

5. *See* 8 C.F.R. § 274a.12(c)(14) (2013) ("An alien who has been granted deferred
action, an act of administrative convenience to the government which gives some cases
lower priority, if the alien establishes an economic necessity for employment.").

6. While one memorandum from DHS on prosecutorial discretion includes some
additional procedures that would include a case to be initiated by the ICE officer,
private attorney, or ICE agent, it does not appear to include a specific method for noti-
fying the noncitizen when he or she has been denied deferred action or prosecutorial
discretion more broadly. *See, e.g.*, Morton Memo I.

7. Notably, Morton Memo I encourages ICE attorneys to review the charging decisions by ICE, CBP, and USCIS. *See, e.g.*, Morton Memo I. By including and amplifying
the role of the ICE attorney, the memo includes an important and new check to the
deferred action process before ICE and prosecutorial discretion generally.

8. (LEGACY) IMMIGRATION AND NATURALIZATION SERVICE, OPERATIONS
INSTRUCTIONS, OI § 103.1(a)(1)(ii) (1975). The 1975 version of internal Operations
Instruction § 103.1(a)(1)(ii) states in part:

(ii) Deferred action. In every case where the district director determines that
adverse action would be unconscionable because of the existence of appealing
humanitarian factors, he shall recommend consideration for deferred action
category. His recommendation shall be made to the regional commissioner
concerned on Form G-312, which shall be signed personally by the district
director. Interim or biennial reviews should be conducted to determine whether
approved cases should be continued or removed from deferred action category.
When determining whether a case should be recommended for deferred action
category, consideration should include the following: (1) advanced or tender age;
(2) many years presence in the United States; (3) physical or mental condition
requiring care or treatment in the United States; (4) family situation in the United

States—effect of expulsion; (5) criminal, immoral or subversive activities or affili-
ations—recent conduct. If the district director's recommendation is approved by
the regional commissioner, the alien shall be notified that no action will be taken
by the Service to disturb his immigration status, or that his departure from the
United States has been deferred indefinitely, whichever is appropriate.

9. Memorandum from Doris Meissner, Commissioner, Immigration and Naturalization Service, on Exercising Prosecutorial Discretion 2 (Nov. 17, 2000) (on file with
author).

10. *See* The REAL ID Act of 2005, Pub. L. No. 109-13, 119 Stat. 302, § 202(c)(2)(B)
(viii).

11. *See, e.g.*, Morton Memo I.

12. *See, e.g.*, Letter from Janet Napolitano, Secretary, U.S. Department of Homeland
Security, to Zoe Lofgren, Representative, U.S. House of Representatives (Aug. 30, 2010)
(on file with author).

13. Press Release, U.S. Citizenship and Immigration Services, USCIS Announces
Interim Relief for Foreign Students Adversely Impacted by Hurricane Katrina (Nov. 25,
2005) (on file with author).

14. Press Release, U.S. Department of Homeland Security, DHS Establishes Interim
Relief for Widows of U.S. Citizens (June 9, 2009), *available at* http://www.dhs.gov/
news/2009/06/09/dhs-establishes-interim-relief-widows-us-citizens.

15. Memorandum from Janet Napolitano, Secretary, U.S. Department of Homeland
Security, on Exercising Prosecutorial Discretion with Respect to Individuals Who
Came to the United States as Children (June 15, 2012), *available at* http://www.dhs.gov/
xlibrary/assets/s1-exercising-prosecutorial-discretion-individuals-who-came-to-us-as
-children.pdf; *see also* Shoba Sivaprasad Wadhia, *Deferred Action in Immigration Law:
The Next Generation*, IMMIGRATIONPROF BLOG (June 28, 2012), *available at* http://
lawprofessors.typepad.com/immigration/2012/06/deferred-action-in-immigration
-law-the-next-generation-by-.html.

16. *See Consideration of Deferred Action.*

17. Ashley Hopkinson, *Somewhere to Turn: The U Visa, a Path to Citizenship for
Domestic Violence Victims*, OAKLAND NORTH (Mar. 9, 2012, 10:00 AM), http://
oaklandnorth.net/2012/03/09/somewhere-to-turn-the-u-visa-a-path-to-citizenship-for
-domestic-violence-victims/.

18. *See, e.g.*, Morton Memo I.

19. Violence Against Women Act, Pub. L. No. 103-322, 108 Stat. 1902 (1994) (codified in scattered sections of the U.S.C.).

20. Memorandum from Michael Cronin, Acting Associate Commissioner of the
Office of Programs, Immigration and Naturalization Service, on Deferred Action for
Self-Petitioning Battered Spouses and Children with Approved I-360 Petitions (Dec.
22, 1998) (on file with author); WILLIAM A. KANDEL, CONG. RESEARCH SERV.,
R42477, IMMIGRATION PROVISIONS OF THE VIOLENCE AGAINST WOMEN ACT
(VAWA) (2012), *available at* www.fas.org/sgp/crs/misc/R42477.pdf.

21. *Battered Spouse, Children, and Parents*, U.S. CITIZENSHIP AND IMMIGRA-TION SERVICES, http://www.uscis.gov/humanitarian/battered-spouse-children -parents (last updated Jan. 16, 2013).

22. Below is a list of the memoranda:

1. Memorandum from Paul Virtue, Acting Active Executive Associate Commis-sioner of the Office of Programs, Immigration and Naturalization Service on Supplemental Guidance on Battered Alien Self-Petitioning Process and Related Issues (May 6, 1997) (describing new ways to handle VAWA Self-Petitions) (on file with author).

2. Memorandum from Michael Cronin, Acting Associate Commissioner of the Office of Programs, Immigration and Naturalization Service, on Deferred Action for Self-Petitioning Battered Spouses and Children with Approved I-360 Petitions (Dec. 22, 1998) (on file with author).

3. Memorandum from Michael Cronin, Acting Associate Commissioner of the Office of Programs, Immigration and Naturalization Service, on Victims of Trafficking and Violence Protection Act of 2000 (VTVPA) Policy Memoran-dum 2—"T" and "U" Nonimmigrant Visas (Aug. 30, 2001) (on file with author).

4. Memorandum from William Yates, Associate Director of Operations, U.S. Citizenship and Immigration Services, on Centralization of Interim Relief for U Nonimmigrant Status Applicants (Oct. 8, 2003) (designating the Vermont Ser-vice Center to serve as a clearing house for the U visa interim relief process and conferred on the Vermont Service Center the ability to grant deferred action in such cases), *available at* http://www.uscis.gov/sites/default/files/USCIS/ Laws/Memoranda/Static_Files_Memoranda/Archives%201998-2008/2003/ ucntrl100803.pdf.

5. Memorandum from William Yates, Associate Director of Operations, U.S. Citizenship and Immigration Services, on Assessment of DA requests for Interim Relief from U nonimmigrant status cases (May 6, 2004), *available at* http://www.uscis.gov/USCIS/Laws/Memoranda/Static_Files_Memoranda/ Archives%201998-2008/2004/uprcd050604.pdf.

23. Memorandum from Paul Virtue, Acting Active Executive Associate Commis-sioner of the Office of Programs, Immigration and Naturalization Service on Supple-mental Guidance on Battered Alien Self-Petitioning Process and Related Issues (May 6, 1997) (on file with author).

24. *Id.*

25. Memorandum from Michael Cronin, Acting Associate Commissioner of the Office of Programs, Immigration and Naturalization Service, on Deferred Action for Self-Petitioning Battered Spouses and Children with Approved I-360 Petitions (Dec. 22, 1998) (on file with author).

26. *See* Leon Wildes, *The Deferred Action Program of the Bureau of Citizenship and Immigration Services: A Possible Remedy for Impossible Cases*, 41 SAN DIEGO L. REV. 835 (2004).

27. *See id.* at 836 n.92.

28. Violence Against Women Act of 2000, Pub. L. No. 106-386, Div. B, 114 Stat. 1464 (2000); Violence Against Women and Department of Justice Reauthorization Act of 2005, Pub. L. No. 109-162, 119 Stat. 2960 (2006); Violence Against Women Reauthorization Act of 2013, Pub. L. No. 113-4, 127 Stat. 54 (2013).

29. KANDEL, CONG. RESEARCH SERV., R42477, IMMIGRATION PROVISIONS OF THE VIOLENCE AGAINST WOMEN ACT.

30. INA § 101(a)(15)(U), 8 U.S.C. § 1101(a)(15)(U) (2013); INA § 1101 (a)(15)(T), 8 U.S.C. § 101(a)(15)(T) (2013).

31. The VTVPA included VAWA 2000 to create a new "U" visa remedy for victims of crime as well as the Trafficking Victims Protection Act of 2000 (TVPA) to create the "T" visa for victims of human trafficking.

32. *See* Victims of Trafficking and Violence Protection Act (VTVPA), Pub. L. No. 106-386 § 1513(a) (2000) (8 U.S.C. § 1101(a)(15)(U)); 8 C.F.R. § 214.14.

33. In addition, the qualifying criminal activity must have occurred on American soil. 8 C.F.R. § 214.14 (b) (describing U visa eligibility requirements).

34. 8 U.S.C. § 1184(p)(2)(A); 8 C.F.R. § 214.14(b) (describing U visa eligibility requirements); 8 C.F.R. § 214.14(d) (stating the annual cap on U visas).

35. 8 U.S.C. § 101(a)(15)(T); 8 C.F.R. § 214.11.

36. 8 U.S.C. § 1184(o)(2); 8 C.F.R. § 214.11(m) (stating the annual cap on T visas).

37. Memorandum from Michael Cronin, Acting Associate Commissioner of the Office of Programs, Immigration and Naturalization Service, on Victims of Trafficking and Violence Protection Act of 2000 (VTVPA) Policy Memorandum 2—"T" and "U" Nonimmigrant Visas (Aug. 30, 2001) (on file with author).

38. *Id.*

39. *Id.*

40. Memorandum from William Yates, Associate Director of Operations, U.S. Citizenship and Immigration Services, on Centralization of Interim Relief for U Nonimmigrant Status Applicants (Oct. 8, 2003), *available at* http://www.uscis.gov/ sites/default/files/USCIS/Laws/Memoranda/Static_Files_Memoranda/Archives%20 1998-2008/2003/ucntrl100803.pdf. *See* Victims of Trafficking and Violence Protection Act (VTVPA), Pub. L. No. 106-386 § 1513(a) (2000) (8 U.S.C. § 1101(a)(15)(U)); 8 C.F.R. § 214.14.

41. Memorandum from William Yates, Associate Director of Operations, U.S. Citizenship and Immigration Services, on Assessment of Deferred Action Requests for Interim Relief from U Nonimmigrant Status Aliens in Removal Proceedings (May 6, 2004), available at http://www.uscis.gov/USCIS/Laws/Memoranda/Static_Files_ Memoranda/Archives%201998-2008/2004/uprcd050604.pdf.

42. Additional guidance was issued by DHS in 2009 to protect pending U visa applicants from deportation, highlighting the use of a stay of removal as a form of prosecutorial discretion ICE should use in appropriate cases, such as a situation where an individual has a final administrative order of removal but indicates having a

pending application for a U visa. The guidance emphasizes the authority given to ICE field officers; *see* Memorandum from David Venturella, Acting Director, U.S. Immigration and Customs Enforcement, on Guidance: Adjudicating Stay Requests Filed by U Nonimmigrant Status (U-visa) Applicants (Sept. 24, 2009), *available at* http://www .ice.gov/doclib/foia/dro_policy_memos/11005_1-hd-stay_requests_filed_by_u_visa_ applicants.pdf; Memorandum from Peter Vincent, Principal Legal Advisor, U.S. Immigration and Customs Enforcement, on Guidance Regarding U Nonimmigrant Status (U visa) Applicants in Removal Proceedings or with Final Orders of Deportation or Removal (Sept. 25, 2009), *available at* http://www.ice.gov/doclib/foia/dro_policy_ memos/vincent_memo.pdf.

43. New Classification for Victims of Criminal Activity; Eligibility for "U" Nonimmigrant Status, 72 Fed. Reg. 53014 (Oct. 17, 2007) (later codified at 8 C.F.R. §§ 103, 212, 214, 248, 274a, and 299) ("Aliens who have been granted interim relief from USCIS are encouraged to file for U nonimmigrant status within 180 days of the effective date of this interim rule. USCIS will no longer issue interim relief upon the effective date of this rule; however, if the alien has properly filed a petition for U nonimmigrant status, but USCIS has not yet adjudicated that petition, interim relief will be extended until USCIS completes its adjudication of the petition.").

44. 8 C.F.R. § 214.14 (2013).

45. Memorandum from William J. Howard, Principal Legal Advisor, U.S. Immigration and Customs Enforcement, on Prosecutorial Discretion (Oct. 24, 2005) (on file with author).

46. *See* USCIS OFFICE OF PERFORMANCE AND QUALITY, FORM I-914 — APPLICATION FOR T NONIMMIGRANT STATUS AND FORM I-918 — PETITION FOR U NONIMMIGRANT STATUS (Dec. 14, 2012), http://www.uscis.gov/USCIS/ Resources/Reports%20and%20Studies/Immigration%20Forms%20Data/Victims/ I914T-I918U-visastatistics-2013-Oct.pdf; 8 C.F.R. § 214.14(a)(9) (2013) (describing the waiting list on which individuals are granted deferred action or parole); email from William Kandel, Analyst in Immigration Policy for the Congressional Research Service (June 6, 2013) (on file with author) (Kandel suggests that the 283 individuals could have received deferred action or could also have been an "administrative aberration whereby persons who should have been processed in 2010 were processed in 2011." He mentioned that such administrative aberrations occur frequently with legal admissions.).

47. *USCIS Approves 10,000 U Visas for the 5th Straight Fiscal Year*, U.S. CITIZENSHIP AND IMMIGRATION SERVICES, http://www.uscis.gov/news/ alerts/uscis-approves-10000-u-visas-5th-straight-fiscal-year (last updated Dec. 11, 2013).

48. U CAP UPDATE FROM USCIS AND ADDITIONAL UPDATES FROM VSC STAKEHOLDER TELECONFERENCE, ASISTA (Dec. 11, 2013), *available at* http:// www.asistahelp.org/documents/news/U_cap_advisory_and_notes_from_stakh_ 60F50EB294846.pdf.

49. *See* USCIS OFFICE OF PERFORMANCE AND QUALITY, FORM I-914.

50. Leslye E. Orloff and Janice V. Kaguyutan, *Offering a Helping Hand: Legal Protections for Battered Immigrant Women: a History of Legislative Responses*, 10 AM. U.J. GENDER SOC. POL'Y AND L. 95 (2002).

51. ROBERT L. GLICKSMAN AND RICHARD E. LEVY, ADMINISTRATIVE LAW: AGENCY ACTION IN LEGAL CONTEXT 247 (2010) (citing to NLRB v. Sears, Roebuck and Co., 421 U.S. 132 (1975)).

52. *See* Leon Wildes, *The Nonpriority Program of the Immigration and Naturalization Service Goes Public: The Litigative Use of the Freedom of Information Act*, 14 SAN DIEGO L. REV. 57 (1976).

53. *Id.* at 57.

54. *Id.* at 53.

55. *Id.* at 58–60.

56. *Id.* at 59.

57. *Id.* at 60 n.45.

58. *Id.* at 55–57.

59. *See* U.S. CITIZENSHIP AND IMMIGRATION SERVICES, CONSIDERATION OF DEFERRED ACTION FOR CHILDHOOD ARRIVALS PROCESS, *available at* http://www.uscis.gov/portal/site/uscis/menuitem.eb1d4c2a3e5b9ac89243c6a7543f6d1a/?vgnextoid=f2ef2f19470f7310VgnVCM100000082ca60aRCRD&vgnextchannel=f2ef2f19470f7310VgnVCM100000082ca60aRCRD.

60. Wildes, *Nonpriority Program of the Immigration and Naturalization Service*, at 57.

61. *Id.* at 51.

62. *Id.* at 52.

63. *See* Wildes, *The Deferred Action Program of the Bureau of Citizenship and Immigration Services.*

64. *See id.* at 826–27.

65. *See id.* at 826.

66. *See id.* at 830.

67. *See id.* at 829.

68. *See id.* at 830.

69. *See id.* at 831.

70. *See id.*

71. *See id.* at 832.

72. *See id.* at 831.

73. *See id.* at 832.

74. *See id.*

75. *See id.* at 830.

76. *See id.* at 835.

77. My initial FOIA request to USCIS headquarters was made on October 6, 2009. USCIS responded on October 9, 2009, in a letter that confirmed the receipt of my request and assigned it a control number. On October 28, 2009, a second letter was sent from USCIS requesting additional information about the records sought. *See* Letter from T. Diane Cejka, Director, U.S. Citizenship and Immigration Services, to author (Oct. 27, 2009) (concerning control number NRC2009057166) (on file with author). More specifically, USCIS required the inquiry be made regarding particular individuals with their consent. On February 9, 2010, the FOIA request was closed. I made a second and more detailed FOIA request on March 30, 2010.

78. USCIS sent a response on April 1, 2010, assigning the request a control number. *See* Letter from T. Diane Cejka, Director, U.S. Citizenship and Immigration Services, to author (Apr. 1, 2010) (concerning control number NRC2009057166) (on file with author). As of August 31, 2010, my FOIA request was listed on the USCIS website as 65 out of 219 requests pending in track 2. After nearly one year without a response, I discussed my request with the Office of the DHS ombudsman on February 25, 2011; the office took an interest in the nature of my request and agreed to assist with moving the FOIA along at USCIS. *See* email from Gary Merson, Office of the Citizenship and Immigration Services Ombudsman (Feb. 25, 2011, 6:41 PM) (on file with author). On March 11, 2011, I received an e-message from a USCIS FOIA officer stating "[we have] received most of the records responsive to your request and are contacting an additional program office to determine if additional records exist on this subject." Email from Tembra Greenwood, Nat'l Records Ctr., Freedom of Info. Act Div., to author (Mar. 11, 2011, 1:48 PM) (referring to NRC2010021400) (on file with the author).

79. Letter from Jill A. Eggleston, Director of FOIA Operations, U.S. Immigration and Customs Enforcement, to author (June 17, 2011), *available at* http://works.bepress .com/cgi/viewcontent.cgi?article=1036&context=shoba_wadhia [hereinafter Response from USCIS on my FOIA re Deferred Action].

80. *Id.*

81. *Id.*

82. u.s. department of homeland security, citizenship and immigration services ombudsman, deferred action.

83. It was difficult to label a case as tender or elder age because much of the data lacked identifiers. However, when a field included the word "minor" or "infant" or a specific age (*e.g.*, eighty-nine years old), the case was calculated as involving tender or elder age for purposes of this analysis. It should also be mentioned that some of the cases approved, pending, or unknown contained little to no factual information and, as a consequence, were not identified as bearing any of the "positive" factors listed above. The outcomes for many of these cases were unknown because the field was blank or there simply was not a field in the log maintained by a particular office. Many of the cases also had outcomes that were marked as "pending." Of the 118 cases, 59 were pending or unknown, 48 were granted, and 11 were denied.

84. Below is a sampling of approved cases involving a serious medical condition, tender or elder age, and/or the presence of U.S. citizen (USC) family members:

- Cerebral palsy victim, Korean orphan with USC sponsors
- Father of eight-year-old child receiving extensive neurological treatment

- Father of eleven-year-old USC daughter with severe heart problems
- Mother of eleven-year-old USC daughter with severe heart problems
- Mother of U.S. national child with progressive muscular dystrophy
- Religious worker denied adjustment due to HIV infection
- Forty-seven-year-old schizophrenic B-2 overstay; son of LPR; USC siblings
- Twenty-two-year-old with Down syndrome unable to care for self; daughter of an LPR
- B-2 overstay, polio survivor, and permanently disabled and in a wheelchair; lives with USC mother and brother who care for him; sister is an LPR
- Deaf, mute, and mentally and learning disabled; permanently disabled and wheelchair-bound for life; requires twenty-four-hour supervision
- Eighty-nine-year-old man suffering from Parkinson's disease, dementia, Alzheimer's disease, glaucoma, hypertension, and hypotension
- Person receiving medical care for a rare and life-threatening disease; parents are helping in his care since he is only twelve years old
- Person came to the United States at the age of four months for medical treatment and has been here ever since
- Person entered the United States as a visitor for pleasure, has moderate mental retardation, and was denied adjustment of status
- Noncitizen has two older siblings born in the United States and a now deceased father who was also a USC
- Couple entered the United States as B-1 and B-2 visitors, are parents to four USC children, two of whom were born with a kidney disease for which they are receiving medical treatment

85. Letter from author to FOIA Officer, U.S. Citizenship and Immigration Services (May 24, 2013), *available at* http://works.bepress.com/cgi/viewcontent.cgi?article=1046&context=shoba_wadhia.

86. Letter from Jill A. Eggleston, Freedom of Information Act Director, U.S. Citizenship and Immigration Services, to author (Sept. 3, 2013), *available at* http://w3.law.psu.edu/_file/Document_2.pdf.

87. *Id.*

88. *Id.*

89. 8 C.F.R. 274a.12(c) (2013).

90. Letter from Jill A. Eggleston, Freedom of Information Act Director, U.S. Customs and Enforcement, to author (July 22, 2013), *available at* http://w3.law.psu.edu/_file/foiadapackage2013.pdf [hereinafter USCIS DEFERRED ACTION BIOGRAPHIES AND DEMOGRAPHICS].

91. Applicants for DACA have been instructed to use a different code and specifically (c)(33) when applying for work authorization pursuant to DACA even though these applications are technically based on discretionary grants of deferred action.

92. *See* USCIS DEFERRED ACTION BIOGRAPHIES AND DEMOGRAPHICS.

93. *See* USCIS OFFICE OF PERFORMANCE AND QUALITY, DEFERRED ACTION FOR CHILDHOOD ARRIVALS (February 6, 2014), http://www.uscis.gov/sites/default/files/USCIS/Resources/Reports%20and%20Studies/Immigration%20Forms%20Data/All%20Form%20Types/DACA/DACA-06-02-14.pdf.

94. *See id.*

95. *See id.*

96. *See, e.g.,* TOM K. WONG ET AL., CENTER FOR AMERICAN PROGRESS, UNDOCUMENTED NO MORE: A NATIONWIDE ANALYSIS OF DEFERRED ACTION FOR CHILDHOOD ARRIVALS, OR DACA (Sept. 20, 2013), *available at* http://www.americanprogress.org/issues/immigration/report/2013/09/20/74599/undocumented-no-more/; JEANNE BATALOVA, SARAH HOOKER, AND RANDY CAPPS, MIGRATION POLICY INSTITUTE, DEFERRED ACTION FOR CHILDHOOD ARRIVALS AT THE ONE YEAR MARK (August 2013), *available at* http://www.migrationpolicy.org/pubs/CIRbrief-DACAatOneYear.pdf.

97. WONG ET AL., CENTER FOR AMERICAN PROGRESS, UNDOCUMENTED NO MORE.

98. *Id.*

99. U.S. IMMIGRATION AND CUSTOMS ENFORCEMENT, NO. OF ACTIVE CASES GRANTED DEFERRED ACTION STATUS SINCE CY 2003 (Undated) (on file with author). *See* Shoba Sivaprasad Wadhia, *Sharing Secrets: Examining Deferred Action and Transparency in Immigration Law*, 10 U.N.H. L. REV. 1, 34–38 (2012).

100. *See* Letter from author to Assoc. Gen. Counsel, Department of Homeland Security (Mar. 29, 2011) (on file with author) (appealing adverse decision in FOIA matter 2011FOIA1845).

101. *See id.*

102. Letter from Catrina M. Pavlik-Kennan, Freedom of Info. Act Dir., U.S. Immigration and Customs Enforcement, to author (Sept. 27, 2011) (on file with author) (regarding matter number OPLA-181, 2011, 2011FOIA14736).

103. Complaint, Wadhia v. United States Dep't. of Homeland Sec. (D.D.C. filed Jan. 3, 2012) (on file with author).

104. *See* series of emails between author and DOJ/ICE attorneys (June 2012 through Sept. 2012) (on file with author).

105. Wadhia v. Dep't of Homeland Sec. (dismissed Oct. 1, 2012).

106. *See* SHOBA SIVAPRASAD WADHIA, DATA FROM ICE ON DEFERRED ACTION, FALL 2012, http://law.psu.edu/_file/Wadhia/FOIA_FOD_Adjudicated_Deferred.xlsx (last updated Aug. 30, 2013).

107. Unlike deferred action, a stay of removal is available to the noncitizen only after a removal order has been entered and may be granted only by ICE (as opposed to USCIS, *e.g.*).

108. *See* Letter from Catrina M. Pavlik-Kennan, FOIA Officer, to author (Sept. 26, 2012) (on file with author). The twenty-four field offices are distributed across the United States and cover certain jurisdictional areas, usually more than one state. The

field offices are located in the following locations: Atlanta, GA; Baltimore, MD; Boston, MA; Buffalo, NY; Chicago, IL; Dallas, TX; Denver, CO; Detroit, MI; El Paso, TX; Houston, TX; Los Angeles, CA; Miami, FL; Newark, NJ; New Orleans, LA; New York, NY; Philadelphia, PA; Phoenix, AZ; Salt Lake City, UT; San Antonio, TX; San Diego, CA; San Francisco, CA; Seattle, WA; St. Paul, MN; and Washington, DC. *See Enforcement and Removal Operations*, U.S. IMMIGRATION AND CUSTOMS ENFORCEMENT, http://www.ice.gov/contact/ero/ (last visited Dec. 20, 2013).

109. *See* Letter from Catrina M. Pavlik-Kennan.

110. *See* U.S. IMMIGRATION AND CUSTOMS ENFORCEMENT, FORM I-246, APPLICATION FOR A STAY OF DEPORTATION OR REMOVAL (Dec. 2010), http://www.ice.gov/doclib/news/library/forms/pdf/i246.pdf; 8 C.F.R. § 241.6 (2013).

111. As part of the settlement agreement, ICE collected seven data points from each field office:

1. Applicant's birth date (as collected from the ENFORCE database)
2. Applicant's citizenship country (as collected from the ENFORCE database)
3. Whether the applicant was represented by counsel (as provided from the GEMS database)
4. Whether the applicant applied for deferred action or a stay of removal
5. Whether the application was granted
6. The date a decision was made
7. The reason the application was granted or denied

112. Since the data provided by ICE lacked identification markers for each individual applicant (such as an alien registration number), I cannot verify if a single applicant submitted multiple applications for deferred action or submitted an application for both deferred action and a stay of removal. Despite this limitation and in light of the deliberations leading to settlement of the lawsuit and the careful research conducted by ICE to create the data leading to such settlement, my analysis assumes that most, if not all, of the 3,837 cases are separate cases.

113. Note that the ICE data differentiate between whether the *applicant* suffered from a serious mental or physical illness and whether the applicant was the *primary caretaker* of someone who suffered from a serious mental or physical illness. The same is true for whether the applicant was a minor or elderly individual, or just the caretaker of a minor or elderly individual. Moreover, though the data from ICE identify "length of presence in the U.S." as the fourth most common factor (excluding "other") for why a deferred action case was granted, the data do not include the length of time each individual has been present in the United States.

114. Note that the total displayed in the graph does not add up to 324 because there were 15 additional reasons for a deferred action grant, totaling 36 occurrences, which were omitted from the graph.

115. *See* MICHAEL HOEFER, NANCY RYTINA, AND BRYAN BAKER, ESTIMATES OF THE UNAUTHORIZED IMMIGRANT POPULATION RESIDING IN THE UNITED STATES: JANUARY 2011, UNITED STATES DEP'T OF HOMELAND

SECURITY, OFFICE OF IMMIGRATION STATISTICS 5 (Mar. 2012), *available at* http://www.dhs.gov/xlibrary/assets/statistics/publications/ois_ill_pe_2011.pdf.

116. *See, e.g.*, Roger C. Cramton, *Administrative Procedure Reform: The Effects of S. 1663 on the Conduct of Federal Rate Proceedings*, 16 ADMIN. L. REV. 108, 112 (1963); *see also* Wadhia, *Sharing Secrets*, at 11–15.

117. For an argument in favor of subjecting some acts of prosecutorial discretion to judicial review under the "arbitrary and capricious" standard of the APA, *see* Wadhia, *Sharing Secrets*, at 11–15. Shoba Sivaprasad Wadhia, *The Immigration Prosecutor and the Judge: Examining the Role of the Judiciary in Prosecutorial Discretion Decisions*, 16 HARV. LATINO L. REV. 39, 53 (2013).

118. Richard Thomas, *Prosecutorial Discretion and Agency Self-Regulation: CNI v. Young and the Aflatoxin Dance*, 44 ADMIN. L. REV. 131, 137–38 (1992) (citing to KENNETH CULP DAVIS, DISCRETIONARY JUSTICE: A PRELIMINARY INQUIRY (1969)); *see also* Ronald M. Levin, *The Administrative Law Legacy of Kenneth Culp Davis*, 42 SAN DIEGO L. REV. 315, 324 (2005) (citing to KENNETH CULP DAVIS, ADMINISTRATIVE LAW TREATISE § 6.15 (Supp. 1970)). Kenneth Culp Davis was a seminal scholar whose Administrative Law Treatise became a leading authority in administrative law. According to his former pupil and administrative law scholar Ronald M. Levin, "With Davis's capacity for broad research, incisive analysis, and moral passion on full display, the treatise immediately overshadowed all prior work in the area." *Id.* at 315.

119. *See, e.g.*, 5 U.C.S. §§ 551, 553, 555 (2009); 7 U.C.S. §§ 701–2, 704, 706 (2009).

120. 5 U.C.S. § 553 (2009).

121. 5 U.C.S. § 553 (2009).

122. 5 U.C.S. § 553 (2009).

123. *See* Robert A. Anthony and David A. Codevilla, *Pro-Ossification: A Harder Look at Agency Policy Statements*, 31 WAKE FOREST L. REV. 667, 671 (1996).

124. Thomas, *Prosecutorial Discretion and Agency Self-Regulation*, at 132; Community Nutrition Inst. v. Young, 818 F.2d 943 (D.C. Cir. 1987).

125. Community Nutrition Inst. v. Young, 818 F.2d 943 (D.C. Cir. 1987).

126. Thomas, *Prosecutorial Discretion and Agency Self-Regulation*, at 152.

127. *See, e.g.*, Pasquini v. Morris, 700 F.2d 658, 661 (11th Cir. 1983); Soon Bok Yoon v. INS, 538 F.2d 1211, 1213 (5th Cir. 1976); Lennon v. INS, 527 F.2d 187 (2d Cir. 1975); Wan Chung Wen v. Ferro, 543 F. Supp. 1016 (W.D.N.Y. 1982); Zacharakis v. Howerton, 517 F.Supp. 1026, 1027–28 (D. Fla. 1981); *see* Velasco-Gutierrez v. Crossland, 732 F.2d 792, 798 (10th Cir. 1984); *see also* Siverts v. Craig, 602 F.Supp. 50, 53 (D. Haw. 1985) (construing 1981 instruction).

128. Nicholas v. INS, 590 F.2d 802, 807 (9th Cir. 1979).

CHAPTER 5. PRESIDENTIAL PORTRAIT

1. For a sampling of President Obama's public discussion about comprehensive immigration reform, *see* President Barack Obama, Remarks on Comprehensive

Immigration Reform (July 1, 2010), *available at* http://www.whitehouse.gov/photos
-and-video/video/president-obama-comprehensive-immigration-reform; Julie Mason,
President Obama Pushes Immigration Overhaul, POLITICO, May 10, 2011, http://www
.politico.com/news/stories/0511/54696.html; David Jackson, *Obama Talks Immigration
with Officials—But No Members of Congress*, USA TODAY, Apr. 19, 2011, http://content
.usatoday.com/communities/theoval/post/2011/04/obama-talks-immigration-with
-officials----but-no-members-of-congress/1. For an analysis of previous congressional
proposals on comprehensive immigration reform, *see* Shoba Sivaprasad Wadhia, *Policy
and Politics of Immigrant Rights*, 16 TEMP. POL. AND CIV. RTS. L. REV. 387 (2007);
Shoba Sivaprasad Wadhia, *Immigration: Mind over Matter*, 5 UNIV. OF MD. L.J. RACE
RELIG., GENDER & CLASS 201 (2005).

    2. IMMIGRATION POLICY: TRANSITION BLUEPRINT, OBAMA-BIDEN TRAN-
SITION PROJECT (2008), *available at* http://www.aila.org/content/fileviewer.aspx?
docid=27611&linkid=188816. For a longer discussion about previous efforts to enact
legislative reform, *see* Wadhia, *Policy and Politics of Immigrant Rights*.

    3. *See, e.g.*, Development, Relief, and Education for Alien Minors Act of 2009,
S.3992, 111th Cong. (2009); Development, Relief, and Education for Alien Minors Act
of 2009, H.R. 6497, 111th Cong. (2009).

    4. *See* Luis Miranda, *Get the Facts on the DREAM Act*, THE WHITE HOUSE
BLOG (Dec. 10, 2012, 7:19 PM), http://www.whitehouse.gov/blog/2010/12/01/get-facts
-dream-act.

    5. *See* Elise Foley, *Dream Act Vote Fails in Senate*, HUFFPOST POLITICS, Dec. 18,
2010, http://www.huffingtonpost.com/2010/12/18/dream-act-vote-senate_n_798631
.html.

    6. *See id.*

    7. Dreamers are people who entered the United States at a minor age who may
have been eligible for relief under the DREAM Act, introduced by Congress but never
passed into law.

    8. *See* U.S. IMMIGRATION AND CUSTOMS ENFORCEMENT, ICE TOTAL
REMOVALS (2012), *available at* http://www.ice.gov/doclib/about/offices/ero/pdf/ero
-removals1.pdf.

    9. LOST IN DETENTION (*Frontline*, Oct. 18, 2011), *transcript available at* http://
www.pbs.org/wgbh/pages/frontline/race-multicultural/lost-in-detention/transcript-11/.

    10. Memorandum from Denise A. Vanison, et al., to Alejandro Mayorkas, on
Administrative Alternatives to Comprehensive Immigration Reform (undated) (on file
with author).

    11. *Id.*

    12. *Id.*

    13. *Id.*

    14 David North, *Leaked USCIS Memo Is a Serious One, Says a Lot about the Agency*,
CENTER FOR IMMIGRATION STUDIES, Aug. 3, 2010, http://www.cis.org/north/uscis
-memo.

15. Robert VerBruggen, *The Amnesty Memo*, NATIONAL REVIEW ONLINE (July 29, 2010, 5:30 PM), http://www.nationalreview.com/corner/233793/amnesty-memo -robert-verbruggen.

16. HOMELAND SECURITY, TESTIMONY OF SECRETARY JANET NAPOLI- TANO U.S. DEPARTMENT OF HOMELAND SECURITY BEFORE THE UNITED STATES SENATE COMMITTEE ON THE JUDICIARY, "DEPARTMENT OF HOME- LAND SECURITY OVERSIGHT," March 9, 2011, *available at* https://www.dhs .gov/news/2011/03/09/testimony-secretary-janet-napolitano-united-states-senate -committee-judiciary.

17. *Id.*

18. *Id.*

19. Letter from AILA and Immigration Council to DHS Secretary Janet Napolitano (Apr. 6, 2011), *available at* http://www.americanimmigrationcouncil.org/sites/default/ files/docs/AILA-AIC-Napolitano-4-6-2011.pdf.

20. *A Sad Comparison: Napolitano's DHS, Tougher than Bush*, AMERICA'S VOICE (Mar. 9, 2011), http://americasvoiceonline.org/press_releases/a_sad_comparison_ napolitanos_dhs_tougher_than_bush/.

21. Letter from Senator Harry Reid et al. to President Barack Obama (Apr. 13, 2011) (on file with author).

22. *Id.* For an example of a DREAM Act student granted deferred action, *see, e.g.*, *Michigan Student's Deportation Put on Hold; Warren Student Wants to Graduate, Continue Schooling at University of Michigan*, CLICKONDETROIT.COM (May 24, 2011, updated May 25, 2011, 9:36 AM) (on file with author).

23. Letter from Senator Harry Reid et al. to President Barack Obama.

24. Letter from the Senate Judiciary Subcommittee on Immigration to DHS Secre- tary Janet Napolitano (Apr. 14, 2011) (on file with author).

25. STATEMENT OF KAREN T. GRISEZ ON BEHALF OF THE AMERICAN BAR ASSOCIATION TO THE COMMITTEE ON THE JUDICIARY UNITED STATES SEN- ATE, AMERICAN BAR ASSOCIATION, 7, *available at* http://www.americanbar.org/ content/dam/aba/uncategorized/2011/2011may18_grisezs_t.authcheckdam.pdf.

26. DONALD M. KERWIN, DORIS MEISSNER, AND MARGIE MCHUGH, MIGRATION POLICY INSTITUTE, EXECUTIVE ACTION ON IMMIGRATION: SIX WAYS TO MAKE THE SYSTEM WORK BETTER 1 (2011), *available at* http://www .migrationpolicy.org/pubs/administrativefixes.pdf.

27. *Id.* at 15. While I agree with the MPI's sound recommendation for greater use of prosecutorial discretion, I disagree that deferred action cases should be limited to a "case by case" basis, a point that is obviated by my recommendation to promulgate a regulation on deferred action.

28. Press Release, NAFSA: Association of International Educators, NAFSA State- ment on Immigration Reform and Undocumented Students (May 10, 2011), *available at* http://www.nafsa.org/PressRoom/PressRelease.aspx?id=26639.

29. *See, e.g.*, DHS Prosecutorial Discretion Initiative Falls Short, American

Immigration Lawyers Association, AILA InfoNet Doc. No. 12060752 (June 7, 2012), http://www.aila.org/content/default.aspx?docid=40035.

30. *New Toolkit Sheds Light on Lesser Known Immigration Remedies*, PENN STATE LAW (May 17, 2011), http://law.psu.edu/news/immigration_toolkit.

31. *Education Not Deportation: A Guide for Undocumented Youth in Removal Proceedings*, ASIAN LAW CAUCUS, Asian Law Caucus, Educators for Fair Consideration, DreamActivist.org, and National Immigrant Youth Alliance, http://www.advancingjustice-alc.org/news-media/publications/guide-undocumented-youth-removal-proceedings (last visited July 18, 2011).

32. Memorandum from John Morton, Director, U.S. Immigration and Customs Enforcement, on Civil Immigration Enforcement: Priorities for the Apprehension, Detention, and Removal of Aliens (Mar. 2, 2011), *available at* http://www.ice.gov/doclib/news/releases/2011/110302washingtondc.pdf [hereinafter Priorities Memo].

33. *Id.*

34. For a more in-depth analysis of the Priorities Memo, *see* SHOBA SIVAPRASAD WADHIA, IMMIGRATION POLICY CENTER, READING THE MORTON MEMO: FEDERAL PRIORITIES AND PROSECUTORIAL DISCRETION, *available at* http://www.immigrationpolicy.org/special-reports/reading-morton-memo-federal-priorities-and-prosecutorial-discretion.

35. The Priorities Memo further explained that individuals convicted of crimes who fall under priority 1 will be classified in three "levels," specifically:

Level 1: "aggravated felonies as defined in [the immigration statute], or two or more crimes each punishable by more than one year."

Level 2: "any felony or three or more crimes punishable by less than one year."

Level 3: "crimes punishable by less than one year."

Priorities Memo, at 2.

36. *Id.* at 1.

37. *Id.* at 4.

38. *Id.* On March 2, 2011, ICE Director John Morton republished the Priorities Memo, and added the following clause at the end: "These guidelines and priorities are not intended to, do not, and may not be relied upon to create any right or benefit, substantive or procedural, enforceable at law by any party in any administrative, civil, or criminal matter." Priorities Memo, at 4. The "no right or benefit" clause embedded in the Priorities Memo was included in every memorandum in 2011.

39. Memorandum from John Morton, Director, U.S. Immigration and Customs Enforcement, on Exercising Prosecutorial Discretion Consistent with the Civil Immigration Enforcement Priorities of the Agency for the Apprehension, Detention, and Removal of Aliens (June 17, 2011), *available at* http://www.ice.gov/doclib/secure-communities/pdf/prosecutorial-discretion-memo.pdf [hereinafter Morton Memo]. For a more in-depth analysis of the Morton Memo, *see* SHOBA SIVAPRASAD WADHIA, IMMIGRATION CENTER, THE MORTON MEMO AND THE PROSECUTORIAL DISCRETION: AN OVERVIEW, *available at* http://www.immigrationpolicy.org/special-reports/morton-memo-and-prosecutorial-discretion-overview. Throughout

this book the shorthand terms "Morton Memo" and "Morton Memo I" are used interchangeably.

40. Morton Memo, at 4.

41. *Id.*

42. *Id.*

43. Leon Wildes and Shoba Sivaprasad Wadhia, *Prosecutorial Discretion and the Legacy of John Lennon*, IMMIGRATIONPROF BLOG (July 14, 2011), http://law professors.typepad.com/immigration/2011/07/prosecutorial-discretion-and-the-legacy -of-john-lennon-by-leon-wildes-and-shoba-sivaprasad-wadhia.html.

44. *Id.*

45. Morton Memo.

46. A second memo published by ICE on June 17, 2011, is titled "Prosecutorial Discretion: Certain Victims, Witnesses, and Plaintiffs" (Morton Memo II) and is aimed at protecting victims and witnesses of crime, including victims of domestic violence and individuals involved in nonfrivolous efforts related to the protection of their civil rights, from removal. Morton Memo II boldly states: "Absent special circumstances or aggravating factors, it is against ICE policy to initiate removal proceedings against an individual known to be the immediate victim or witness to a crime." Morton Memo II reminds ICE officers about the availability of the U, T, and VAWA Self-Petition and lists victims of crime, domestic violence, and trafficking as among the groups who must receive particular consideration for a favorable exercise of prosecutorial discretion. The memo reiterates that cases to prosecute criminals, felons, and individuals endangering national security should take priority over cases where an illegal alien poses no threat to society and is in desperate need of relief. Memorandum from John Morton, Director, U.S. Immigration and Customs Enforcement, on Prosecutorial Discretion: Certain Crime Victims, Witnesses and Plaintiffs (June 17, 2011), *available at* http://www.ice.gov/doclib/secure-communities/pdf/domestic-violence.pdf.

47. *See, e.g.*, R. Cort Kirkwood, *Circumventing Congress: Failed Dream Act Mandated by ICE Director*, NEW AMERICAN (June 27, 2011), *available at* http://www .thenewamerican.com/usnews/immigration/8015-circumventing-congress-failed -dream-act-mandated-by-ice-director; Letter from Rep. Lamar Smith, Prevent the Obama Administration from Bypassing Congress and Legalizing Millions of Illegal Immigrants Co-Sponsor the HALT Act (June 23, 2011), *available at* http://big.assets .huffingtonpost.com/Smith_DearColleague.pdf; *Obama Administration Bypasses Congress; Grants Amnesty to DREAM Act Students*, FEDERATION FOR AMERICAN IMMIGRATION REFORM, *available at* http://www.fairus.org/site/News2/1245052251? page=NewsArticle&id=24229&security=1601&news_iv_ctrl=1012 (last visited July 1, 2011); *ICE Agent's Union Speaks Out on Director's "Discretionary Memo" Calls on the Public to Take Action*, AFG NATIONAL COUNCIL (June 23, 2011), *available at* http:// www.iceunion.org/news/ice-agent%E2%80%99s-union-speaks-out-director%E2%80% 99s-%E2%80%9Cdiscretionary-memo%E2%80%9D-calls-public-take-action-click-her.

48. Letter from House Judiciary Committee Chairman Lamar Smith, to Members of Congress (June 23, 2011) (on file with author).

49. *Id.; see also* H.R. 2497, 112th Cong. (2011), *available at* http://www.gpo.gov/fdsys/pkg/BILLS-112hr2497ih/pdf/BILLS-112hr2497ih.pdf; S. 1380, 112th Cong. (2011), *available at* http://www.gpo.gov/fdsys/pkg/BILLS-112s1380is/pdf/BILLS-112s1380is.pdf. On a historical note, in 1999, Representative Lamar Smith went on the record supporting prosecutorial discretion by coauthoring a letter from select members of Congress to the immigration agency. For a copy of the letter and commentary about Representative Smith's reverse position on prosecutorial discretion, *see Editorial, The Forgetful Mr. Smith*, N.Y. TIMES, July 12, 2011, http://www.nytimes.com/2011/07/13/opinion/13wed3.html.

50. Letter from House Judiciary Committee Chairman Lamar Smith, to Members of Congress; *see also Hearing Information*, U.S. HOUSE OF REPRESENTATIVES COMMITTEE ON THE JUDICIARY, http://judiciary.house.gov/hearings/hear_07262011_2.html (last visited Dec. 20, 2013).

51. *Hearing Information*, U.S. HOUSE OF REPRESENTATIVES COMMITTEE ON THE JUDICIARY.

52. Statement of Chris Crane, President of National Immigration and Customs Enforcement Council 118 of the American Federation of Government Employees, before the Judiciary Subcommittee on Immigration and Policy Enforcement (July 26, 2011), *available at* http://judiciary.house.gov/hearings/pdf/Crane07262011.pdf. Beyond the scope of this article but noteworthy are Crane's remarks about the importance of training, and the ostentatious lack of training or guidance field officers received on the Morton Memo on Prosecutorial Discretion prior to its publication.

53. Letter from Democratic Members from the House of Representatives, to President Barack Obama (July 21, 2011), *available at* http://clarke.house.gov/sites/clarke.house.gov/files/wysiwyg_uploaded/HALT_Act_letter_complete.pdf.

54. The Hinder the Administration's Legalization Temptation Act: Hearing on H.R. 2497 before the Subcomm. on Immigration Policy and Enforcement of the House Comm. on the Judiciary, 112th Cong. 3–4 (2011), http://www.gpo.gov/fdsys/pkg/CHRG-112hhrg67575/html/CHRG-112hhrg67575.htm.

55. *Id.*

56. *See* Susan Carroll, *Report: Feds Downplayed ICE Case Dismissals; Documents Show Agency Had Approval to Dismiss Some Deportation Cases*, HOUSTON CHRONICLE, June 27, 2011, http://www.chron.com/disp/story.mpl/chronicle/7627737.html; Susan Carroll, *Cornyn Presses Napolitano over Immigration Case Dismissals*, HOUSTON CHRONICLE, June 28, 2011, http://www.chron.com/disp/story.mpl/chronicle/7631394.html.

57. Susan Carroll, *The Dismissal Records*, HOUSTON CHRONICLE, June 28, 2011, http://blog.chron.com/immigration/2011/06/the-dismissal-records/.

58. *Id.*

59. Letter from House Judiciary Committee Chairman Lamar Smith and Homeland Security Subcommittee Chairman Robert Aderholt, to DHS Secretary Janet Napolitano (July 5, 2011), *available at* http://judiciary.house.gov/index.cfm/2011/7/smithandaderholttoadministrationstopadministrativeamnesty.

60. Press Release, Sen. Orrin Hatch, Hatch, Senate Colleagues Press U.S. Immigration and Customs Enforcement to Enforce Immigration Laws (July 13, 2011), *available at* http://www.hatch.senate.gov/public/index.cfm/releases?ID=86f43fd7-bb7c-4d03-8bb8-f83ea8468843.

61. *See generally* LEXISNEXIS LEGAL NEWSROOM IMMIGRATION LAW, http://www.lexisnexis.com/legalnewsroom/immigration/tags/Shoba+Sivaprasad+Wadhia/default.aspx (last visited Dec. 20, 2013).

62. Policy Memorandum from U.S. Citizenship and Immigration Services on Revised Guidance for the Referral of Cases and Issuance of Notices to Appear (NTAs) in Cases Involving Inadmissible and Removable Aliens (Nov. 7, 2011), *available at* http://www.uscis.gov/sites/default/files/USCIS/Laws/Memoranda/Static_Files_Memoranda/NTA%20PM%20%28Approved%20as%20final%2011-7-11%29.pdf.

63. Memorandum from Gary Mead, Executive Associate Director, U.S. Citizenship and Immigration Services, on Applicability of Prosecutorial Discretion Memoranda to Certain Family Relationships (Oct. 5, 2012), *available at* http://www.immigrationequality.org/wp-content/uploads/2012/11/PD-memo-10-5-2012-2.pdf.

64. *Id.*

65. *Id.*

66. Mahwish Khan, *ICE Director Morton's Prosecutorial Discretion Memo Offered Hope, Yet to be Realized*, America's Voice (Apr. 17, 2012, 10:26 AM), http://americasvoiceonline.org/blog/ice-director-mortons-prosecutorial-discretion-memo-offered-hope-yet-to-be-realized/.

67. FAIR IMMIGRATION REFORM MOVEMENT, RESTORE THE PROMISE OF PROSECUTORIAL DISCRETION (June 2012), *available at* http://fairimmigration.files.wordpress.com/2012/06/restore-the-promise-full-report.pdf.

68. CASE-BY-CASE REVIEW STATISTICS, U.S. IMMIGRATION AND CUSTOMS ENFORCEMENT (2012), *available at* http://www.ilw.com/immigrationdaily/news/2012,0430-prosecutorialdiscretion.pdf.

69. CASE-BY-CASE REVIEW STATISTICS, U.S. IMMIGRATION AND CUSTOMS ENFORCEMENT (2012), *available at* http://www.immigrationpolicy.org/sites/default/files/docs/DHS-PD-stats-6-6-2012.pdf. "Administrative closure" has been conflated with "prosecutorial discretion" insofar as DHS—and ICE in particular—has identified this exercise of prosecutorial discretion (which as a technical matter would be limited to ICE joining in a motion, filing a separate motion, or not opposing a respondent's motion to administratively close a removal case). The conflation is inaccurate for two reasons: First, ICE's support through a motion to administratively close a case is but one among several exercises of prosecutorial discretion available to DHS. Second, the actual decision to administratively close a removal case rests with the immigration judge within the Department of Justice, not with the ICE prosecutor.

70. CASE-BY-CASE REVIEW STATISTICS, U.S. IMMIGRATION AND CUSTOMS ENFORCEMENT (2012), available at http://www.ilw.com/immigrationdaily/news/2012,0430-prosecutorialdiscretion.pdf.

71. *Id.*

72. *Id.; see also* Shoba Sivaprasad Wadhia, *Board Offers New Standard for Administrative Closure, and Highlights the Importance of Decisional Independence,* AILA IMMIGRATION SLIP OPINION BLOG (Feb. 2, 2012) (on file with author).

73. DHS Prosecutorial Discretion Initiative Falls Short.

74. Julia Preston, *Deportations Continue Despite U.S. Review of Backlog,* N.Y. TIMES, June 6, 2012, at A13, http://www.nytimes.com/2012/06/07/us/politics/deportations-continue-despite-us-review-of-backlog.html; Julia Preston, *Deportations under New U.S. Policy Are Inconsistent,* N.Y. TIMES, Nov. 12, 2011, at A16; *see also* Editorial, *A Failure of Discretion,* N.Y. TIMES, June 7, 2012, at A26; CASE-BY-CASE REVIEW STATISTICS, U.S. IMMIGRATION AND CUSTOMS ENFORCEMENT (2012), available at http://www.ilw.com/immigrationdaily/news/2012,0430-prosecutorialdiscretion.pdf; DHS Prosecutorial Discretion Initiative Falls Short.

75. *See, e.g.,* Preston, *Deportations Continue.*

76. *See, e.g.,* JOAN FRIEDLAND, AMERICAN IMMIGRATION COUNCIL, FALLING THROUGH THE CRACKS (May 14, 2012), *available at* http://www.americanimmigrationcouncil.org/perspectives/falling-through-cracks.

77. *See* CASE-BY-CASE REVIEW STATISTICS, U.S. IMMIGRATION AND CUSTOMS ENFORCEMENT (2012), *available at* http://www.ilw.com/immigrationdaily/news/2012,0430-prosecutorialdiscretion.pdf.

78. Wadhia, *Board Offers New Standard for Administrative Closure.*

79. Mandeep Chahal, *A DREAMer's Take: Why Obama Has Failed Us,* NEXTGEN JOURNAL (Jan. 22, 2012), http://www.nextgenjournal.com/2012/01/a-dreamers-take-why-obama-has-failed-us/.

80. Julia Preston, *Students Press for Action on Immigration,* N.Y. TIMES, May 30, 2012, at A14, *available at* http://www.nytimes.com/2012/05/31/us/students-press-for-action-on-immigration.html.

81. Memorandum from Janet Napolitano, Secretary of U.S. Department of Homeland Security, on Exercising Prosecutorial Discretion with Respect to Individuals Who Came to the United States as Children (June 15, 2012), *available at* http://www.dhs.gov/xlibrary/assets/s1-exercising-prosecutorial-discretion-individuals-who-came-to-us-as-children.pdf; *see also* Shoba Sivaprasad Wadhia, *Deferred Action in Immigration Law: The Next Generation,* IMMIGRATIONPROF BLOG (June 28, 2012), http://lawprofessors.typepad.com/immigration/2012/06/deferred-action-in-immigration-law-the-next-generation-by-.html.

82. *Consideration of Deferred Action for Childhood Arrival Process,* U.S. CITIZENSHIP AND IMMIGRATION SERVICES, http://www.uscis.gov/humanitarian/consideration-deferred-action-childhood-arrivals-process (last updated July 2, 2013).

83. *See, e.g.,* UNITED WE DREAM, http://unitedwedream.org/ (last visited Oct. 13, 2012); *Dream Activist,* UNDOCUMENTED YOUTH ACTION AND RESOURCE NETWORK, http://www.dreamactivist.org/ (last visited Oct. 13, 2012); Jose Antonio Vargas, *Not Legal Not Leaving,* TIME (June 25, 2012), *available at* http://www.time.com/time/magazine/article/0,9171,2117243,00.html.

84. *See, e.g., AILA Resources on Deferred Action,* AMERICAN IMMIGRATION LAWYERS ASSOCIATION, http://www.aila.org/content/default.aspx?docid=40291 (last visited Dec. 20, 2013); *Dreamer Resource Hub,* NATIONAL IMMIGRANT JUSTICE CENTER, http://www.immigrantjustice.org/DREAMers#Eligibility (last visited Oct. 13, 2012); *DREAMer Resources,* NORTHWEST IMMIGRANT RIGHTS PROJECT, http://www.nwirp.org/resources/dreamer (last visited Dec. 20, 2013); *FAQ: Deferred Action for Certain Immigrant Youth,* NATIONAL IMMIGRATION LAW CENTER, http://www.nilc.org/FAQdeferredactionyouth.html (last visited Dec. 20, 2013); *About Deferred Action,* NYC MAYOR'S OFFICE OF IMMIGRANT AFFAIRS, http://www.nyc.gov/html/imm/html/deferred/about-deffered.shtml (last visited Dec. 20, 2013); *see also* BEST PRACTICES AND RESOURCES FOR CONDUCTING COMMUNITY EDUCATION WORKSHOPS FOR DEFERRED ACTION FOR CHILDHOOD ARRIVALS, PENN STATE LAW (2013), *available at* http://law.psu.edu/_file/Immigrants/Best_Practices_for_Conducting_Community_Workshops_on_DACA.pdf.

85. *See Deferred Action for Childhood Arrivals UT Law Assistance Clinics,* UNIVERSITY OF TEXAS SCHOOL OF LAW, http://www.utexas.edu/law/clinics/immigration/daca.php (last visited Dec. 10, 2013).

86. Elise Foley, *Deferred Action Immigration Event Draws Thousands of DREAMers on First Day,* HUFFINGTON POST, Aug. 16, 2012, http://www.huffingtonpost.com/2012/08/15/deferred-action-immigration_n_1785443.html.

87. *See, e.g., Find Helpful Resources,* UNITED WE DREAM, http://unitedwedream.org/toolbox (last visited Dec. 10, 2013).

88. *See, e.g., Deferred Action for Childhood Arrivals,* LEGAL ACTION CENTER, http://www.legalactioncenter.org/practice-advisories/deferred-action-childhood-arrivals (last visited Dec. 10, 2013).

89. *See* USCIS OFFICE OF PERFORMANCE AND QUALITY, DEFERRED ACTION FOR CHILDHOOD ARRIVALS (February 6, 2014), http://www.uscis.gov/sites/default/files/USCIS/Resources/Reports%20and%20Studies/Immigration%20Forms%20Data/All%20Form%20Types/DACA/DACA-06-02-14.pdf.

90. *See, e.g.,* Elise Foley, *Kris Kobach Represents Immigration Agents in Lawsuit Against Obama Administration,* HUFFINGTON POST, Aug. 23, 2012, http://www.huffingtonpost.com/2012/08/23/kris-kobach-immigration-lawsuit-obama_n_1825272.html; Complaint, Crane v. Napolitano, No. 12CV03247 (N.D. Tex. filed Aug. 23, 2012), 2012 WL 3629252.

91. *See, e.g.,* Elise Foley, *Kris Kobach Represents Immigration Agents.*

92. Complaint, Crane v. Napolitano, No. 12CV03247 (N.D. Tex. filed Aug. 23, 2012), 2012 WL 3629252.

93. John Yoo and Robert J. Delahunty, *Dream On: The Obama Administration's Non-enforcement of Immigration Laws, the Dream Act, and the Take Care Clause,* 91 TEX. L. REV. 781 (2013), *available at* http://www.texaslrev.com/wp-content/uploads/DelahuntyYoo.pdf.; *see also* Shoba Sivaprasad Wadhia, *Response, the Obama Administration, In Defense of DACA, Deferred Action, and the DREAM Act,* 91 TEX. L. REV. SEE ALSO 59 (2013).

94. Yoo and Delahunty, *Dream On.*

95. U.S. Const. art. II, §3.

96. Yoo and Delahunty also question the Obama administration's motivations in creating the DACA program and related costs. The analysis falls short because the authors misidentify ICE (instead of USCIS) as the agency absorbing the costs of DACA, failing to explain how the fees generated by the DACA program (DACA applicants must pay $465 with their application) interacts with the USCIS's funding of the program. Perhaps most important, the authors misunderstand that alongside the economic considerations are the humanitarian factors that have driven prosecutorial discretion decisions for years. I agree with Yoo and Delahunty that cost savings alone cannot explain the DACA program, but I also believe that creating nonenforcement alternatives for people who have resided in the United States from their childhood and exhibit intellectual promise is an acceptable motivation for enacting the program.

97. Delahunty and Yoo examine *Youngstown Sheet & Tube Co. v. Sawyer* (1952) to analyze whether the Obama administration has the prerogative power to violate the law. Known as the "Steel Seizure Case," *Youngstown* dealt with President Truman's power to seize and operate most of the steel mills during a labor strike even though such seizure was not authorized by the Constitution or a statute. Writing for the majority, Justice Hugo Black held that President Truman had no prerogative power because, among other things, "[t]he President's power, if any, to issue the order must stem either from an act of Congress or from the Constitution itself. There is no statute that expressly authorizes the President to take possession of property as he did here." Youngstown Sheet & Tube Co. v. Sawyer, 343 U.S. 579, 585 (1952). At least under this point and without conceding that the Obama administration has violated any law, the DACA program appears to satisfy the threshold requirement under *Youngstown,* namely that deferred action stems from a congressional act or the Constitution.

98. *See, e.g.,* H.R. 1842 Development, Relief, and Education for Alien Minors Act of 2011; S. 952 Development, Relief, and Education for Alien Minors Act of 2011.

99. *See generally* Michael Olivas, *Dreams Deferred: Deferred Action, Prosecutorial Discretion, and the Vexing Case(s) of DREAM Act Students,* 21 WM. & MARY BILL RTS. J. 463 (2012).

100. *See, e.g.,* MARK HUGO LOPEZ AND ANA GONZALEZ-BARRERA, INSIDE THE 2012 LATINO ELECTORATE (2013), *available at* http://www.pewhispanic.org/2013/06/03/inside-the-2012-latino-electorate/; *Obama's Re-election Sets Record Support for Latino Voters,* AMERICA'S VOICE (Nov. 13, 2012, 11:27 AM), http://americasvoiceonline.org/blog/obamas-re-election-sets-record-support-for-latino-voters.

101. *See* Deirdre Walsh and Tom Cohen, *House GOP Split over Immigration Reform,* CNN, July 11, 2013, http://www.cnn.com/2013/07/10/politics/immigration-reform/; *see also* Elise Foley, *Senate Immigration Reform Bill Passes with Strong Majority,* HUFFPOST POLITICS, June 27, 2013, *available at* http://www.huffingtonpost.com/2013/06/27/senate-immigration-reform-bill_n_3511664.html.

102. *See, e.g.,* Katie Sanders, *PolitiFact: Rubio's Immigration Warning about Obama Ignores Legal Reality,* TAMPA BAY TIMES, Aug. 23, 2013, http://www.tampabay.com/

news/politics/stateroundup/can-obama-legalize-immigrants-in-one-fell-swoop/
2138050.

103. *Goodlatte Goes Off the Rails on Modest Administrative Policy Directive*,
AMERICA'S VOICE (Aug. 26, 2013, 3:56 PM), http://americasvoiceonline.org/blog/
goodlatte-goes-off-the-rails-on-modest-administrative-policy-directive/.

104. *See, e.g.*, Greg Sargent, *The Morning Plum: On Immigration, Obama Is in a Jam*,
WASHINGTON POST, March 14, 2014, http://www.washingtonpost.com/blogs/plum
-line/wp/2014/03/14/the-morning-plum-on-immigration-obama-is-in-a-jam/; *see also*
David Nakamura, *Under Pressure, Obama Calls for Immigration-Enforcement Review*,
WASHINGTON POST, March 13, 2014 ("The Obama administration has deported
nearly 2 million undocumented immigrants, according to figures from the Department of Homeland Security. In the announcement, the White House said the president
asked Homeland Security Secretary Jeh Johnson to take an "inventory" of immigration
enforcement policies, though no specifics were included about what changes might
be made.").

CHAPTER 6. GOING TO COURT

1. Hirokazu Yoshikawa and Carola Suárez-Orozco, *Deporting Parents Hurts Kids*,
N.Y. TIMES, April 20, 2012, http://www.nytimes.com/2012/04/21/opinion/deporting
-parents-ruins-kids.html?_r=1&ref=opinion.

2. *See, e.g.*, Padilla v. Kentucky, 130 S. Ct. 1473, 1484 (2010) ("When attorneys know
that their clients face possible exile from this country and separation from their families, they should not be encouraged to say nothing at all."); Delgadillo v. Carmichael,
332 U. S. 388, 391 (1947) ("Deportation can be the equivalent of banishment or exile.").
Notably and somewhat distinguishable from the past, and starting in November 2011,
ICE appears to have exercised prosecutorial discretion favorably (or offered to do so)
in more cases in which the respondent appears to be eligible for relief from removal.
See, e.g., email from Mary Kenney to author (Apr. 3, 2012) (on file with author).

3. INA § 212(a)(9)(A), 8 U.S.C. § 1182(a)(9)(A) (2006).

4. KENNETH CULP DAVIS, DISCRETIONARY JUSTICE: A PRELIMINARY
INQUIRY 152 (1969).

5. *Id.* at 154.

6. Chae Chan Ping v. United States, 130 U.S. 581 (1889).

7. Chevron U.S.A. Inc. v. Natural Resources Defense Council, Inc., 467 U.S. 837
(1984).

8. *See* ROBERT L. GLICKSMAN AND RICHARD E. LEVY, ADMINISTRATIVE
LAW: AGENCY ACTION IN LEGAL CONTEXT 146–47 (1st ed. 2010).

9. To illustrate, the June 17 Morton Memo elucidates nineteen factors that ICE
employees and attorneys should take into account when deciding whether or not to
exercise prosecutorial discretion favorably. Memorandum from John Morton, Director,
U.S. Immigration and Customs Enforcement, on Exercising Prosecutorial Discretion Consistent with the Civil Immigration Enforcement Priorities of the Agency for
the Apprehension, Detention, and Removal of Aliens, 4–5 (June 17, 2011), *available at*

http://www.ice.gov/doclib/secure-communities/pdf/prosecutorial-discretion-memo
.pdf [hereinafter Morton Memo I].

10. *See, e.g.*, Reno v. ADC, 525 U.S. 471, 492 (1999). The facts involved a group of noncitizens who believed they were selectively charged with violating the immigration laws based on their affiliation with a politically unpopular group. The respondents argued that the doctrine of constitutional doubt required the Court to interpret section 242(g) to permit the immediate review of selective enforcement claims because of the potential "chilling effect" on First Amendment rights. Justice Scalia disagreed with the respondents and concluded "an alien unlawfully in this country has no constitutional right to assert selective enforcement as a defense against his deportation." Though Justice Scalia read section 242(g) to preclude review of prosecutorial discretion decisions involving the commencement of removal proceedings, adjudication cases, and execution of removal orders, he stated, "To resolve the present controversy, we need not rule out the possibility of a rare case in which the alleged basis of discrimination is so outrageous that the foregoing considerations can be overcome."

11. *See, e.g.*, Memorandum from Doris Meissner, Commissioner, Immigration and Naturalization Service, on Exercising Prosecutorial Discretion 3 (Nov. 17, 2000) (on file with author) [hereinafter Meissner Memo]. Prior to *Heckler v. Chaney* and *ADC v. Reno*, several federal circuit courts took up the question of whether the former Operations Instruction governing "deferred action" operates as a substantive right to the noncitizen. *See, e.g.*, Pasquini v. Morris, 700 F.2d 658, 662 (11th Cir. 1983); Nicholas v. INS, 590 F.2d 802, 807 (9th Cir. 1979).

12. Meissner Memo, at 3.

13. *Id.* at 1.

14. *Id.* at 7.

15. *See* Homeland Security Act of 2002, Pub. L. No. 107-296, 116 Stat. 2135 (2002); INA § 103, 8 U.S.C. § 1103 (2006).

16. Administrative Procedure Act (APA), 5 U.S.C. § 702 (2006).

17. *Id.* at § 704.

18. *See* Gary J. Edles, *The Continuing Need for an Administrative Conference*, 50 ADMIN. L. REV. 101, 107 (1998). The judicial review provisions of the APA are codified at 5 U.S.C. §§ 701–6.

19. Abbott Laboratories v. Gardner, 387 U.S. 136, 137–38 (1967).

20. *Id.* at 152.

21. *Id.* at 140.

22. 8 CFR §§ 1003.2(c)(2), 1003.23 (2013).

23. 8 CFR §§ 1003.23(3) (2013).

24. *See, e.g.*, Matter of Velarde-Pacheco, 23 I&N Dec. 253 (BIA 2002); Matter of J-J-, 21 I&N Dec. 976 (BIA 1997); Matter of L-O-G-, 21 I&N Dec. 413 (BIA 1996).

25. INS v. Abudu, 485 U.S. 94, 105 (1988).

26. Kucana v. Holder, 130 S. Ct. 827, 840 (2010).

27. *Id.* at 831.

28. *See* INA § 242(a)(2)(B), 8 U.S.C. § 1252(a)(2)(B) (2006) ("Denials of Discretionary Relief.-Notwithstanding any other provision of law (statutory or nonstatutory), including section 2241 of title 28, United States Code, or any other habeas corpus provision, and sections 1361 and 1651 of such title, and except as provided in subparagraph (D), and regardless of whether the judgment, decision or action is made in removal proceedings, no court shall have jurisdiction to review—

(i) any judgment regarding the granting of relief under section 212(h), 212(i), 240A, 240B, or 245, or

(ii) any other decision or action of the Attorney General or the Secretary of Homeland Security the authority for which is specified under this title to be in the discretion of the Attorney General or the Secretary of Homeland Security, other than the granting of relief under section 208(a).").

29. Kucana v. Holder, 130 S. Ct. 827, 831 (2010).

30. *Id.* at 839.

31. The Court went on, "Finally, we stress a paramount factor in the decision we render today. By defining the various jurisdictional bars by reference to other provisions in the INA itself, Congress ensured that it, and only it, would limit the federal courts' jurisdiction. To read §1252(a)(2)(B)(ii) to apply to matters where discretion is conferred on the Board by regulation, rather than on the Attorney General by statute, would ignore that congressional design. If the Seventh Circuit's construction of §1252(a)(2)(B)(ii) were to prevail, the Executive would have a free hand to shelter its own decisions from abuse-of-discretion appellate court review simply by issuing a regulation declaring those decisions 'discretionary.' Such an extraordinary delegation of authority cannot be extracted from the statute Congress enacted." Kucana v. Holder, 130 S. Ct. 827, 839–40 (2010).

32. APA, 5 U.S.C. § 706 (2006). The governing section of APA reads in full: "To the extent necessary to decision and when presented, the reviewing court shall decide all relevant questions of law, interpret constitutional and statutory provisions, and determine the meaning or applicability of the terms of an agency action. The reviewing court shall—

(1) compel agency action unlawfully withheld or unreasonably delayed; and

(2) hold unlawful and set aside agency action, findings and conclusions found to be—

(A) arbitrary, capricious, an abuse of discretion or otherwise not in accordance with law;

(B) contrary to constitutional right, power, privilege or immunity;

(C) in excess of statutory jurisdiction, authority or limitations, or short of statutory right;

(D) without observance of procedure required by law;

(E) unsupported by substantial evidence in a case subject to sections 556 and 557 of this title or otherwise reviewed on the record of an agency hearing provided by statute; or

(F) unwarranted by the facts to the extent that the facts are subject to trial de novo by the reviewing court."

Notably, the Supreme Court recently applied this standard in *Judulang v. Holder*, and specifically found that the "[t]he BIA's policy for applying §212(c) in deportation cases is 'arbitrary and capricious' under the Administrative Procedure Act." Though *Judulang* dealt with an agency's interpretation of a statute as opposed to a discretionary decision, the case highlights the fundamental role of the judiciary and gives meaning to the standard of review outlined in the APA.

33. 8 CFR § 1003.29 (2013). Continuances have been analogized by some courts to "administrative closure." *See* Garza-Moreno v. Gonzales, 489 F.3d 239, 242 (6th Cir. 2007).

34. EOIR, IMMIGRATION COURT PRACTICE MANUAL 96 (Apr. 1, 2008), *available at* http://www.justice.gov/eoir/vll/OCIJPracManual/Practice_Manual_1-27-14.pdf#page=99 (*"(a) Motion to continue.* — A request for a continuance of any hearing should be made by written motion. Oral motions to continue are discouraged. The motion should set forth in detail the reasons for the request and, if appropriate, be supported by evidence. *See* Chapter 5.2(e) (Evidence). It should also include the date and time of the hearing, as well as preferred dates that the party is available to re-schedule the hearing. However, parties should be mindful that the Immigration Court retains discretion to schedule continued cases on dates that the court deems appropriate.").

35. *See* Matter of Hashmi, 24 I&N Dec. 785, 788 (BIA 2009); *see also* Matter of Rajah, 25 I&N Dec. 127, 130 (BIA 2009).

36. *See, e.g.*, Masih v. Mukasey, 536 F.3d 370, 376 (5th Cir. 2008); Hashmi v. Att'y Gen. of U.S. 531 F.3d 256, 262 (3rd Cir. 2008); Biwot v. Gonzales, 403 F.3d 1094, 1099 (9th Cir. 2005); Herbert v. Ashcroft, 325 F.3d 68, 72 (1st Cir. 2003).

37. *See* Executive Office for Immigration Review's Operating Policies and Procedures Memorandum 13-01: Continuances and Administrative Closure, March 7, 2013; *see also* Matter of Sibrun, 18 I & N Dec. 354 (BIA 1983).

38. Hashmi v. Attorney General of the U.S., 531 F.3d 256, 257 (3rd Cir. 2008).

39. *Id.* at 247–48.

40. *Id.* at 258.

41. *See* Morton Memo I, at 4–5. For example, following a listing of the positive factors offices may utilize in making prosecutorial decisions, the June 17 Morton Memo I advises "[t]his list is not exhaustive and no one factor is determinative. ICE officers, agents, and attorneys should always consider prosecutorial discretion on a case-by-case basis. The decisions should be based on the totality of the circumstances, with the goal of conforming to ICE's enforcement priorities."

42. APA, 5 U.S.C. § 701 (2006).

43. Citizens to Preserve Overton Park v. Volpe, 401 U.S. 402, 410 (1971).

44. *Id.* at 404–6.

45. *Id.* at 405.

46. *Id.* at 410.

47. Heckler v. Chaney, 470 U.S. 821, 826 (1985).

48. Citizens to Preserve Overton Park v. Volpe, 401 U.S. 402, 414 (1971) (internal citations omitted).

49. Heckler v. Chaney, 470 U.S. 821, 823–25 (1985).

50. *Id.* at 830. This passage has been affirmed and cited to by the Court in subsequent decisions including but not limited to Lincoln v. Vigil, 508 U.S. 182, 191 (1993). Justice Thurgood Marshall issued a concurrence, criticizing the majority's "presumption of unreviewability" and detailing the jurisprudence in support of judicial review over prosecutorial discretion. Justice Marshall stated:

> And in rejecting on the merits of a claim of improper prosecutorial conduct in [citation omitted] we clearly laid to rest any notion that prosecutorial discretion is unreviewable no matter what the basis is upon which it is exercised: "There is no doubt that the breadth of discretion that our country's legal system vests in prosecuting attorneys carries with it the potential for both individual and institutional abuse. And broad though that discretion may be, there is undoubtedly constitutional limits upon its exercise."

Heckler v. Chaney, 470 U.S. 821, 846–47 (1985) (Marshall, J., concurring in the judgment) (quoting Bordenkircher v. Hayes, 434 U.S. 357, 365 (1978)).

51. Heckler v. Chaney, 470 U.S. 821, 837–38 (1985).

52. *Id.* at 831. The Court further noted that "the agency must not only assess whether a violation has occurred, but whether agency resources are best spent on this violation or another, whether the agency is likely to succeed if it acts, whether the particular enforcement action requested best fits the agency's overall policies, and, indeed, whether the agency has enough resources to undertake the action at all. An agency generally cannot act against each technical violation of the statute it is charged with enforcing."

53. *Id.* at 832–33.

54. Admittedly, there are some agency decisions that are technically "inactions" that I would like to see reviewable under the APA, but most of the situations I envision for my argument involve prosecutorial discretion "denials" that result in the agency taking an enforcement action against the individual.

55. *Id.* at 832.

56. *See, e.g.*, Meissner Memo, at 3.

57. To illustrate, the June 17 Morton Memo elucidates nineteen factors that ICE employees and attorneys should take into account when deciding whether or not to exercise prosecutorial discretion favorably. Morton Memo I, at 4–5.

58. U.S. Dep't of Justice, *Board of Immigration Appeals*, JUSTICE.GOV, *available at* http://www.justice.gov/eoir/biainfo.htm (last updated Nov. 2011).

59. 64 Fed. Reg. 56135 (Oct. 18, 1999).

60. *See* 67 Fed. Reg. 54878 (Aug. 26, 2002). *See* 8 C.F.R. § 1003(e)(4) (2012) ("Affirmance without opinion. (i) The Board member to whom a case is assigned shall affirm the decision of the Service or the immigration judge, without opinion, if the Board member determines that the result reached in the decision under review was correct; that any errors in the decision under review were harmless or nonmaterial; and that

(A) The issues on appeal are squarely controlled by existing Board or federal court precedent and do not involve the application of precedent to a novel factual situation; or

(B) The factual and legal issues raised on appeal are not so substantial that the case warrants the issuance of a written opinion in the case.

(ii) If the Board member determines that the decision should be affirmed without opinion, the Board shall issue an order that reads as follows: 'The Board affirms, without opinion, the result of the decision below. The decision below is, therefore, the final agency determination. See 8 CFR 1003.1(e)(4).' An order affirming without opinion, issued under authority of this provision, shall not include further explanation or reasoning. Such an order approves the result reached in the decision below; it does not necessarily imply approval of all of the reasoning of that decision, but does signify the Board's conclusion that any errors in the decision of the immigration judge or the Service were harmless or nonmaterial.").

61. ARNOLD AND PORTER, LLP, AMERICAN BAR ASSOCIATION COMMIS-SION ON IMMIGRATION, *Part 3: Board of Immigration Appeals*, in REFORMING THE IMMIGRATION SYSTEM (2010), *available at* http://www.americanbar.org/content/dam/aba/migrated/Immigration/PublicDocuments/full_report_part3.authcheckdam.pdf.

62. *See, e.g.*, Haoud v. Ashcroft, 350 F.3d 201, 206 (1st Cir. 2003); Smriko v. Ashcroft, 387 F.3d 279, 292 (3d Cir. 2004); Chen v. Ashcroft, 378 F.3d 1081, 1087 (9th Cir. 2004).

63. *See* Haoud v. Ashcroft, 350 F.3d 201, 206 (1st Cir. 2003); Smriko v. Ashcroft, 387 F.3d 279, 292 (3d Cir. 2004); Chen v. Ashcroft, 378 F.3d 1081, 1087 (9th Cir. 2004).

64. Haoud v. Ashcroft, 350 F.3d 201, 206 (1st Cir. 2003).

65. *See, e.g., id.* at 201; Smriko v. Ashcroft, 387 F.3d 279 (3d Cir. 2004); Chen v. Ashcroft, 378 F.3d 1081 (9th Cir. 2004).

66. Matter of Gutierrez, 21 I&N Dec. 479, 480 (BIA 1996), *available at* http://www.justice.gov/eoir/vll/intdec/vol21/3286.pdf; *see also* Matter of Peugnet, 20 I&N Dec. 233 (BIA 1991); Matter of Munoz-Santos, 20 I&N Dec. 205, 206 (BIA 1990).

67. Matter of Avetisyan, 25 I&N Dec. 688, 690 (BIA 2012), *available at* http://www.justice.gov/eoir/vll/intdec/vol25/3740.pdf.

68. *Id.*

69 Alcaraz v. INS, 384 F.3d 1150, 1158–62 (9th Cir. 2004). "Repapering" is a form of a relief because it enables certain noncitizens to become eligible for removal relief by postponing or repapering the date of their removal proceedings. The court cited to a series of memoranda issued by INS and EOIR regarding the procedures by which cases should be administratively closed for persons eligible for repapering.

70. Alcaraz v. INS, 384 F.3d 1150, 1156 (9th Cir. 2004).

71. *Id.* at 1162–63.

72. *Id.* (recognizing that "[t]he legal proposition that agencies may be required to abide by certain internal policies is well-established."). For a nice analysis about the role of subregulatory guidance in immigration law, *see* Jill Family, *Administrative Law through the Lens of Immigration Law*, Widener Law School Legal Studies

Research Paper No. 12-04 (February 22, 2012), *available at* SSRN: http://ssrn.com/abstract=2009436 or http://dx.doi.org/10.2139/ssrn.2009436.

73. Alcaraz v. INS, 384 F.3d 1150, 1161 (9th Cir. 2004) (quoting Heckler v. Chaney, 470 U.S. 821, 830 (1985)).

74. *Id.* at 1161 (quoting Heckler v. Chaney, 470 U.S. 821, 830 (1985)). The court also cites to Mendez-Gutierrez v. Ashcroft, 340 F.3d 865, 868 (9th Cir. 2003) (stating the "no law to apply" rule is applicable where there are "no statutes, regulations, established agency policies or judicial decisions that provide a meaningful standard against which to assess" the agency's actions).

75. Alcaraz v. INS, 384 F.3d 1150, 1161 (9th Cir. 2004) (quoting Heckler v. Chaney, 470 U.S. 821, 830 (1985)). Note that the Ninth Circuit came down with a different position in Diaz-Covarrubias v. Mukasey, 551 F.3d 1114, 1120 (9th Cir. 2009) (finding that judicial review is precluded in general administrative closure decisions because courts have no legal standard to apply). In Garza-Moreno v. Gonzales, the court also found that it had jurisdiction to review a denial of administrative closure by the BIA. The court reasoned:

> The decision to administratively close a case is, in this context, not distinguishable from a continuance. Following Abu-Khaliel, we hold that § 1252 does not strip us of jurisdiction to review the denial of an administrative closure. Having jurisdiction, we review for abuse of discretion, disturbing the BIA's decision only if the refusal to administratively close the case "was made without a rational explanation, inexplicably departed from established policies, or rested on an impermissible basis such as invidious discrimination."

Garza-Moreno v. Gonzales, 489 F.3d 239, 242 (6th Cir. 2007) (citing Abu-Khaliel v. Gonzales, 436 F.3d 627, 630–31 (6th Cir. 2006)). The court did not discuss the application of *Heckler v. Chaney* and the APA exemption for decisions "committed to agency discretion."

76. Webster v. Doe, 486 U.S. 592, 594 (1988) (quoting the National Security Act of 1947, 50 U.S.C. § 403(c)).

77. Webster v. Doe, 486 U.S. 592, 594–95 (1988).

78. *Id.* at 596.

79. *Id.* at 599–601.

80. *Id.* at 592–93.

81. Some of the scenarios identified in this chapter involve the review of adjudicatory decisions by immigration judges as opposed to the prosecutorial judgments of DHS officers and attorneys. However, this distinction is less relevant to this chapter's examination of whether federal judges have "enough law" against which to analyze and review prosecutorial discretion decisions for abuse, arbitrariness, or whatever the standard of review may be.

82. APA, 5 U.S.C. § 701 (2006).

83. Illegal Immigration Reform and Immigrant Responsibility Act of 1996, 8 U.S.C.S. § 1103 (2008).

84. Immigration and Nationality Act (INA) § 242(g), 8 U.S.C. § 1252 (2006).

85. Reno v. ADC, 525 U.S. 471, 492 (1999).

86. Reno v. ADC, 525 U.S. 471, 484 (1999). Specifically, the Court stated:
The provision applies only to three discrete actions that the Attorney General may take: her "decision or action" to "*commence* proceedings, *adjudicate* cases, or *execute* removal orders." [Emphasis added.] There are of course many other decisions or actions that may be part of the deportation process—such as the decisions to open an investigation, to surveil the suspected violator, to reschedule the deportation hearing, to include various provisions in the final order that is the product of the adjudication, and to refuse reconsideration of that order. It is implausible that the mention of three discrete events along the road to deportation was a shorthand way of referring to all claims arising from deportation proceedings.
Reno v. ADC, 525 U.S. 471, 482 (1999).

87. Alcaraz v. INS, 384 F.3d 1150, 1160–61 (9th Cir. 2004).

88. Morton Memo I, at 2–3. *See also* SHOBA SIVAPRASAD WADHIA, IMMIGRATION POLICY CENTER, THE MORTON MEMO AND PROSECUTORIAL DISCRETION: AN OVERVIEW (July 20, 2011), *available at* http://www.immigrationpolicy.org/special-reports/morton-memo-and-prosecutorial-discretion-overview.

89. *See, e.g.*, 8 C.F.R. § 239.2 ("Any officer authorized by § 239.1(a) to issue a notice to appear may cancel such notice prior to jurisdiction vesting with the immigration judge pursuant to § 3.14 of this chapter provided the officer is satisfied that:
   (1) The respondent is a national of the United States;
   (2) The respondent is not deportable or inadmissible under immigration laws;
   (3) The respondent is deceased;
   (4) The respondent is not in the United States;
   (5) The notice was issued for the respondent's failure to file a timely petition as required by section 216(c) of the Act, but his or her failure to file a timely petition was excused in accordance with section 216(d)(2)(B) of the Act;
   (6) The notice to appear was improvidently issued; or
   (7) Circumstances of the case have changed after the notice to appear was issued to such an extent that continuation is no longer in the best interest of the government.
(c) Motion to dismiss. After commencement of proceedings pursuant to 8 CFR 1003.14, ICE counsel, or any officer enumerated in paragraph (a) of this section, may move for dismissal of the matter on the grounds set out under paragraph (a) of this section.
(d) Motion for remand. After commencement of the hearing, ICE counsel or any officer enumerated in paragraph (a) of this section may move for remand of the matter to district jurisdiction on the ground that the foreign relations of the United States are involved and require further consideration.")

90. *See, e.g.*, Matter of Avetisyan, 25 I&N Dec. 688, 694 (BIA 2012), *available at* http://www.justice.gov/eoir/vll/intdec/vol25/3740.pdf; Matter of GNC, 22 I&N Dec. 281, 284 (BIA 1998), *available at* www.justice.gov/eoir/vll/intdec/vol22/3366.pdf. In the case of *Matter of GNC* the board held:

We recognize that the decision to institute deportation proceedings involves the exercise of prosecutorial discretion and is not a decision which the Immigration Judge or the Board may review. Matter of Ramirez-Sanchez, 17 I&N Dec. 503, 505 (BIA 1980). Likewise, a Service officer authorized to issue a Notice to Appear has complete power to cancel such notice prior to jurisdiction vesting with the Immigration Judge. 8 C.F.R. § 239.2(a). However, after commencement of proceedings in the Immigration Court, Service counsel "may move for dismissal of the matter on the grounds set out [in] this section." 8 C.F.R. § 239.2(c). This language marks a clear boundary between the time prior to commencement of proceedings, where a Service officer has decisive power to cancel proceedings, and the time following commencement, where the Service officer merely has the privilege to move for dismissal of proceedings. By this distinction, the regulation presumably contemplates not just the automatic grant of a motion to terminate, but an informed adjudication by the Immigration Judge or this Board based on an evaluation of the factors underlying the Service's motion. *See* Matter of Vizcarra-Delgadillo, 13 I&N Dec. 51, 54 (BIA 1968); *see also* Matter of Wong, 13 I&N Dec. 701, 703 (BIA 1971) (stating that Service officials may move the Immigration Judge for termination of proceedings as a matter of prosecutive discretion); *cf.* Matter of Andrade, 14 I&N Dec. 651, 652 (BIA 1974) (finding that the Service motion to terminate, if granted, would benefit the alien, and assuming there would be no opposition from the alien's attorney).

Matter of GNC, 22 I&N Dec. 281, 284 (BIA 1998), *available at* www.justice.gov/eoir/vll/intdec/vol22/3366.pdf. Also relevant to the prosecutorial decisions governed by regulation is the BIA standard that regulatory violations can invalidate removal proceedings if the procedure or regulation benefits the noncitizen and the violation of the regulation prejudiced the noncitizen. Matter of Hernandez, 21 I&N Dec. 224, 228 (BIA 1996), *available at* http://www.justice.gov/eoir/vll/intdec/vol21/3265.pdf.

91. INA § 242(a)(2)(B), 8 U.S.C. § 1252(a)(2)(B) (2013).

92. INA § 240A(b)(1), 8 U.S.C. § 1229b(b)(1) (2013).

93. Arizona v. United States, 132 S. Ct. 2492 (2012), *available at* http://scholar.google.com/scholar_case?case=17891750818453472454&hl=en&as_sdt=2&as_vis=1&oi=scholarr.

94. INA § 242(a)(2)(D), 8 U.S.C. § 1252 (2006).

95. *See, e.g.,* Kucana v. Holder, 130 S. Ct. 827 (2010).

96. *See, e.g.,* Stephen H. Legomsky, *Fear and Loathing in Congress and the Courts: Immigration and Judicial Review*, 78 TEX. L. REV. 1615 (2000); Lenni B. Benson, *You Can't Get There from Here: Managing Judicial Review of Immigration Cases*, 2007 U. CHI. LEGAL FORUM 405 (2007); Lenni B. Benson, *Back to the Future: Congress Attacks the Right to Judicial Review of Immigration Proceedings*, 29 CONN. L. REV. 1411 (1997); Nancy Morawetz, *Back to Back to the Future? Lessons Learned from Litigation over the 1996 Restrictions on Judicial Review*, 51 N.Y.L. SCH. L. REV. 113 (2006–7); Stephen H. Legomsky, *Deportation and the War on Independence*, 91 CORNELL L. REV.

369 (2006); Shoba Sivaprasad Wadhia, *The Role Of Prosecutorial Discretion in Immigration Law*, 9 CONN. PUB. INT. L.J. 243, 293 (2010).

97. Stephen H. Legomsky, *Political Asylum and the Theory of Judicial Review*, 73 MINN. L. REV. 1205, 1210–11 (1989); *see also, e.g.*, Legomsky, *Fear and Loathing*, at 1631; Shoba Sivaprasad Wadhia, *Sharing Secrets: Examining Deferred Action and Transparency in Immigration Law*, 10 U.N.H. L. REV. 1 (2011).

98. Benson, *You Can't Get There from Here*, at 431.

99. *Id.* at 432.

100. *Id.* at 410.

101. *Id.* at 405.

102. Legomsky, *Fear and Loathing*, at 1629.

103. *See, e.g.*, Daniel Kanstroom, *Surrounding the Hole in the Doughnut: Discretion and Deference in U.S. Immigration Law*, 71 TUL. L. REV. 703 (1997), *available* at http://works.bepress.com/daniel_kanstroom/24; Legomsky, *Fear and Loathing*, at 1630.

104. Legomsky, *Fear and Loathing*, at 1630. I am less persuaded that uniformity is a real problem when discussing review over prosecutorial discretion decisions, in part because the review I envision is founded on arbitrary decisions or abuse of discretion by the agency. A sampling of recent prosecutorial discretion decisions illustrates a lack of consistency from one region to the next, and further suggests that a review function over these decisions would only enhance uniformity. *See, e.g.*, AMERICAN IMMIGRA-TION LAWYERS ASSOCIATION AND THE AMERICAN IMMIGRATION COUNCIL LEGAL ACTION CENTER, HOLDING DHS ACCOUNTABLE ON PROSECUTORIAL DISCRETION (Nov. 2011), *available at* http://www.aila.org/content/default.aspx?bc= 6755|25667|37615.

105. Posting of David A. Martin, dam3r@virginia.edu, to Immigration Law Professors Listserve, immprof@lists.ucla.edu (Feb. 16, 2012 3:06 PM) (on file with author).

106. *See* Cheruku v. Attorney General of the United States, 662 F.3d 198, 209 (3d Cir. 2011).

107. *See id.* at 200–201.

108. Matter of Arrabally and Yerrabelly, 25 I&N Dec. 771 (BIA 2012).

109. *See* Cheruku v. Attorney General of the United States, 662 F.3d 211 (3d Cir. 2011).

110. *See* Mata-Fasardo v. Holder, 668 F.3d 675, 676 (9th Cir. 2012); Pocasangre v. Holder, 668 F.3d 674, 675 (9th Cir. 2012); Jex v. Holder, 668 F.3d 673, 673–74 (9th Cir. 2012); San Agustin v. Holder, 668 F.3d 672 (9th Cir. 2012); Rodriguez v. Holder, 668 F.3d 670, 671 (9th Cir. 2012).

111 *See, e.g.*, http://cdn.ca9.uscourts.gov/datastore/opinions/2012/02/06/06-74444 .pdf.

112. *See* Mata-Fasardo v. Holder, 668 F.3d 675, 676 (9th Cir. 2012); Pocasangre v. Holder, 668 F.3d 674, 675 (9th Cir. 2012); Jex v. Holder, 668 F.3d 673, 673–74 (9th Cir. 2012); San Agustin v. Holder, 668 F.3d 672 (9th Cir. 2012); Rodriguez v. Holder, 668 F.3d 670, 671 (9th Cir. 2012).

113. MARGARET STOCK, SUB-REGULATORY GUIDANCE IN IMMIGRATION MATTERS, HOW TO USE IT WISELY (2013) (on file with author).

114. In the Matter of Immigration Petitions for Review Pending in the United States Court of Appeals for the Second Circuit, No. 12-4096 (2d Cir. decided Oct. 16, 2012).

115. Gasparian v. Holder, 700 F.3d 611, 615 (1st Cir. 2012).

116. Bridges v. Wixon, 326 U.S. 135, 162 (1945).

CHAPTER 7. OPEN GOVERNMENT

1. There is no shortage of literature scrutinizing an administrative process against a set of normative values. *See, e.g.*, Stephen H. Legomsky, *Forum Choices for the Review of Agency Adjudication: A Study of the Immigration Process*, 71 IOWA L. REV. 1297, 1313–14 (1986); Roger C. Cramton, *Administrative Procedure Reform: The Effects of S. 1663 on the Conduct of Federal Rate Proceedings*, 16 ADMIN. L. REV. 108, 112 (1963); Roger C. Cramton, *A Comment on Trial-Type Hearings in Nuclear Power Plant Siting*, 58 VA. L. REV. 585, 592–93 (1972); Lenni B. Benson, *Breaking Bureaucratic Borders: A Necessary Step toward Immigration Law Reform*, 54 ADMIN. L. REV. 203, 263–64 (2002); Abraham D. Sofaer, *The Change-of-Status Adjudication: A Case Study of the Informal Agency Process*, 1 J. LEGAL STUD. 349 (1972); Lenni B. Benson, *Making Paper Dolls: How Restrictions on Judicial Review and the Administrative Process Increase Immigration Cases in the Federal Courts*, 51 N.Y.L. SCH. L. REV. 37 (2006); David A. Martin, *Reforming Asylum Adjudication: On Navigating the Coast of Bohemia*, 138 U. PA. L. REV. 1247, 1322 (1990); Colin Diver, *The Optimal Precision of Administrative Rules*, 93 YALE L.J. 65 (1983); Jill E. Family, *A Broader View of the Immigration Adjudication Problem*, 23 GEO. IMMIGR. L.J. 595 (2009).

2. *See* Jill E. Family, *Murky Immigration Law and the Challenges Facing Immigration Removal and Benefits Adjudication*, 31 J. NAT'L ASS'N ADMIN. L. JUDICIARY 46, 75 (2011).

3. Letter from Shoba Sivaprasad Wadhia to USCIS, ICE and CBP about FOIA Request for Deferred Action and Prosecutorial Discretion Records (Mar. 30, 2010) (on file with author); Letter from Shoba Sivaprasad Wadhia to USCIS, ICE and CBP about FOIA Request for Prosecutorial Discretion Records (Oct. 6, 2009) (on file with author).

4. Letter from Jill A. Eggleston, Director of FOIA Operations, U.S. Citizenship and Immigration Services, to author (June 17, 2011) (on file with author). A subsequent conversation with the FOIA officer responsible for responding to my FOIA request indicated that deferred action records from FY 2003 through FY 2010 were requested from every USCIS regional service center and field office. Phone conversation with National Records Center FOIA Division (June 28, 2011).

5. January Contreras, U.S. Citizenship and Immigration Services Ombudsman, Deferred Action: Recommendations to Improve Transparency and Consistency in the USCIS Process (July 11, 2011), available at http://www.dhs.gov/xlibrary/assets/cisomb -combined-dar.pdf.

6. Letter from Jill A. Eggleston, Freedom of Information Act Director, U.S. Customs and Enforcement, to author (July 22, 2013), *available at* http://w3.law.psu.edu/_file/foiadapackage2013.pdf.

7. Letter from Jill A. Eggleston, Freedom of Information Act Director, U.S. Citizenship and Immigration Services, to author (Sept. 3, 2013), *available at* http://w3.law.psu.edu/_file/Document_2.pdf.

8. SHOBA SIVAPRASAD WADHIA, FOIA RESPONSE/REQUEST FROM USCIS ON DEFERRED ACTION CASES (2013), *available at* http://works.bepress.com/shoba_wadhia/24.

9. *Id.*

10. Wadhia v. Dep't of Homeland Security (dismissed and settled on October 1, 2012).

11. Letter from FOIA Officer Catrina M. Pavlik-Kennan to author (Sept. 26, 2012) (on file with author).

12. *See, e.g.*, Jaya Ramji-Nogales, Andrew I. Schoenholtz, and Philip G. Schrag, *Refugee Roulette: Disparities in Asylum Adjudication*, 60 STAN. L. REV. 295 (2007).

13. Letter from FOIA Officer Catrina M. Pavlik-Kennan to author.

14. *See* Shoba Sivaprasad Wadhia, *Sharing Secrets: Examining Deferred Action and Transparency in Immigration Law*, 10 U.N.H. L. REV. 1, 34–38 (2012).

15. *See, e.g.*, John Morton, Director, U.S. Immigration and Customs Enforcement, on Exercising Prosecutorial Discretion Consistent with the Civil Immigration Enforcement Priorities of the Agency for the Apprehension, Detention, and Removal of Aliens 5 (June 17, 2011), *available at* http://www.ice.gov/doclib/secure-communities/pdf/prosecutorial-discretion-memo.pdf [hereinafter Morton Memo I].

16. Wadhia, *Sharing Secrets*.

17. *Id.* at 49.

18. SHOBA SIVAPRASAD WADHIA, FOIA RESPONSE FROM CBP ON NOTICE TO APPEAR (2013), *available at* http://works.bepress.com/shoba_wadhia/28/.

19. *Id.*

20. AILA 8 for September 19, 2013, So How Discreet Is CBP? (on file with author).

21. *See id. See also* AILA InfoNet Doc. No. 14031849. (Posted 3/18/14).

22. Email from Margaret Stock to author (Sept. 24, 2013) (on file with author).

23. *See* U.S. CITIZENSHIP AND IMMIGRATION SERVICES, CONSIDERATION OF DEFERRED ACTION FOR CHILDHOOD ARRIVALS PROCESS (Sept. 14, 2012), *available at* http://www.uscis.gov/portal/site/uscis/menuitem.eb1d4c2a3e5b9ac89243c6a7543f6d1a/?vgnextoid=f2ef2f19470f7310VgnVCM100000082ca60aRCRD&vgnextchannel=f2ef2f19470f7310VgnVCM100000082ca60aRCRD.

24. *See id.*

25. *See id.*; Michael Olivas, *Dreams Deferred: Deferred Action, Prosecutorial Discretion, and the Vexing Case(s) of DREAM Act Students*, 21 WM. & MARY BILL RTS. J. 463 (2012), *available at* http://scholarship.law.wm.edu/cgi/viewcontent.cgi?article=1640&context=wmborj; Shoba Sivaprasad Wadhia, *The Immigration Prosecutor and the Judge: Examining the Role of the Judiciary in Prosecutorial Discretion Decisions*, 16 HARV. LATINO L. REV. 39 (2013).

26. *See, e.g.*, UNITED STATES CITIZENSHIP AND IMMIGRATION SERVICES, USCIS Processing Time Information, https://egov.uscis.gov/cris/processTimesDisplay Init.do;jsessionid=bacXD1OC9RCyFagQNRyeu (last visited March 18, 2014) (use drop-down menus at the bottom of the page to ascertain processing times for various types of applications at field offices, service centers, or the national benefits center).

27. *See, e.g.*, UNITED STATES CITIZENSHIP AND IMMIGRATION SERVICES, Data on Individual Applications and Petitions, http://www.uscis.gov/portal/site/uscis/menuitem.eb1d4c2a3e5b9ac89243c6a7543f6d1a/?vgnextoid=1b52d725f5501310VgnVCM 100000082ca60aRCRD&vgnextchannel=1b52d725f5501310VgnVCM100000082ca60a RCRD (last visited March 18, 2014) (providing various performance data from most months dating back to June 2012).

28. *See*, UNITED STATES CITIZENSHIP AND IMMIGRATION SERVICES, What You Need to Know: Filing Tips for Deferred Action for Childhood Arrivals, http://www.uscis.gov/humanitarian/consideration-deferred-action-childhood-arrivals -process/what-you-need-know-filing-tips-deferred-action-childhood-arrivals (last visited March 23, 2014).

29. *See* USCIS OFFICE OF PERFORMANCE AND QUALITY, DEFERRED ACTION FOR CHILDHOOD ARRIVALS (February 6, 2014), *available at* http://www.uscis.gov/sites/default/files/USCIS/Resources/Reports%20and%20Studies/Immigration%20 Forms%20Data/All%20Form%20Types/DACA/DACA-06-02-14.pdf.

30. *See id.*

31. SHOBA SIVAPRASAD WADHIA, DHS RESPONSE ON FOIA RE DEFERRED ACTION FOR CHILDHOOD ARRIVALS (DACA), *available at* http://works.bepress .com/shoba_wadhia/19/.

32. U.S. Citizenship and Immigration Services, Revised Guidance for the Referral of Cases and Issuance of Notices to Appear (NTAs) in Cases Involving Inadmissible and Removable Aliens (Nov. 17, 2011), http://www.uscis.gov/sites/default/files/USCIS/ Laws/Memoranda/Static_Files_Memoranda/NTA%20PM%20%28Approved%20as%20 final%2011-7-11%29.pdf.

33. PENNSYLVANIA STATE UNIVERSITY DICKINSON SCHOOL OF LAW'S CENTER FOR IMMIGRANTS' RIGHTS, TO FILE OR NOT TO FILE A NOTICE TO APPEAR: IMPROVING THE GOVERNMENT'S USE OF PROSECUTORIAL DISCRETION 15 (Oct. 2013) (prepared for the American Bar Association Commission on Immigration), *available at* https://law.psu.edu/sites/default/files/documents/ pdfs/NTAReportFinal.pdf. *See also* WADHIA, FOIA RESPONSE FROM USCIS ON NOTICES TO APPEAR.

34. WADHIA, FOIA RESPONSE FROM USCIS ON NOTICES TO APPEAR.

35. *Id.*

36. DEPARTMENT OF HOMELAND SECURITY, Freedom of Information Act (FOIA) and Privacy Act: Your Rights to DHS Information under FOIA, http://www .dhs.gov/freedom-information-act-foia-and-privacy-act (last visited March 18, 2014).

37. Cramton, *Administrative Procedure Reform.*

38. Recommendation from Prakash Khatri, Citizenship and Immigration Services

Ombudsman, to Director, on Recommendation to USCIS That It 1) Post General Information on Deferred Action on Its Website; 2) Maintain Statistics on the Issuance and Denial of Deferred Action Requests; and 3) Designate a Headquarters Official to Review Grants and Denials of Deferred Action Requests on a Quarterly Basis to Ensure That Like Cases Are Decided in Like Manner 3–4 (Apr. 6, 2007), *available at* http://www.dhs.gov/xlibrary/assets/CISOmbudsman_RR_32_O_Deferred_Action_04 -06-07.pdf.

39. *See, e.g.*, Legomsky, *Forum Choices for the Review of Agency Adjudication.*

40. Stephen H. Legomsky, *Learning to Live with Unequal Justice: Asylum and the Limits to Consistency*, 60 STAN. L. REV. 413, 426 (2007).

41. Cramton, *Administrative Procedure Reform.*

42. *See, e.g.*, Letter from Shoba Sivaprasad Wadhia to USCIS, ICE and CBP on FOIA Request for Deferred Action and Prosecutorial Discretion Records (Mar. 30, 2010) (on file with author); Letter from Shoba Sivaprasad Wadhia to USCIS, ICE and CBP about FOIA Request for Prosecutorial Discretion Records (Oct. 6, 2009) (on file with author); *see also* Daniel M. Kowalski, *NIJC Sues DHS re FOIA, Prosecutorial Discretion*, LEXISNEXIS LEGAL NEWSROOM, June 18, 2012, http://www.lexisnexis. com/legalnewsroom/immigration/b/insidenews/archive/2012/06/18/nijc-sues-dhs-re -foia-prosecutorial-discretion.aspx.

43. Zadvydas v. Davis, 533 U.S. 678, 693 (2001).

44. Fong Haw Tan v. Phelan, 333 U.S. 6, 10 (1948) ("We resolve the doubts in favor of that construction because deportation is a drastic measure and at times the equivalent of banishment or exile. . . . [W]e will not assume that Congress meant to trench on [the individual's] freedom beyond that which is required by the narrowest of several possible meanings of the words used.").

CHAPTER 8. REFORM

1. John Morton, Director, U.S. Immigration and Customs Enforcement, on Civil Immigration Enforcement: Priorities for the Apprehension, Detention, and Removal of Aliens (Mar. 2, 2011), *available at* http://www.ice.gov/doclib/news/releases/2011/110302 washingtondc.pdf.

2. FY 2013 ICE REMOVAL NUMBERS, ERO ANNUAL REPORT, ICE, available at https://www.ice.gov/doclib/about/offices/ero/pdf/2013-ice-immigration-removals.pdf.

3. *See, e.g.*, John Morton, Director, U.S. Immigration and Customs Enforcement, on Exercising Prosecutorial Discretion Consistent with the Civil Immigration Enforce- ment Priorities of the Agency for the Apprehension, Detention, and Removal of Aliens (June 17, 2011), *available at* http://www.ice.gov/doclib/secure-communities/pdf/ prosecutorial-discretion-memo.pdf [hereinafter Morton Memo I].

4. FY 2013 ICE REMOVAL NUMBERS.

5. *See generally* chapter 5.

6. *See, e.g.*, Memorandum from Doris Meissner, Commissioner, Immigration and Naturalization Service, on Exercising Prosecutorial Discretion 4 (Nov. 17, 2000) (on file with author).

7. PENNSYLVANIA STATE UNIVERSITY DICKINSON SCHOOL OF LAW'S CENTER FOR IMMIGRANTS' RIGHTS, TO FILE OR NOT TO FILE A NOTICE TO APPEAR: IMPROVING THE GOVERNMENT'S USE OF PROSECUTORIAL DISCRETION (Oct. 2013) (prepared for the American Bar Association Commission on Immigration), *available at* https://law.psu.edu/sites/default/files/documents/pdfs/NTAReportFinal.pdf [hereinafter TO FILE OR NOT TO FILE].

8. *Id.*

9. A similar recommendation appears in TO FILE OR NOT TO FILE, at 59–60.

10. Similar recommendations appear in *id.* at 60–62; ABA Commission on Immigration, *Reforming the Immigration System: Proposals to Promote Independence, Fairness, Efficiency, and Professionalism in the Adjudication of Removal Cases*, 1–12 (2010), *available at* http://www.americanbar.org/content/dam/aba/publications/commission_on_immigration/coi_complete_full_report.pdf.

11. TO FILE OR NOT TO FILE.

12. *See* INA § 241(a)(5) (providing that "[i]f the Attorney General finds that an alien has reentered the United States illegally after having been removed or having departed voluntarily, under an order of removal, the prior order of removal is reinstated from its original date and is not subject to being reopened or reviewed, the alien is not eligible and may not apply for any relief under this Act, and the alien shall be removed under the prior order at any time after the reentry").

13. *See* INA § 240A (listing the criteria for eligibility for cancellation of removal).

14. *See* INA § 240(c)(4)(A) (in formal removal proceedings, the noncitizen carries the burden of proving statutory eligibility and that he or she merits a favorable exercise of discretion).

15. Memorandum from Brian M. O'Leary, Chief Immigration Judge, Executive Office for Immigration Review, on Operating Policies and Procedures Memorandum 13-01: Continuances and Administrative Closures (Mar. 7, 2013), *available at* http://www.justice.gov/eoir/efoia/ocij/oppm13/13-01.pdf.

16. *Wong Wing Hang v. Immigration & Naturalization Serv.*, 360 F.2d 715, 719 (2d Cir. 1966).

17. *See* Stephen H. Legomsky, *Political Asylum and the Theory of Judicial Review*, 73 MINN. L. REV. 1205, 1209–12 (1989); Stephen H. Legomsky, *Fear and Loathing in Congress and the Courts: Immigration and Judicial Review*, 78 TEX. L. REV. 1615 (2000); Shoba Sivaprasad Wadhia, *Sharing Secrets: Examining Deferred Action and Transparency in Immigration Law*, 10 U.N.H. L. REV. 1, 34–38 (2012).

18. *Office of the Secretary*, U.S. DEP'T OF HOMELAND SECURITY, *available at* http://www.dhs.gov/xabout/structure/office-of-the-secretary.shtm (last visited Dec. 20, 2013).

19. *See* Shoba Sivaprasad Wadhia, *The Role of Prosecutorial Discretion in Immigration Law*, 9 CONN. PUB. INT. L.J. 243 (2010). *See also* AILA's comments on the Department of Homeland Security's implementation of Executive Order 13563, "Improving Regulation and Regulatory Review." Special thanks to the AILA Interagency Liaison Committee. AILA Doc. No. 11041463 ("Guidance on deferred action

was contained in the now withdrawn INS Operating Instructions. Though the relief is still available, there are currently no regulations that would facilitate a more meaningful and consistent application of prosecutorial discretion in context of deferred action. We ask that such regulations be promulgated.").

20. For an argument on what "Good Guidance" practices might look like, *see* Jill E. Family, *Easing the Guidance Document Dilemma Agency by Agency: Immigration Law and Not Really* Binding Rules, 47 U. MICH. J.L. REFORM 1 (2013).

21. *See, e.g.,* Abraham D. Sofaer, *The Change-of-Status Adjudication: A Case Study of the Informal Agency Process,* 1 J. LEGAL STUD. 349 (1972); Paul R. Verkuil, *A Study of Immigration Procedures,* 31 UCLA L. REV. 1141 (1984).

22. Colin S. Diver, *The Optimal Precision of Administrative Rules,* 93 YALE L.J. 65, 95 (1983); Stephen H. Legomsky, *Learning to Live with Unequal Justice: Asylum and the Limits to Consistency,* 60 STAN. L. REV. 413, 463 (2007).

23. Morton Memo I.

24. A legacy INS memo from Johnny Williams indicates that, while an individual is in deferred action, he or she does not accrue unlawful presence. *See* Memorandum from Johnny Williams, Office of Field Operations of INS, to Regional Directors about Unlawful Presence, AILA Doc. No. 02062040 (June 12, 2002).

25. *Statement of Robert L. Glicksman to the House Judiciary Committee's Subcommittee on Courts, Commercial and Administrative Law,* HOUSE JUDICIARY COMMITTEE (2011), *available at* http://judiciary.house.gov/_files/hearings/pdf/Glicksman03292011.pdf, citing to Robert L. Glicksman and Sidney A. Shapiro, *Improving Regulation Through Incremental Adjustment,* 52 U. KAN. L. REV. 1179 (2004).

26. *See* Factors to Be Considered in the Exercise of Administrative Discretion, 44 Fed. Reg. 36,187, 36,191 (June 21, 1979) (proposing 8 C.F.R. 245.8). *See also* Wadhia, *Role of Prosecutorial Discretion in Immigration Law,* at 284–86 ("Several provisions of these proposed regulations would have required a favorable exercise of discretion in the absence of adverse factors. For example, with regard to the exercise of discretion under the former 212(c) waiver, the rule identified the following factors for consideration in the exercise of discretion: 'alien is likely to continue type of activity which gave rise to the grounds of excludability; alien has a history of criminal, immoral, narcotic, or subversive activity; act giving rise to grounds of excludability was relatively recent; no unusual hardship would accrue to alien or family members if the waiver is denied.'") (internal citations omitted); Diver, *The Optimal Precision of Administrative Rules,* at 94.

27. *Id.*

28. INA § 240A, 8 U.S.C. § 1229b (2006).

INDEX

Figures and tables are indicated by "*f*" and "*t*" following page numbers.

Obama administration (*continued*)
reform attempts, 88–89, 207n104;
statistics, 103; and terrorism, 94–95;
in USCIS, 90–91, 101, 106. *See also*
Deferred Action for Childhood
Arrivals
Office for Civil Rights and Civil
Liberties, 10
Office of Attorney General, 34
Office of Field Operations, 49
Office of Immigration Statistics, 49
Ono, Yoko, ix, xi, 14–17, 19*f*
Open government. *See* Transparency in
prosecutorial discretion
Operations Instructions (OI): and
deferred action, 55, 87, 175n49,
187–88n8; defined, 159; and deporta-
tion, 21–22; historical background,
17–18, 20–22, 162; and Meissner
Memo, 24
O'Scannlain, Diarmuid, 132
"Overcriminalization," 37, 47

Parole, 29–31
Parole in Place (PIP), 31, 105
Parole Memo (2013), 165
Penn State Law's Center for Immigrants'
Rights, 93, 140, 142
Plea bargaining, 35, 42, 43, 50, 182–83n51
Plenary power, 110, 172n30
"Policies for Apprehension, Deten-
tion, and Removal of Undocumented
Immigrants" (effective January 2015),
156
Political persecution. *See* Asylum
Politics, 8, 18; in criminal prosecutions,
38, 45; and DREAM Act, 89; and
Lennon case, 15; and Obama adminis-
tration, 147, 156
Priorities Memo (June 2010), 94–96,
200n35, 200n38
Professional code of conduct, recommen-
dations regarding, 151

Pro se applicants, 138–39, 159
Prosecutorial discretion: ABA on, 92–93;
absolute discretion, 110–11; during
arrest, 11; categorical grants of, 28–32;
in CBP, 7, 9–11, 27, 48–49; during
charging process, 11, 48–50; and Constitution, 36; in current immigration
structure, 9–13; defined, 159; during
deportation, 11–13, 172n32; during
detention, 11, 51–52, 185n100; in DHS,
1–2, 5–7, 9–13, 26–28, 48–53, 148–50,
169–70n2, 171n21, 172n25; discretionary points, 47–52; economic rationale,
8; and evolution of, 14–22; in ICE, 1–2,
7, 9–11, 27–28, 47–49, 51–52; under
INA, 10; in INS, 9, 13, 46–47; during
interrogation, 11; and 9/11, 4, 9; and
NTAs, 48–50, 49*f*; and "overcriminalization," 47; overview, 7–13; political
rationale, 8; and State Department, 9;
and terrorism, 4, 9, 94–95; during trial,
11; in USCIS, 7, 9–11, 27, 48–49; for
victims of crime and abuse, 57–62; and
voluntary departure, 50–51; and witnesses, 8, 44–45. *See also* Criminal law,
prosecutorial discretion in; Deferred
action; Humanitarian factors; Judicial
review of prosecutorial discretion;
Obama administration, prosecutorial
discretion under; Recommendations
regarding prosecutorial discretion;
Transparency in prosecutorial discretion; *specific memos*
Public interest as basis for prosecutorial
discretion, 36–38, 43–45

Raben, Robert, 23–24
Race discrimination, 30, 45, 150
REAL ID Act of 2005, 107, 176n61
Recommendations regarding prosecutorial discretion, 5, 146–56; abuse of
process, 150–51; administrative review,
151; code of conduct, 151; deferred

ABOUT THE AUTHOR

Shoba Sivaprasad Wadhia is Samuel Weiss Faculty Scholar and Director of the Center for Immigrants' Rights at Penn State Law. Previously, Wadhia was Deputy Director for Legal Affairs at the National Immigration Forum and an associate with Maggio Kattar P.C., both in Washington, D.C.